Banking for Family Business

Stefano Caselli · Stefano Gatti
(Editors)

Banking for Family Business

A New Challenge for Wealth Management

With 46 Figures and 26 Tables

🍷 Springer

Professor Stefano Caselli
Professor Stefano Gatti
IEMIF
Bocconi University
Via Sarfatti 25
20136 Milan
Italy
stefano.caselli@uni-bocconi.it
stefano.gatti@uni-bocconi.it

Cataloging-in-Publication Data
Library of Congress Control Number: 2004115459

ISBN 3-540-22798-9 Springer Berlin Heidelberg New York

Springer is a part of Springer Science+Business Media

springeronline.com

© Springer Berlin · Heidelberg 2005
Printed in Germany

Hardcover-Design: Erich Kirchner, Heidelberg

SPIN 11310860   43/3130-5 4 3 2 1 0 – Printed on acid-free paper

Preface

Laurent Huck[1] and Sergio Trezzi[2]

During the last 5 years the asset management industry has been constantly invested by events which have required top management of major companies to rethink their business model, while preserving their company's mission.

From the Internet bubble easy growth model to a strong cost control environment in 2000-2003, many financial institutions have undertaken structural changes in order to reap the opportunities offered by the "new" market.

Hints of globalization have actually been around for several decades, even though they made only a modest impact; however, the availability of global capital and advances in communication technology have emphasized the process of internationalization and the tools available to connect and integrate business activities to answer to more complex needs of clients. Moreover, the financial scandals and the review of mutual fund trade activity in the US by the Attorney General Elliot Spitzer have highlighted the importance to focus all efforts on renewing the confidence of professional investors and their clients who have entrusted their capital to asset managers. Therefore, there is a growing need in the market to reinforce the concept of "Shared Positive Values" among the entire industry and among its stakeholders.

The European market can still be viewed as a puzzle of different "markets" within a very large territory; however, in the more sophisticated segments of asset management the transition from an "offer market" to a "demand market" is also a fact. From the multi-national companies to pure domestic entrepreneurs the need of financial integrated solutions seems to be evident. Both global and domestic players have the opportunity to fulfill this demand in order to create concrete business opportunities.

This book offers an interesting and thoughtful analysis of the segment of family offices within the private banking business by analyzing synergies among the various activities and by offering ideas on how to develop new business opportunities. Europe's tapestry is still characterized by the fact

[1] Chief Business Development Officer – Continental Europe
Managing Director. INVESCO, Milan
[2] Head of Business Development – Southern Europe
INVESCO. Milan

that there is really no one single business model in each country. Nevertheless, there seems to be a growing understanding of the need to find the right balance between global synergies and local empowerment. The following pages illustrate how organizations can bridge the gap still present in the market, helping us to understand current needs and behaviors and by giving concrete examples of business ideas in a changing environment.

Foreword

Stefano Caselli and Stefano Gatti

"Giordano Dell'Amore" Institute of Financial Markets and Financial Intermediaries – "L. Bocconi" University

No issue is more antique and traditional than family business banking. This is because in the European and, above all, Anglo-Saxon tradition numerous banks have been set up by entrepreneurs just as numerous banks have quite often focused their activities on the management of businesses and wealth owned by entrepreneurial families.

The necessity to dedicate a research study to an issue which is not aligned with our time is therefore contradictory and not appropriate. Yet, the new and important stimulus emerging from this apparent contrast takes into account relevant signals coming from the financial and the production system.

As for the financial system, the divisional path pursued with strong determination by Italian and most of the banks in Continental Europe has on the one hand allowed banks to reach deep down customer needs thanks to their differentiating organizational structures, but on the other it has not enabled them to reach the needs of interlocutors that are characterized by a different profile compared to the traditional corporate-private bipartition. As for the production system, the relevance of the family business, which is typical of the Italian, German, French and partially American context, stimulates interlocutors from the financial system to find appropriate solutions, above all in view of the challenges emerging from the generational change, the dimensional growth and internationalization.

The quest of replies and organizational models for family business banking cannot be confined to the mere bank-family business relation as the complexity of needs and the constantly interweaving occurrences between the firm and the family involve a number of differentiated actors belonging to the professional world, to that of consulting and the financial system. This means that the bank willing to compete in the market of family business should not only face different competencies but also define a dedicated strategy, which may range from counter-position, to cooperation or the exit from the market itself.

Owing to the presence of several development courses for the bank-family business relationship, the goal of our research is twofold. On the one hand, define the characteristics of the requirements within the family business system and the typology of the best suiting financial services, irrespective of the organizational solution or the proposing subject. On the other hand, proceed with a review of the existing market trends in Italy and abroad, in terns of organizational choices and solutions for a correct management of family business banking. Along this path, special stress will be placed on the structure of family office, which is viewed as the unitary management solution for the relationship with the family-owned firm.

The development of a banking activity specifically designed for entrepreneurial families represents the challenge consistent with the development of a supply function oriented to partnership and problem solving of customer financial needs. From this point of view, the more the bank is able to present itself as assistance and support provider for family financial choices, the better its image, its perception and its actual positioning as "relation-bank" and "home-bank". The above competitive model is grounded on four relevant aspects which must be present concurrently and structurally: repeated and satisfactory matching between the firm requirement system, the family requirement system and the bank service system; high degree of service co-ordination thanks to dedicated organizational structures; high degree of continuity of bank-customer exchange process in the course of time; mutual, though not formalized, commitment toward medium-term consolidation of relationship as value adding element.

The success of a banking model designed for family business requires the bank concurrent control over the four aspects described above, as unbalanced development-paths might undermine the effectiveness and the efficiency of the bank competitive positioning. For example, solutions characterized by high diversification of the bank product-portfolio and by a low degree of co-ordination do not produce a significant increase in the relationship value added for the target customer, thus limiting the possibility of providing an overall customized service. Or, a low degree of continuity of the exchange process combined with high product diversification and a remarkable degree of supply co-ordination reduce the bank chances of taking action during the change phases in the life-cycle of the firm and the family, thus compromising the steadiness and the profitability of the customer relationship in the medium term.

An organic approach to family business should rely not only on the concurrent development of firm and family requirement matching, supply co-ordination, exchange continuity and medium-term relation commitment, but should be supported by the control of significantly different competencies and management technologies.

As for requirement matching, the bank wider-ranging supply requires the availability of sophisticated managerial and technical-production com-

petencies, totally different from traditional competencies of credit intermediation. The supply of advisory products or, for example, capital market
services can be developed exclusively by employing specialized resources
that, on the one hand, have a deep knowledge of the product specific nature and, on the other hand, allow managing the supply in relation to customer needs. It's worth noticing that the increase in the service supply does
not necessarily imply a symmetrical increase in the production capacity:
specialized products can be produced in specific product companies and
distributed by banks, which manage the customer sale process.

As for supply co-ordination, the possibility for the bank to enter the
market by supplying service systems that are not overlapping and consistent with family and firm needs must be supported by a keen development
of interface and customer portfolio management resources as well as by
the design of effective IT systems allowing the bank to follow the evolution of customer needs on a regular basis. This leads directly to the aspect
of exchange continuity in the course of time: the bank capacity to satisfy a
growing amount of requirements, without leaving evident discontinuity in
the overall circuit of financial flows generated by the business and invested
by the family, is closely connected with the availability of timely and
flexible action means as well as with the ability of contact and management roles to strengthen a visible presence within the entrepreneurial family.

Finally, with reference to medium-term relation consolidation, the prospect of building constant exchange forms offering commercial opportunities and anyway relying on counterparts' loyalty has long distinguished
and defined the concept of "relationship" orientation as a conceptual category opposing that of "transaction" orientation, attributed to the historical
tradition of Italian commercial banks. However, operationally, the above
contrast does not match banking actual correlated as the relational content
of the exchange and the tension toward relationship consolidation must be
referred to any customer segment as the minimum condition for survival in
the market.

On the contrary, segment differentiation implies a distinction based on
three different parameters which define and distinguish the approach to
family business. The three parameters regard the following: human requisites, professional requisites and contractual requisites.

The human requisites that characterize the value creation orientation in
the relationship regard the human profile, the standing and the availability
of the resources involved in the management of the same relations. This
means that the organizational solution dedicated to family business must
choose, as contact roles, people who stand out not only for their good
communication skills and their ability to create a trustful climate in the ex-

change but also because they have the qualities that are indispensable for the performance of complex transactions, such as discretion, confidentiality, assertiveness, timely solutions and ability to focus the production process onto customer needs. As a result, bank recruiting must be grounded on these parameters for the purpose of skimming and identifying the resources with highest potential.

Professional requisites define market competencies human resources must be familiar with. Too often this element is confused with the quite vague definition of "advisory orientation", which should indicate a sort of generic propensity to high-standing customer relations. Such generic character should be overcome by analytically specifying the professional content contact roles should use and demonstrate in their relations with customers. In addition, the content specification should be tuned with the bank entire production process, for maximum consistency is to be pursued between the typologies of diagnosis made by the client manager and the chances of solution within the bank supply system. When diagnosis skills are higher than supply capacity, the resulting gaps are bound to produce not only role's frustration but also a decline in bank trustworthiness. On the contrary, when solution capacity is higher than diagnosis skills, the resulting gaps are bound to reduce client managers' authority and to prevent the bank production capacity from being fully exploited. This might be extremely penalizing in the startup phases of new product industries and in those of development of product areas as break-even achievement in due time is slowed down or even precluded.

Finally, contractual requisites regard the product typology proposed by the bank as the contractual specifications of the different financial services significantly condition the chances of growth in terms of exchange commitment, loyalty and continuity. This can be verified under two different aspects. On the one hand, the intrinsic characteristics of each product differently condition the degree of interaction and interdependence between the bank and the customer in the medium term: corporate finance and nonfinancial asset management for their own nature establish complex contracts – where the bank professional image is at stake – that are also binding in the course of time owing to the nature of the rights included and to the pervasiveness of the financial service within the asset system of the owner-family. On the other hand, when product contractual specifications are identical, the characteristics of collaterals and packaging define the bank attitude toward the development of a trustworthy climate. Decisive indicators in this sense are the indiscriminate or calibrated use of guarantees, covenant imposition style, transparency of service pricing conditions and more or less flexible contractual terms.

The path pursued by our research study represents the "project" the bank should design and implement in order to define a supply system designed for family business. This effort is absolutely necessary to overcome intermediate or partial solutions that would emerge from a stiff divisional approach segmented into private and corporate market. In this sense, the bank that consciously chooses to enter family business will proceed along a logic path leading through the issues of organizational and strategic structures, organizational roles and involved competencies, relation management modes, market positioning depending on the selected segmentation criteria.

The internal consistency of the sequence of issues tackled by the bank and the resulting strategic choices is not sufficient to guarantee a successful and effective project but it may represent an essential reference benchmark. As a result, attention should be finally focused on the critical aspects for the success of the family business "project".

For the purpose of a clear representation and a correct focus on the specific features of the critical aspects, a preliminary distinction should be made between inside and outside critical aspects. The former regard the bank organization in terms of strategy, management and production as well as the typology of connections the bank must develop with the entire financial system for entrepreneurial families in order to find the best suiting and most effective solutions also in terms of performance. The latter regard the relationship and the contact with customers and rely on bank interaction modes with family demand functions in order to improve problem solving and customer satisfaction skills.

With reference to inside critical aspects, the debate is focused on the following issues: well-defined processes of requirement segmentation and mapping; constant and determined quest of human, professional and contractual requisites in management roles; major relevance of educational processes; tension toward the governance of the financial network, irrespective of the institutional-organizational model chosen by the bank.

Market segmentation is crucial as it allows the bank to achieve substantial consistency between the bank organizational structure and family business demand specifications. Consequently, the choice the bank is obliged to make should avoid any standardized and systemized solution which, by replicating the same specifications in most of Italian banks, are bound to flatten competition down to low-value-added elements and produce frequently inadequate and outsized choices in relation to bank characteristics so as to have a negative impact on effective and efficient competition. On the contrary, the adoption of a personal market vision resulting from explicit and sometimes radical management choices represents a potential source of competitive advantage and a correct choice of fine tuning with the relative reference market.

The constant pursuit of appropriate human, professional and contractual requisites for the roles involved in family business banking is closely connected with the selected segmentation model as such roles are responsible for the good quality and the functional continuity of the model in the course of time. The role-segmentation link must rely on the concurrent presence of three different elements: activity content, activity process, process engineering of all the activities in family business banking.

As for the content, resources' skills must lead the bank to a concrete, substantial and exhaustive management of contents regarding products, services and activities designed for family business customers. Unlike the retail or private market approach, the wholesale attitude emerging from the organization of a dedicated management cannot lead to the availability of content competencies thanks to the good quality of the production structure. On the contrary, human resources are the differentiating element and, as such, they are responsible for making the service supply system constantly adjustable to the customer requirement system.

As for the process, the supply system must rely on production mechanisms that are able to lead to the actual execution of the solution designed for the customer. This is possible only when both the procedural structure and the resources' habit and frequency of defining deals are congruous and significant. As a result, the process relevance grows increasingly critical as the supply function moves away from the traditional control of asset management and lending services to enter all the other business areas. It is worth noticing that the process acquires great relevance and independence thanks to its contribution to the success of family business banking. This can be understood because the bank, despite the availability of appropriate contents in the area, for example, of company re-structuring, is not able to actually execute solutions due to the lack of either clearly defined procedures or of fluent execution or because resources are not accustomed to developing the above business.

As for process engineering, the overall supply system of family business banking must be provided not only with objective operative competencies and skills, but above all with teamworking and qualitative competencies, which allow identifying the real source of value production in the requirement system of the entrepreneurial family on a continuous basis. This means that if content and process represent the "mechanics" of the organization producing services and products for family business, process engineering represents the "chemistry" of the organization, which generates customer contextual solutions by the summation of mechanical processes. This path inevitably warns the bank that not only the construction of a family business tailored solution requires constant investment in team-building and teamworking, but that the organizational structure evolves toward the professional team logic, pretty far from the productive and cultural archetype of the traditional commercial bank.

The key relevance of educational processes represents the third critical aspect inside the bank and the strong correlate to the issue of content, process and process engineering management. This is due to that the cultural and professional profile of resources is the only point of junction between the variety and good quality of production processes and the complexity of demand functions. Therefore, the educational process must be characterized by: relevance as primary and strategic investment in family business banking; continuity of such investment in the course of time; pursuit of absolute consistency with the set of necessary contents for overall startup of the supply system; ability to educate customers in order to increase customer satisfaction and potential market spaces for more complex products.

According to such requisites, the educational activity should permeate the entire design and the entire operating cycle of family business banking. The high variety of necessary competencies, which require an effective time-to-market updating system, forces the bank to opt for either "make" or "buy" production choices. If supply diversification tends to increase and thus deny the neat superiority of traditional asset management and lending, such choices will lean toward the "buy" logic, which will be followed by a professional and organizational growth of the bank by discontinuity. Although such approach leads directly to the result and to bridging the competencies gap, it does expose the bank to significant risks, related to the possible rejection of the structure and the emergence of substantial differences in the way of acting and communicating which may finally lead to a substantial production paralysis.

The tension toward the governance of the financial network is the fourth and last critical aspect involving the bank during the design of the banking area dedicated to family business. At first sight, this issue seems to have a larger scope than the previous ones and involve the traditional problem of the link between the selected institutional model and the strategic and organizational model that has been adopted. More analytically, apart from the choices banks are due to make in order to find the internalization/externalization junction of production activities, the presence of a financial system with heterogeneous actors dedicated to family-owned firms (advisors, accountants, legal firms, merchant banks, etc...) urges for the design and management of a network of relations and alliances which may have quite different contractual and content aspects. This is due to that some activities have such distinctive attributes that they can be hardly replicated or returned to the bank through the processes of internalization and externalization. Let us think of the activity developed by professional agencies or by private equity funds, where the condition of success is often the distance and, somehow, the contrast of interests in comparison to bank objectives. The issues of independence, discretion and confidentiality are at the same time the physiological limits of the concept of universal banking - but also of divisional banking if seen as bank self-sufficient solution – and the principles of internal diversification of the financial system in relation to the requirements of family business. Such evaluations lead the bank not to consider a policy solely aimed at the mere replication of external activities, but to pursue a policy of networking and selective alliances, which relies on an appropriate mapping of the value chain connecting the bank with family business. This is carried out for the purpose of conveying the image of distance in the case of conflict situations and of unity given by an explicit and strong business idea. In the future this challenge is likely to lead the bank to work on networking and on the "bank-net" in terms of research and operationally, but also to implement stronger solutions recalling the image of the financial district.

With reference to outside critical aspects, the debate is focused on the following issues: the development of supply policies for family office; specific definition of packaging strategies.

As for family office supply policies, it should be noticed that the family's view of market relations between banks and family-owned companies is an element breaking off with the traditional logic of relations with customer companies as, on the one hand, it broadens the available market and, on the other, multiplies the relevant variables for the development of a profitable relationship. Risks in this respect, and not only opportunities, are quite high. This is due to that considering the entrepreneurial family as the center of production of financial requirements and as the element conditioning the firm choices generates overlapping and conflict of assignments between corporate and private division. In addition the family is likely to need a partner characterized by independence, confidentiality and discretion who can qualify the market relation professionally.

The solution to such critical aspects cannot be the arbitrary assignment of the customer control to either of the two divisions as risks and efficiency gaps would probably be the same. After assigning the firm to the corporate division, the path to be pursued consists in identifying the contractual and production "environments" dedicated to the management of the relationship with the entrepreneurial family. The family office offers both a production solution (a specialized production center) and a contractual solution (the stipulation of the family office contract), in which the bank undertakes to structurally manage family members, risks and assets in the long and medium term. This solution tends to position the bank as the supporting, trustworthy and exclusively operative structure designed to satisfy the whole range of family needs. Due to the "delicacy" of matters, the bank-customer relationship tends to grow stronger, binding and heralding exchange opportunities; moreover the bank inevitably benefits from the knowledge of the family dynamics, which means credit risk protection. Finally, the bank positioning in the family office logic forces the bank to make a "final" choice which may be the result of conscious indifference but also that of supplying external family offices created by the same entrepreneurs.

As for the explicit definition of packaging strategies, the complexity of segmentation models will inevitably require a re-distribution of responsibilities among client managers and production structures. This means that back-office activities must be extended to become "marketing labs" or to create innovation- dedicated centers, which not only design the specifications of new and old product but also define the criteria for product combinations and packaging. This is relevant as the package approach represents the link between the product system and that of customer needs and, together with the client manager, contributes to matching the two systems. To this aim, product packaging must be performed in relation with customer requirement areas or with specific contextual situations where the key element is not the client manager's diagnosis skill but the appropriate functionality of solutions, execution speed and overall effectiveness. Examples in this sense can be packaging for real asset operations, financial risk management or development of export activities. There are no indications against extending the packaging approach to more complex situations, such as startup lending. To conclude, packaging relies on two important assumptions: first of all, the client manager cannot effectively develop the same tasks as the global player in the case of family business bank supply; the availability of packaging provides spaces and times for action; secondly, the bank decides to make ex ante aggregations based on the mapping of product-market mixes and supported by success expectations and recurrence.

The research includes nine chapters which can be divided into three different areas of analysis: the relationship system between family business and financial intermediaries (chapter 1 and 2); the management of financial services and relations with family business to develop family business banking (chapter 3, 4, and 5); the specificity of the family office solution in the light of market trends and operators' experience (chapter 7, 8 and 9).

The first chapter tackles the issue of family business from an evolutionary and dynamic view by highlighting its distinctive features in order to understand the resulting financial and non-financial requirements in view of their evaluation by the financial system. In this respect, the analysis of the distinctive features of family business mainly develops through the study of governing mechanisms and the diagnosis of the critical aspects for long lasting success, considering the system of relations the entrepreneurial family establishes with its own reference environment. The second chapter intends to analyze the "state of the art" of the supply of private banking services, by outlining the possible modes of evolution and conflict between wealth management and family business banking.

The third chapter introduces the issue of the implementation of family business banking by coordinating the needs expressed by the entrepreneurial family with the range of financial and non-financial services designed to satisfy them. In this context, the major critical areas in the field of both organization and production are pointed out in order to have them implemented in the bank. The fourth chapter deepens the themes developed in the previous one by focusing the operating logic of financial and asset connections between the family and the firm as well as the presence of spaces for synergies between corporate and private banking services. The aim consists in identifying the dynamics characterizing the system of governance, relations and development of family and firm requirements. Special stress is placed on the link between the firm external financial requirements, family capacity of action and typology of asset relations among the members of the family. The fifth chapter deals with the relation between corporate finance services and business shareholders. Here the traditional classification of extraordinary finance operations is completely changed in order to create best practices of interaction not so much with the equity side of the firm as with the asset side of the family, considering the existing financial and asset connections between the family and the firm. The sixth chapter concludes the area of analysis regarding the management issues of family business banking by reviewing the different modes of relation between banking and family office from the organizational and strategic point of view.

The seventh chapter offers an accurate analysis of the family office phenomenon at an international level by reporting the relevant data emerging from a sample survey carried out with questionnaires that had been sent to the major operators in the sector. The aim of the survey consists in seizing the basic elements of family office competitive advantage, the prevailing structures (mono or multi family, independent or captive, etc...) and the characteristics of the profit and loss account, with reference to the typology of operating costs and the typology of fees charged on customers. The eighth and ninth chapters compare the cases of two operators in the market of family office: the first at an international level through a bank structure; the second at a domestic level in the logic of the independent structure.

At the end of this introduction, the editors have to thank many people, starting from Professors Paolo Mottura and Francesco Saita, respectively Director and Co-Director of Newfin Bocconi (Financial Innovation Research Centre of Bocconi University in Milan), who have sponsored and funded the research on which this book is based. Then, a special thank goes to Alberto Frisiero for his help and patience in reviewing the text layout. Last but not least, a sincere thank you to the persons this book is dedicated to: Brother Marco (my big brother, Stefano Gatti is writing) and to Anna, Elisa and Lorenzo (Stefano Caselli is writing now) for all the time we didn't allow them during the long days spent in writing and reviewing the chapters of the book.

Milan, October 2004

Table of Contents

1 Family Business as Viewed by Financial Intermediaries

Guido Corbetta and Gaia Marchisio

1.1 The Importance of Family Business and Definition of the Entrepreneurial Family

In Italy in the manufacturing and service industries there are 4.1m firms, of which 2.8m are in the service industry (Istat 2001). Only a few dozen thousand firms count more than 50 employees (large and medium enterprises). On the whole, however, these firms employ about 30% of the working population.

Despite the possible distortions created by the well-known phenomenon of groups, the above data point out the great fragmentation of the Italian entrepreneurial system and the enterprises' difficulty in growing beyond a certain size.

Among small-sized firms the importance of family business is obviously very high and almost all of the people hired by under-50-employee enterprises work for family-owned firms. If we use the weights proposed by Banca d'Italia, about 70% of over-50-employee enterprises fall in the category of family business. Moreover, according to a survey carried out by SDA Bocconi on the first 150 groups in Italy, 69 are family owned (46%). Hence we can conclude:

1. family-owned firms are not exclusively small or medium sized;

2. large and medium sized family-owned firms are an important wealth for the development of the country.

What do we mean exactly by family-owned firms? Literature about family business has often dealt with this subject (see Barnes and Hershon 1976, Corbetta 1995, Aronoff et al. 1996, Neubauer and Lank 1998). According to most of the authors family business indicates differently sized firms held by one or more owners linked by family connections, affinity or strong alliances.

On the basis of such definition we can now define the entrepreneurial family as a group of people composed by all the descendants from a family founder who jointly own shares directly or indirectly in one or more companies operating in the manufacturing, commercial or service industry. More generally, the entrepreneurial family may include husbands and wives of current or future partners as well as other relatives-in-law.

1.2 Taxonomy of Entrepreneurial Families: Structural Variables

Though operating in the same geographical context, entrepreneurial families may be highly different and different criteria may be used for their classification (Table 1.1):

1. family members: age, number and differentiation of family members in terms of possible roles inside the firm (e.g. ownership, governance, management, etc.) or activities developed outside it;

2. net worth: total value, origins, diversification, assets distribution among individual members of the family;

3. controlled company: current economic/financial situation and future strategy.[1]

Different typologies of family business have been distinguished on the basis of the above variables in order to identify the different financial or non-financial requirements[2]. Thanks to the identification of the requirements, in fact, it will be easier to identify the possible services which might be provided by the financial intermediary.

1. Family members

The age of the owners is an important element for the resulting consequences at three levels. First of all, age can be taken as family members' risk propensity proxy. In fact, the older the individuals, the lower their risk propensity in front of corporate decisions or investment decisions regarding extra-corporate assets. The second aspect concerns young members' different perspectives and activities compared with those of old members of the family and their different financial needs. For example, a thirty-

---

[1] When we deal with a controlled company, we refer to the company (or group of companies) making up the typical business of the entrepreneurial family. The identification of the typical business is not particularly difficult except for some entrepreneurial families that have control over various businesses in the manufacturing, commercial or financial industry.

[2] See Par. 1.5

year-old man needs to purchase a house, afford an expensive standard of living or invest resources for his sons; on the contrary, very old owners might have far more limited but more frequent necessities. Finally, the third aspect regards the different standard of education: now personal education requires higher investment compared with the past and, as a result, the higher educational standard makes the young members of the family more competent as to financial issues compared to the members of the previous generations.

As for the composition of the entrepreneurial family, on the one hand there are families that include a sole component with no sons or only young sons (e.g. the Squinzi);[3] on the other, there are families that include dozens of components (e.g. the Marzotto or the Frescobaldi), where roles are distributed among ownership, governance, management and executive positions. In the middle there are families that include just a few components with a varying degree of differentiation: take the Ferrarini, for example, with 5 members from the second generation, all of them engaged in ownership, governance and management roles or the Alessi, with 6 members from the third generation: some of them are engaged as owners and carry out other activities outside the firm, others develop more roles within the firm.

The higher the number of members and the degree of age and roles differentiation, the more likely the presence of different remuneration expectations often characterized by different levels of business knowledge. The co-existence of such diversities among the same group of shareholders is liable to produce remarkable complexity which requires more sophisticated and complex governance tools.

2. Family net worth

When the family is analyzed as a group of individuals that own a certain amount of assets, the first classification variable to be considered is the value of such assets. The assets value is to be calculated by including the value of the firm/s controlled by the family as a whole. From this point of view, different thresholds can be utilized for the classification of the family. Despite the obvious difficulties (and without entering the definition of quantitative thresholds)[4], it seems useful to distinguish big families (i.e. the

---

[3] Information about entrepreneurial families in this volume is collected from public sources.

[4] According to the *World Wealth Report 2003* published by Cap Gemini and Ernts&Young and Merrill Lynch, in Italy there are about 110,000 HNWI; according to Eurisko Finanza, about 200,000 individuals own financial assets amounting to 1m Euros.

leading 150-200 entrepreneurial families in Italy) from locally famous families and rich families. The first ones might be looking for highly sophisticated services and their national visibility is source of specific behaviors; the second ones (a sort of local champions) are important as they are often cases other entrepreneurial families, the so-called "rich" ones, consider examples to be followed for their investment decisions.[5]

The origins of the family assets are the second relevant variable and can be viewed in two different ways. First, assets can have more or less recent origins: in the case of ancient origins the family is likely to have developed better expertise in wealth management and, sometimes, a sort of detachment from it. Secondly, assets may have been produced to a larger extent by the controlled company or by other activities and this generally defines the critical competencies of the family as well as the focus of its attention.

The third variable is assets degree of diversification. The more diversified the assets (business income, real assets, securities, art works, liquid assets) the more complex the investment decisions as more interlocutors will be involved with different competencies.

Empirical evidence suggests this variable might be correlated with the first one: locally or nationally most famous families usually have a larger share of their assets not invested in the original firm. This is also due to the fact that these families are often involved by the various actors in multiple diversification undertakings, which are not always successful.

Finally, a fourth element is necessary: the distribution of assets among the different types of businesses for each member of the family. The mapping of individual investments within large entrepreneurial families is a key aspect for those who intend to provide financial services: in fact it enables the financial intermediary to provide customized services able to attract single investors.

3. Family-controlled firm

With reference to the third typology of criteria for the classification of entrepreneurial families, since the business income of the company or group of companies controlled by the family accounts for a significant share of the total assets of a large number of families, it is relevant to analyze the situation of such companies. An important classification variable is the current economic-financial situation; more specifically it is necessary to distinguish companies requiring financial resources from their partners (e.g. in the form of guarantees for the lending system) from compa-

---

[5] According to Eurisko Finanza report, only 19% of Italian HNWI live in cities exceeding 500,000 inhabitants.

nies potentially able to distribute financial resources among their partners. A second variable regards prospective strategy. According to this variable, three typical situations can be outlined: a growth strategy which is bound to draw attention and resources from the entrepreneurial family into the company; a maintenance strategy which should not produce significant changes in family assets outside the company; a squeeze strategy which might bring about the transfer of the company with the obvious intake of financial resources which will be invested in other businesses. Always with reference to the company situation, it might be useful to analyze company assets: the analysis allows distinguishing situations in which no management can be attempted on assets from situations in which there can be interesting margins (e.g. for operations involving real assets owned by the company). Finally, the level of business risk should be considered: a high level of business risk might suggest safer investment policies outside the company.

1.3 Taxonomy of Entrepreneurial Families: Social Variables

To fully understand entrepreneurial families' decision processes, a number of social variables should be used, such as:

1. family internal cohesion;

2. leadership nature;

3. financial culture and service utilization mode;[6]

4. family members' risk propensity;

5. life-style.

The higher the number of family members involved, the more relevant the degree of cohesion among them. In fact, the degree of cohesion defines the borders of the family area to be considered by financial intermediaries. Cohesion depends on relationship elements and on net worth elements. The actual degree of cohesion can be fully appreciated only through deep knowledge of family behaviors. Experience suggests the necessity of the so-called "third stage". At the first stage the family appears cohesive; at a deeper stage of knowledge there are signs of disagreement among family members which might indicate a divided family; the third stage of knowledge allows detecting whether such divisions represent the normal dialec-

---

[6] See Garofalo 2002-2003.

tic exchange within the family or rather a deep inner conflict. Some legal tools, such as holdings or family agreements, can serve to maintain a higher degree of cohesion at least in terms of entrepreneurial decisions.

Leadership nature allows distinguishing two major groups of entrepreneurial families: in the first group one or two individuals have a strong influence on other members' decisions, also in areas differing from that of business (e.g. personal investments, life choices, etc.); in the second group there is not such a strong "center", one leader may be responsible for business matters, but extra-business issues are left to multiple "decision centers": people responsible for individual family branches, for their subsystems and individual heads of family. Another aspect is leadership lifecycle: in some families the leaders have just asserted their role and their young age heralds a long lasting "service" for the family; elsewhere consolidated leadership has been performing its functions for years and is still far from considering a replacement; elsewhere the family is experiencing a phase of transition at the end of which perhaps there will be a new leader.

Financial culture and service utilization mode (active or passive investor) have a strong impact on the kind of relationship that will be established between the family and the financial intermediary. Good financial culture and active attitude require the financial intermediary to have at least an identical degree of competence or the capacity to involve more competent collaborators. Moreover, he must be able to discuss best investment solutions with no signs of unwelcome superiority but highly frequent and professional communication instances.

Family members' risk propensity is obviously quite relevant for the issues discussed in this study. In fact family members with a different degree of risk propensity tend to make different investment choices regarding the portion of assets for which they can take independent decisions. Less obvious are another two considerations about risk: in the first place, if members' risk propensity is highly different, deep discussions are likely to occur when decisions must be taken about common assets; in the second place, if some members of the family show strong risk propensity, investments in new businesses or actual spin-offs are likely to be made.

Finally, sophisticated life-style is a strong differentiation element among entrepreneurial families. Different life-styles can be classified by considering how much of the annual income is invested in consumer goods by the single individual or the family as a whole. At one end there are styles where ostentation is the primary element of consumer attitudes; at the opposite end there are families that, despite their wealth, opt for discretion and reserve and thus choose not to show off and sometimes hide their financial means.

Table 1.1 Taxonomy variables for the entrepreneurial family

Structural variables			Social variables
Family Members	**Family Net Worth**	**Family-Controlled Firm**	family internal cohesion
age	total value	current economic-financial situation	leadership nature
number of members	origins		culture and service utilization mode
family members differentiation (roles or activities)	diversification degree	future strategy	family members' risk propensity
	assets distribution among family members		life-style

1.4 Current Trends in Italian Entrepreneurial Families

Some "structural forces" are changing Italian family business. Let us not analyze these forces by focusing our attention on how they can affect family structure and net worth.

Property succession

The first dynamic changing the entrepreneurial family is the high number of successions from the first to the second generation that is expected in the next few years by empirical research carried out on this issue. According to a recent survey by SDA Bocconi, over 40% of Italian entrepreneurs are over 55; thus a lot of entrepreneurs will have to manage a generation takeover within the next 10 years.

This will produce three consequences. In the first place, in view of the succession process, some families may have to diversify their net worth into extra-business monetary or anyway easily cashable assets. Diversification is sometimes necessary to meet the rights of relatives-in-law, who are usually excluded from business capital also due to marriage increased instability. Diversification can also be used to liquidate members of the family who prefer to employ their capital in a different way. Finally, it allows the family to face the succession process more safely and with some fiscal advantages.

In the second place, the succession process takes young members of the family to the lead of the company. These may be more independent than their parents when it comes to some consolidated business management models and to the family net worth. The presence of new leaders and the resulting changes in front of competitive challenges influence corporate strategy. Sometimes the maintenance strategy adopted by senior family members shifts to growth strategy, as claimed by young generations. Sometimes, on the contrary, the young opt for a consolidation strategy to avoid the risk of dispersing the capital so skillfully accumulated by the previous generation. Such behaviors have an impact on corporate financial requirements and therefore result in different investment choices.

In the third place, the senior members who have reduced their commitment inside the company may decide to employ their energies in other activities. There are cases, especially in families with a long-dated tradition and deep involvement in the social area, where senior members dedicate themselves to philanthropic or artistic foundations.

Partnership re-structuring

Another important dynamic is partnership re-structuring that has become too extended as a result of "generation drifting" processes[7]. Due to the growing presence of multi-member partnerships, re-structuring processes are likely to increase in the next few years. Some partners may decide to exit because of a loss of interest in pursuing any business undertaking or because of different strategic views or deep discrepancies regarding business conceptions and family-firm relationships or finally due to lack of trust. Such processes are always accompanied by high emotional strain. When partners' exit results from non-negotiated processes, the remaining partners feel the necessity to introduce formal governance processes and mechanisms.

Competitive dynamics

Finally, a third "force" is connected with competitive dynamics. The pressure for business growth is becoming stronger in many sectors: growing internationalization, growing medium size, growing investment in research and technology, the need for a new contractual balance in relation-

---

[7] Generation drifting indicates the increase in the number of family members due to generation changes.

ships with customers and suppliers are the main reasons for the growth pressure.

The urgency varies according to the characteristics of the specific sector, the enterprise absolute dimensions and the ratio between growth rate and financial/managerial resources available.

Up to certain dimensions (approximately €25-50m annual turnover for companies in traditional manufacturing sectors) growth is essentially based on already known development factors. Beyond such dimensions, business growth must also rely on less known factors with deferred return (internationalization, acquisitions and joint ventures) and necessary investments can be extremely high.

1.5 The Requirements of the Entrepreneurial Family and the Financial Intermediary

Variables and current trends may help the financial intermediary to identify the financial or non-financial services to be provided. In each entrepreneurial family the combination of the above described variables and the configuration of current trends produce specific needs or different priorities among the various needs.

Hereinafter we shall try and synthesize the variety of existing situations and propose a comprehensive profile of the requirements of the entrepreneurial family.

First of all, entrepreneurial families express *the need to increase their total net worth* or at least not to lose their real purchasing power in the course time. As a result, they express the following specific requirements:

- availability of financial resources in the form of debt and equity for the growth of the controlled company;

- advice on financial issues regarding the controlled company;

- availability of financial resources for startup processes of other companies promoted by family members;

- advice on investment of family's or family members' liquid assets in the controlled company;

- information about investment opportunities in non-liquid assets, such as competitors, suppliers or customers, companies operating in different industries, private equity investments, real estate and art investments;

- availability of financial resources to make investments in non-liquid assets.

In the second place, entrepreneurial families express *the need to manage their net worth*[8]. The following specific requirements fall into this area:

- management of shareholding in controlled companies through fiduciaries or trusts;

- management of real assets and other goods such as boats or art works;

- management of family or family members' liquid assets in the controlled company.

In the third place, entrepreneurial families *express the need to preserve their net worth in the course of time*. This implies the following specific requirements:

- insurance of company goods and assets as well as of extra-company components of family net worth;

- advice about business risk management (rate, exchange, etc.);

- advice about partnership re-organization aimed at reducing fiscal charges and risks as well as risks resulting from possible family conflicts;

- advice about succession different aspects (ownership and management) aimed at reducing fiscal charges and at favoring suitable entrepreneurial and managerial turnover.

- In the fourth place, entrepreneurial families express *the need to re-structure their existing net worth*. This implies the following specific requirements:

- advice about the transfer of the company or other family assets;

- scouting of operators possibly interested in partial or total purchase of the controlled company equity;

- scouting of operators possibly interested in purchasing the other family assets;

- financial resources to liquidate one or more family members.

---

[8] Here the term includes also the activities dedicated to measuring and checking the available net worth.

Needless to say entrepreneurial families express other kinds of requirements, such as education for young family members, property governance, security, household staff management and so on. Such requirements, however, do not represent a relevant area for financial intermediaries.

1.6 Families and Their Relations with Other Advisors

Financial intermediaries willing to successfully provide entrepreneurial families with financial and non-financial products and services should focus their attention onto the process to be followed in customer acquisition and in customer relation management. For this reason, apart from making reference to the previously described social variables, which are the fundamental elements when planning how to establish a relation with the entrepreneurial family, we shall proceed with a short review of the other consultants.

Entrepreneurial families that have been able not to split in the course of events have been always assisted by one or more "third actors" - that is people or institutions other than the family or the family members among whom a difficult situation had been created - who helped the family to overcome a particularly delicate phase. Financial intermediaries are, in fact, one of the third actors that can accompany the entrepreneurial family.

To identify third actors' roles it is advisable to make reference to the contribution of a renowned management author (De Geus 1997), who identifies four typical stages in learning and change processes: perception of the problem or of the opportunity, exchange of ideas for the solution to be adopted, decision-making, resulting action. Third actors may in fact play a role as per the following:

- perception stage: the third actor identifies the problem or the opportunity ahead of time and points it out to the people directly involved in the transition process. In these instances, the nature of the relationship is non-contractual (in relation to the operation being developed) and, to play this role, the third actor has already established a relation with the company or the family as proposing an opportunity or reporting a problem are actions that must be rooted in the prior knowledge of the firm-family system;

- exchange of ideas: here the third actor's role is two-fold. He can provide specific know-how which is not known to the parties directly involved in the process and/or present the experience of other companies where similar transition processes have already been faced;

- decision-making: apart from that the third actor is not entitled to take any decision, he can only help to find a common decision in the event it has to be made by more individuals;

- action taking: at this point the third actor can provide specific skills or resources by contributing to the development of certain stages of the process or by playing the role of the facilitator. At this stage the third actor usually holds a specific contractual mandate.

Therefore, the third actor's role consists in the first place in bridging a gap of knowledge or resources on the part of the entrepreneur or of the other decision-makers. Secondly, his role consists in reducing the emotional area, which is typically quite extended in the case of entrepreneurial families, and finally broadening the area of technical and economic evaluations. In other words, the third actor's contribution lies in reducing the conditions of partiality (Corticell, 1979; Simon 1996). As a matter of fact, the distinction between the two contributions meets an analytical necessity rather than a faithful representation of reality; those who provide process management skills usually provide technical competencies and those who provide technical competencies in situations as those described in our study must also possess good management skills in terms of negotiation processes.

Third actors must have a deep knowledge of the firm-family system and of the people involved in transition processes. As a result, the key requisite for the third actor's successful involvement is that he is fully trusted by all the parties involved and, above all, by the leader of the firm or the family (La Chapelle and Barnes 1998). To gain and preserve such trust, the third actor is expected to have the following distinguishing attributes:

- the technical competence he has been called for or at least the capacity to trigger competent individuals and guarantee their contribution high standard;

- the willingness to deal with the transition process by devoting the time that is necessary, by adopting sharing attitudes in front of the gradually appearing issues and avoiding the mere respect of the rules contractually agreed upon. This quality is quite important as it is extremely difficult to establish *a priori* the difficulty of a transition process in entrepreneurial families;

- transparent behavior and timely indication of areas of possible conflicts of interest;

- independent judgement, above all when responding to various clashing pressures from the different parties in the entrepreneurial family.

The third actor works in close contact with the people involved in the process and with whom he may have to spend a lot of time. For this reason, a second key requisite for the third actor's success is his esteem for these people, his sharing their basic values and his appreciating their human and professional qualities. If not so, the third actor is obliged to make a clear distinction between his convictions and beliefs and the contribution to be given: in the course of time this attitude will lead to break or reduce the importance of the relation for the parties involved. Finally, the advisor must have some personal features which make him acceptable to the commissioner (the entrepreneur or the family); this may regard such aspects as language, attitude towards time, wealth, people and so on.

A large portion of transition processes may have an erratic development subject to sudden slow-downs and just as sudden speed-ups, which are not always rationally justifiable. As a result, another key requisite for the third actor's success is his adopting a very patient attitude without getting discouraged (Gersick 1998), thus carefully avoiding any technocratic approach based on the dominance of technical specialists, which fails to understand the sometimes slow nature of decision-making processes in entrepreneurial families and therefore often turns out to be completely useless (Magretta 1998).

1.7 The Financial Intermediary as the "Third Actor"

The financial intermediary, above all if involved in medium and long term loans, in equity and asset management or private banking, can certainly play the role of the third actor in some processes.[9]. To allow this, it is important to create some organizational conditions inside and outside the institution. The following actions seem to be of crucial importance for the former:

- foster collection of information about the specific situation of the entrepreneurial family as well as about the enterprise/s by assigning officers the task to "keep in close contact" with entrepreneurs, even when no contractual relations have been established yet, so as to seize ahead of time possible chances of collaboration and to be able

---

[9] See. Par. 1.5.

to supply customized services on the basis of customer needs and preferences. More specifically, the financial intermediary is to know the family genotype, how the control on the main business is distributed among family members, partnership structure, information about the roles of family members involved in the company, information about the activities of family members who are not involved in the company, the major historical events, the elements of the family culture;

- foster officers' low turnover in their relation with entrepreneurs and families so as to encourage mutual trust, an element of major importance for sharing information that is not strictly binding under the contractual profile;

- adopt a performance valuation system which takes into account the results obtained over a relatively long period so as to enable officers to reap the fruits of the relations established with entrepreneurs;

- develop third actors' distinctive attributes in officers, by improving above all their capacity to listen to customer needs and avoiding any standardized logic and products. A further aspect of major importance is the officer's personal and cultural profile. Within the context of inside career profiles, officers coming from provincial contexts and thus accustomed to interacting with local entrepreneurs in a retail logic may in fact be transferred to big urban centers and placed in contact with larger-sized customers used to quite different, even personal, profiles;

- facilitate information conveyance within the institution so as to encourage the exchange of experiences among officers from different units (retail, investment banking, private banking) and exploit customer information synergies. At this stage it is of utmost importance not only to avoid losing the information collected at different levels but also to guarantee the strictly confidential use of such data;

- provide customers with user-friendly, accurate and continual reporting regarding current transactions, managed assets, performance valuation and comparative analysis of different portfolios.

With reference to outside organizational conditions, financial intermediaries should collaborate with other third actors so as to overcome entrepreneurs' resistance and integrate their contributions. To this aim, it is important to create a network of relations with accountants, lawyers and national or local advisors by developing ad hoc actions, such as tailored presentations or joint visits to customers.

1.8 Financial Intermediaries as Viewed by Entrepreneurial Families and Development of Family Offices

A number of entrepreneurial families have been interviewed to carry out this research and thanks to the long-dating collaboration with the Italian Association of Family Firms. In this paragraph, it seems useful to offer financial intermediaries some of the evaluations carried out by entrepreneurial families to try and seize the reason why some of them have decided to set up internal or market family offices for one or more families (see Fig. 1.1).

Italian (and not only Italian) entrepreneurial families show a rather critical attitude toward financial intermediaries. The reasons for such criticisms seem to be the following:

- negative returns obtained by even the most blazoned asset managers in the past few years. This has considerably undermined the reputation of such interlocutors by making entrepreneurial families far more sensitive to results achieved;

- the proven existence of conflicts of interest on the part of asset managers who tend to propose products that are more appealing to the manager than to the customer family;

- the service provided by intermediaries is not sufficiently customized; services are differentiated according to total net worth, whereas other qualitative aspects regarding either the net worth or the family are totally neglected;

- the widespread attitude of "intellectual superiority", which is particularly annoying in the presence of the above mentioned negative performances when, may be, the entrepreneurial family has been able to obtain positive performances in their controlled companies.

All of these elements, along with the growing financial culture of younger members in entrepreneurial families, have led some families, individually or with others, to import the so-called family offices from abroad. These are offices or companies (controlled by entrepreneurial families owning or formerly owning one or more businesses in the manufacturing, commercial or service industry) providing assistance in financial and non-financial matters to the members of entrepreneurial families. Four types of family offices can be identified by using two dimensions (Fig. 1.1): i) the number of families owning one or more family offices; ii) family office customer families that can be exclusively the owners or also others.

Fig. 1.1 Types of family offices

	NUMBER OF OWNER FAMILIES	
	1	**>1**
Only Owners	Mono internal family office	Multi Internal family office
FAMILIES AS CUSTOMES		
Owners and others	Mono multi family office	Market multi family office

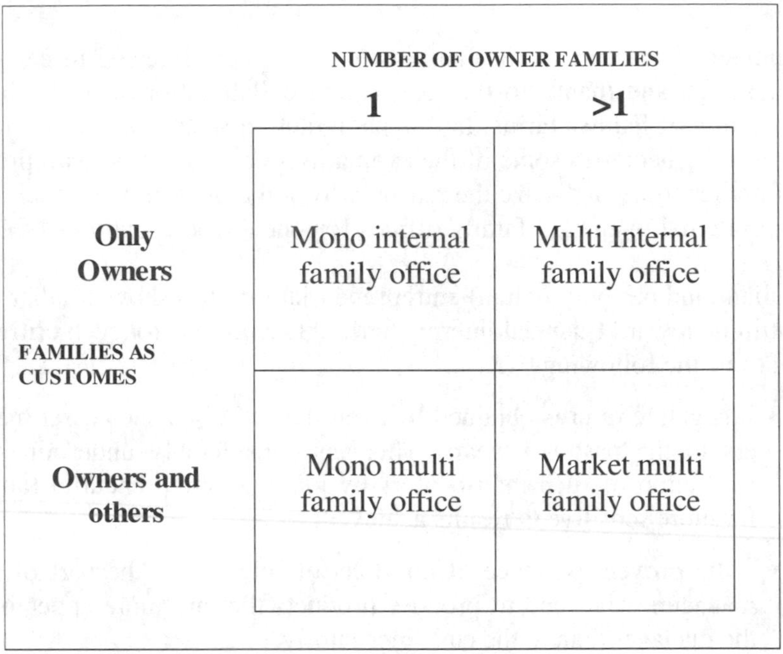

The four types of family offices can be described as follows:

- "internal mono-family office": the structure is usually non-profit and provides services exclusively to the family that has founded it, bears the expenses and not rarely fully owns it. Sometimes it can be founded by more families holding common interests (for example shareholdings in the same family firm);

- "internal multi-family office": the structure is usually non-profit and provides services exclusively to the families that have founded it, bear the expenses and not rarely fully own it;

- "market mono-family office": the structure is usually profit oriented, controlled by an entrepreneurial family and sells services to the partner family and to other families as well;

- "market multi-family office": the structure is usually profit oriented, controlled by more entrepreneurial families and sells services to partner families and to other families as well.

There exist other kinds of family offices: they are controlled by independent partners with or without entrepreneurial families in the capital, they are profit oriented and provide services to more non-interconnected families.

Entrepreneurial families who have decided to set up their own family offices, or to use family office services, always aim at satisfying two major requirements: improve the management of their net worth and create a unitary family spirit. In some cases, with the family office, the entrepreneurial family aims at a profit.

As for the first requirement, the family office presents the following advantages in comparison to the decision to have family assets managed by one or more financial intermediaries:

- independence: the family looks for interlocutors that are free to choose the products they consider most suitable for the management of family assets;

- competence: the family can gather round their assets a group of highly qualified professionals who can be timely replaced, if necessary;

- a team of managers and professionals who collaborate by sharing their expertise above all on financial, legal and fiscal matters, thus ensuring specialized and complementary knowledge;

- customization can be offered as the family office is set up in order to meet the needs of one or just a few families and usually the number of customers is quite limited;

- familiar relation: the family office is like a partner with whom the family can interact with great opening, intensity and express their opinion freely. Moreover, the family office staff use the same language as the entrepreneurial families, which undoubtedly encourages a profitable dialogue;

- unique interlocutor: the family office may become the sole interlocutor for all the questions related to assets management, thus facilitating time saving and a unitary vision of issues and performances;

- timely decision and action: the family office can dialogue with the entrepreneurial family with great timeliness and thus proceed with no hesitation to the accomplishment of steps agreed as all the authorizations that are typical of financial institutions needn't overcoming.

The elements analyzed so far represent the main reasons why the entrepreneurial family may decide to resort to the collaboration of the family office. A second decisional step consists in choosing whether to set up internal or market family office (make) or use the services provided by third parties (buy) (Fig. 1.2).

Fig. 1.2 Key decisions regarding the family office

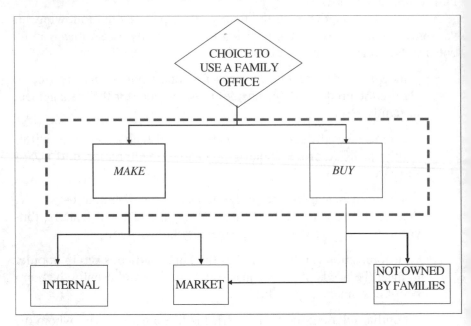

The decision to set up an "internal mono-family office", according to our respondents, depends on the total assets available that have not been invested in the family firm as well as on the do-it-myself attitude and the presence of one or more family members interested in dealing with the matter directly. The decision to set up an "internal multi-family office" along with other entrepreneurial families essentially depends on existing connections with other families, which must be characterized by extreme familiarity and complete trust. On the contrary, the decision to set up a "market family office" essentially results from a diversification choice of the owner families who believe in their capacity to understand the needs of similar families. Some entrepreneurial families make the less demanding decision to resort to the services provided by family offices owned by third parties.

2 Private Banking and Family Business: Positioning and Development

Paola Musile Tanzi

2.1 Introduction

"Family firms are enterprises in which one or more families interconnected by family links and sound alliances detain the power to appoint governance bodies". This is how the Associazione Italiana delle Imprese Familiari defines family business.

In this chapter the field of investigation is limited to the typology of services provided by financial intermediaries operating, in particular, in the areas of private banking and wealth management, to assist this specific market segment, where the complexity of private needs is bound to grow as a result of their interweaving with the evolution of business dynamics and vice versa.

Family business designed services require the effort and the capacity to adopt an integrated view of the "family" and the "business" originated by the family itself.

The analysis of client requirements through comprehensive view and planning is part of the mission of several private banking and wealth management structures, both for the nature of recipients and the typology of the contents. This goal can be pursued through processes able to develop synergies among the bank different business areas.

In this chapter we shall review the reasons leading banks to create a structure where initially highly specialized business areas are later subject to integration not to miss growth opportunities in this sector. In particular, the perspective adopted is that of the evolution of private banking services toward family wealth management criteria, thus trying to identify necessary competencies and feasible organizational solutions.

2.2 The Development of Banking Between Specialization and Integration

The attempt at best serving client needs led banks toward a process of specialization by customer segments with the resulting creation of structures dedicated to retail, private and corporate banking.

In Italy this process started developing in the early '90s and a number of highly differentiated organization structures have been originated. The same variety can be observed in other countries and it is the natural result of enterprises capable of gradually adjusting to external changes always seeking for solutions consistent with their historical background and resources.

Choices and business processes can be interpreted in the light of three aspects that contribute to developing different models of organizational behavior:

- complexity;

- degree of formalization;

- degree of centralization.

"The complexity of an organization depends on the number of activities, functions and tasks, on the degree of diversity and the type of interdependence among the same. Coordination and control are more problematic in highly complex organizations, where activities are multiple and highly interdependent and interpersonal relations are more frequent. Complexity is usually higher in larger-sized organizations.

The degree of formalization refers to the frequency of utilization of policies, routine procedures, formal and written rules, which restrict the choices of the organization members.

The term centralization refers to the distribution of power and authority within the organization"[1].

In a highly dynamic market environment, the complexity of the organization tends to grow, whereas the degree of formalization and centralization may vary in the course of time and different degrees may co-exist within the same organization depending of the activity being developed.

The identification of client segments with different requirements has induced banks to design segment-differentiated and specialized organization units. The degree of formalization of these units and the distribution of power and authority vary from bank to bank, but the degree of organiza-

---

[1] Tosi, Pilati, Mero, Rizzo 2002.

tion complexity as well as the need for coordination among the different units has certainly increased.

Specialization may be restricted to the identification of dedicated functions and services or rather fostered to such an extent to create a divisional structure, where each division - retail banking, private banking and corporate banking - represents an independent income and cost center with its own independence in sales and investment policies. This segment-specialization does not exclude the joint utilization of other specialization criteria for business areas where technical competencies are quite high, like investment banking, asset management...[2].

In Italy the extreme concept of segment specialization led *Gruppo Unicredito* to create three different banks respectively focused on a sole client segment: *Unicredit Banca, Unicredit Private Banking* and *Unicredit Banca d'Impresa*[3]. The Group aims at growing by exploiting the specialization of the new divisional business model, which was adopted in 2003, as well as the interdivisional synergies between "production" and "distribution".

Once the specialization process has been accomplished, regardless of the adopted organization structure, the pursuit of integration is started not to miss the opportunity for creating synergies among the units. Once again, possible coordination mechanisms are multiple and their different combination contributes to organization diverse development.

Coordination mechanisms can be in fact standardized into rules and procedures or instead grounded on plans and programs (budget, strategic plans,...) or on principles of mutual adjustment (lateral relations, groups, integration bodies, organization culture...). In particular, these processes

---

[2] "No choice or criteria can be absolutely valid or applied to all of the organization structures. The choice of the criterion depends on environmental conditions and management preferences...", Tosi, Pilati, Mero, Rizzo 2002. As for the multiple segmentation criteria and relative organizational consequences, see Chapter 3 by Caselli.

[3] "Unicredit Banca d'Impresa has the mission to become the reference bank of corporate clients. These include private and public owned enterprises and organizations whose sizes, legal structures and organizational behaviors require specialist services and dedicated assistance for the business activity... Unicredit Private Banking has the mission to take the lead in the Italian market of services dedicated to highest-standing private clients through highly qualified advisory competencies. Unicredit Banca has the mission to control the market of families and small business and to provide basic services (transactions and operating assistance) to Private and Corporate Banks in the areas where they have no direct operative branches", Unicredito Italiano, Bilancio e Relazione 2002.

trigger inter-functional working teams capable of accomplishing projects that require interdisciplinary competencies or involve joint targets.

With reference to family business, the segment is extremely wide: small family business and professionals fall into the bank retail target, whereas for medium or large family businesses the synergy that might lead to integrated service offering is between private banking and corporate banking[4].

In the case of large family firms with very high personal wealth, the concept of the interdisciplinary team can be fostered up to create task forces dedicated to solving unique, particular and hardly ever repeatable matters[5].

The complexity of structures and coordination mechanisms thus depends on the nature of the target market, the first critical aspect in the design of the range of services to be proposed to clients. On this subject, the lack of well defined borders in the area of private banking, allows outlining different positioning hypotheses with respect to private customers. Ambiguity extends beyond the borders and affects the lexicon: the broadness of the target segment leads in fact to utilize the term *wealth management,* sometimes to underline the intermediary's wish to manage the entire family wealth, sometimes to indicate the top section of the private market.

2.3 The Target Market for Private Banking and Wealth Management

As for the nature of recipients, in private banking client segmentation is made by "family nuclei". The approach to client analysis starts from the "family" as an entity and not from the single individual. This is confirmed by that the Italian potential market of private banking is estimated on the basis of the "family" population distributed over the national territory and that the potential market represented by *Affluent* and *Top* clients is extrapolated from this figure (Fig. 2.1).

---

[4] For the variety of the segment of family business depending on the size and wealth of the business and the family, see Chapter 5 by Gatti.

[5] "…Organizations designed to tackle unique and non-repetitive tasks will organize specialists into homogeneous groups for "internal management" purposes and into task forces for operative purposes", Thompson 2002. The family office is the structured application of the concept of the task force dedicated to the problems of one or more big families.

Fig. 2.1 Estimate of private banking potential market in Italy

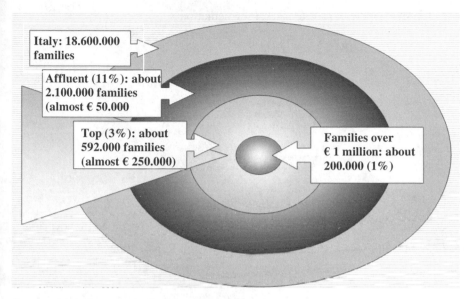

Italy: 18.600.000 families

Affluent (11%): about 2.100.000 families (almost € 50.000

Top (3%): about 592.000 families (almost € 250.000)

Families over € 1 million: about 200.000 (1%)

Source: Multifinanziaria Eurisko, 2003

That being stated, it should be underlined that private banking target market may be re-organized into very large groups of clients on the basis of:

- presence of manageable assets or wealth size;

- customization degree of service demand and complexity degree of requirements.

As for manageable assets, a model proposed at international level by Merrill Lynch identifies the following segments:

- *Affluent* over US$100,000;

- *High Net Worth Individuals (HNWIs)* from US$500,000;

- *Very-High Net Worth Individuals* over US$5million;

- *Ultra-High Net Worth Individuals* over US$50million (Fig. 2.2).

Segmentation depending on manageable assets is extremely limited and it may help to understand the need for further market segmentation. Moreover, the same segmentation criteria are subject to variations; an international estimate of the number of HNWIs by Merrill Lynch uses different segmentation criteria by indicating US$30m instead of 50m net assets for Ultra-High Net Worth Individuals (Fig. 2.3).

Fig. 2.2 An example of private market segmentation

Source: Merrill Lynch – Cap Gemini, World Wealth Report 2002

Fig. 2.3 Number of High Net Worth Individuals by manageable assets; a world estimate, 2002 (thousands)

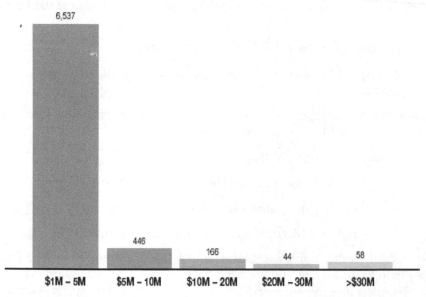

Source: Merrill Lynch-Cap Gemini Ernst&Young, World Wealth Report 2003

In Italy, the target market of private banking services provided by domestic banks is the segment of *High Net Worth Individuals;* this does not exclude a great interest for the *Affluent* segment. The matching of the *Affluent* segment with that of *HNWIs* is connected with the path pursued by Italian banks since the mid-Nineties and with a number of relevant factors, among which:

- in the first place, the original retail vocation of most of the Italian banks. The result of this matrix is the natural closeness to the *Affluent* market and the gradual acquisition of legitimization as interlocutor and service provider of private clients;

- in the second place, the definition of the market borders can be explained as an organizational necessity, but the differences between the requirements perceived by the clients in the *Affluent* and *HNWI* segments are very subtle. This leads to adopt a flexible approach to segmentation. For example, the family with a €500,000 net worth does not show very different requirements from the family with a €1m net worth. That being stated, the *Affluent* segment is sometimes squeezed back into the private client segment as they are characterized by similar complexity of requirements, potential, income, status and represent the prospect market capable of feeding the private segment in the future;

- finally, the positioning of private banking services in a medium-high range of private clients, allows holding a stronger bargaining power within the customer relation than with client segments in the high-very high range that are characterized by a bargaining power comparable to that of institutional clients. Customers in the *Very* or *Ultra-High Net Worth* segments, thanks to the volumes they represent, may demand for special pricing conditions that force banks to heavily reduce their gains, down to the paradoxical instance of complete annulment. Only the bank with strong presence and experience in the institutional market can actually offset the bargaining power of *Ultra-HNW* customers; this explains the positioning in the high-very high range of private customers by foreign banks with a long-dated tradition in investment banking.

With regard to the degree of customization of the demanded service, some considerations should be made about the meaning and the consequences of highly customized services.

In the first place, the term "customization" is frequently opposed to the expression "standardization", where the former is usually assigned a positive meaning and the latter a negative one. As a matter of fact, the identification of standards implies the existence of processes in which quality parameters must be complied with and this does not represent a negative element at all. On the contrary, service customization may hide a handicraft view which allows a lot of discretionary margins with not necessarily positive consequences on the control over service quality.

The difficulty in quality control is to be attributed to the fact that higher levels of customization enable clients to tailor their own services to their specific requirements. Customer contribution to the production process makes it more complicated and slower and leads to the formulation of unique solutions. Uniqueness has a very high cost both during "production" and in the following monitoring of adopted solutions, given the impossibility of making "standard" controls.

Pricing differentiation should enable each client segment to obtain the degree of customization they can actually sustain. If the preference goes to the handicraft model, resulting pros and cons should also be accepted along with positive and negative deviations from "average standards", including price.

What seems to be quite inconsistent is that providers face the challenge of a highly diversified market due to client needs complexity and strong bargaining power with a sole model of supply (Fig. 2.4). The private market requires detailed segmentation and differentiated solutions. The degree of customization must be economically sustainable; hence, it is reasonable to think of growing client focus and provide unique services to *Ultra-High Net Worth* individuals, where one-to-one segmentation criteria can be applied.[6]

---

[6] "The segment of 58,000 ultra-HNWIs around the world, a particular and exclusive segment, illustrates the importance of segmentation. To serve this group, providers have traditionally formed exclusive multi-disciplinary teams armed with a diverse set of capabilities to serve an individual's needs. Typically, ultra-HNWIs are a leading indicator of emerging HNWI needs and demands. Consequently, providers are increasingly facing the challenge of balancing client expectations for tailored offering with economic sustainability and effectiveness.", Merrill Lynch-Cap Gemini Ernst&Young, World Wealth Report 2003.

Fig. 2.4 Private market segmentation by client needs complexity and bargaining power

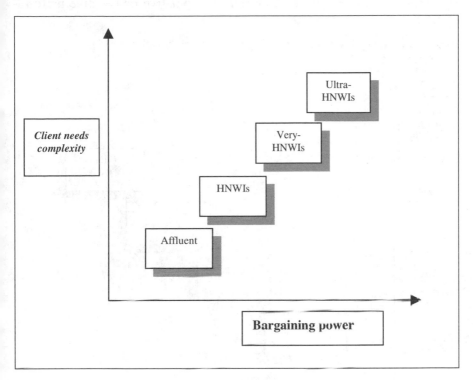

The possibility of service standardization decreases as client needs complexity grows and professional competencies involved in the offering process increase.

When private banking services are positioned in the *Affluent* and *HNWI* segments, task specialization criteria prevail in organization units. In other words, goal achievement is divided into sub-processes assigned to different managers. In this perspective, the relationship manager is usually assigned the responsibility of the relationship with the client, while the asset management unit is responsible for client portfolio performance.

Due to task specialization, there is a coordination effort of roles and responsibilities between the distribution unit of private banking services and the production unit of asset management services, whereas mechanisms favoring integration with other specialized units within the bank are far less common.

The problem is that the wide-ranging service offering is not always accompanied by client asset/liability integrated view. This does not facilitate the adoption of a financial planning approach that, instead, would lead the client to assess the value added of the service received on the basis of elements not exclusively focused on portfolio positive or negative performances.

Fig. 2.5 Client needs complexity and specialized organization

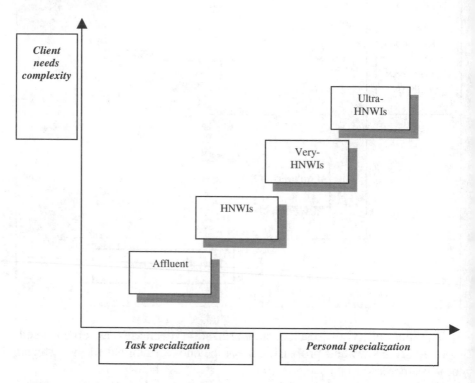

When private banking services are positioned in the *Very-HNWI* and *Ultra-HNWI* segments, personal specialization criteria prevail in the organization. In other words, units are composed by professionals, capable of controlling the entire process they are assigned, from distribution to production. This does not mean the service is actually produced by the team of professionals, but that they can control the whole process thanks to their competencies and expertise.

For this reason, in the design of functions within the organization unit dedicated to the *Ultra-HNWI* segment, the relationship manager is supported or even substituted by the portfolio manager. The latter is directly responsible for the portfolio performances as to financial investments. As for the other services, necessary competencies and professionals are sought inside[7] and outside the bank.

When the wealth grows larger, not always, but frequently, family needs become more complex as regards their estates, their entrepreneurial businesses, their fiscal and succession position... In fact family business services designed for families owning large-sized enterprises are also provided by law and taxation firms capable of tackling issues of governance, legal structure, tax rationalization, succession.

The supply of integrated services leads to the adoption of a planning approach within the family dynamic. For example, in Italy Unicredit Private Bank propose their clients the service of wealth planning, that is *"a detailed analysis of all the components of the family and personal wealth: real assets, financial assets, business assets."*

When client needs complexity requires extremely customized services, the bank may succeed in matching client expectations with bank expected remuneration by dropping the bank approach and taking up family office structures, where the integrated competencies of more professionals are entirely dedicated to one or more families.

2.4 The Financial Offer for Family Wealth Management

With reference to the typology of contents, the evolution of the service offering in the area of private banking leads to a comprehensive view of client needs in the perspective of global financial planning.

To "unhinge" Swiss banks' monopoly, Anglo-Saxon banks entered this business area trying to identify the weakness of market leaders. Despite their secular tradition as portfolio managers, Swiss banks confined their offer to assets management. As a result, the policy pursued by American banks to acquire reliability and reputation among private clients lay in differentiating services dedicated to entrepreneurs and chief executives, by proposing services based upon an asset/liability integrated view. The logic of asset/liability management, which had already been applied in bank management, was thus applied to highest standing private clients[8].

---

[7] In this respect, Unicredit Private Banking uses the services provided by Unicredit Consulting, the unit specialized in legal, fiscal and company advisory, controlled by Gruppo Unicredit.

[8] JPMorgan proposes their clients customized solutions for liability optimization: "...When deciding how to raise needed capital, you often face a choice between liquidating invested assets and using leverage. We can help you compare the costs and risks associated with both alternatives, taking into account interest expense,

Therefore the Anglo-Saxon model of private banking is based on the "all-round" management of client wealth and favors long-term client relationships, where evaluation factors are not exclusively focused on portfolio performances, but also on the value added resulting from a set of services with contents regarding tax and succession matters or legal, real estate, insurance, social security issues or problems connected with the management of art works or any particular events in the course of client lives...

The implementation of this fully comprehensive approach is facilitated by the adoption of some typical activities of personal financial planning. Since the Seventies, personal financial planning has been proposed by a number of independent professional firms to *Ultra-HNW* families. This methodology is an ideal integrating mechanism in the production process of solutions for private clients. This has induced some banks, like Bank of New York, to arrange a team of professionals dedicated to this activity. The loss of independence resulting from the development of this activity within the bank, occurs under circumstances of absolute transparency for the client and is partially offset by the possibility of finding the best solutions in the market that are provided by external firms in a logic of open architecture.

Nowadays the Anglo-Saxon approach to the private market characterizes major global players in the sector, independently from their original matrix. Swiss banks too have definitely overcome the model limited to asset portfolio management and propose a broad range of services supported by systematic global financial planning. For example, *UBS Private Banking*, *Credit Suisse Private Banking*, *Julius Baer* describe financial planning as the "basic" process on which the bank can build a differentiated range of customized solutions.

This model is characterized by elements of unquestionable appeal both for the client and the bank but remarkable organizational efforts have to be made to guarantee high-standard quality. What appeals to the client is the availability of a sole interlocutor upon analysis of needs and the offering of a wide range of solutions. On the other hand, this business model appeals

---

transaction costs, capital gains tax exposure, and the potential investment return that you may forego. Whatever your purpose, we can provide advice in the context of your overall objectives and wealth plan, and we can customize a solution with an optimal debt structure. JPMorgan is a leading provider of credit to private clients. We can lend against almost any type of asset, including art, real estate, aircraft, restricted stock, concentrated stock positions, and certain stock options. If you face an unusual or complex situation – a cross-border transaction, a challenging legal or tax structure, a liquidity need at a closely held company – we have the expertise and global presence to address it". www.jpm.com.

to the bank because it allows achieving client fidelity, diversifying income sources, being judged not only on the basis of performances and becoming the client partner in areas where performance valuation is by definition in the medium-long term, for example, in real estate, succession planning...

The possibility of receiving comprehensive solutions and the need for a customized design are very high among *Very-HNW* and *Ultra-HNW* clients. For this reason, there are roles, services and structures specifically dedicated to these segments within private banking. The complexity of the service reaches its maximum degree when the target market is represented by clients characterized by family business sharing.

As for this market, *Bank of New York* underlines that the approach philosophy to family business requirements must produce unique solutions since the needs expressed by families are just as unique. *"Families who have achieved a substantial level of prosperity have very unique needs. Given the complex and multi-faceted nature of their financial situation, growing, managing and preserving their assets presents a challenge in itself. The greater challenge for many successful families lies in creating a lasting legacy through the business enterprises they have built, the charitable causes they have supported, and their ability to impart to future generations the lesson that with wealth comes opportunity as well as responsibility."*

To tackle the complexity and the multiplicity of the needs expressed by this typology of families, *Bank of New York* offers multi-disciplinary competencies of professionals with long-dated experience: *"Established exclusively to meet the needs of wealthy families, our Family Wealth Management group provides a multi-disciplinary resource. We have assembled a specialized team comprised of seasoned professionals with backgrounds in financial, tax and estate planning, investment consulting, asset management, trusts, accounting, banking and customized lending. Responsible for a limited number of relationships, the team devotes time and expertise to understand the unique goals of each family and provide comprehensive solutions that are distinct and individualized as the families themselves. Through this personalized approach, we can guide you with insight to help you achieve your objective"*.

To these families *Bank of New York* provides services of:

- *Wealth Transition*, i.e. solutions relating to specific moments that may create temporary needs of liquidity connected with changes in the structure or the management of the family business;

- *Wealth Management*, custody and reporting, investment consulting, asset management, risk management, customized lending and banking.

- *Wealth Preservation,* fiduciary services, succession planning, charitable gifting, tax and estate and insurance planning, assistance in the education process of future generations.

In family wealth management the main goal lies in assisting clients with reference to the ownership, governance and management of the family business as well as in growing the family nucleus. This ambitious goal urges the bank to identify which organization structure should be adopted for services supply in order to maximize customer satisfaction and preserve an adequate income profile for the bank.

Bank of New York provides this service in the area of *"Private Client Services"*, which belongs to *"Servicing and Fiduciary Businesses"*, one of the four businesses making up the Bank activity[9], along with Corporate banking, Retail banking and Financial markets.

A different choice characterizes the positioning of the Group *Credit Suisse*. To guarantee utmost independence of proposed solutions and separate the activity designed for international highly complex clients from that provided to the private market as a whole, *Credit Suisse Private Banking* proposes family office services to customers characterized by an over US$50m net worth through the held company *Credit Suisse Trust*. In October 2002 this company was re-organized so as to guarantee maximum independence and provide wealth management integrated solutions for *Ultra-HNWIs*. Their presence in this segment is being enhanced by providing family office services designed for customers living particular periods of transition (sale of corporate assets, mergers and acquisitions, succession plans or re-allocations) at their branches in London and Zurich. Moreover, Frye-Louis Capital Management, a company based in Chicago and specialized in the US segment of family office, was acquired in October 2001.

---

[9] "Servicing and Fiduciary business comprise the Company's core services, including securities servicing, global payment services, and private client services and asset management. These businesses all share certain favorable attributes: they are well diversified and fee based; the Company serves the role of an intermediary rather than principal, thereby limiting risk and generating stable earning streams, and businesses are scalable, which result in higher margins as revenues grow. Long-term trends that favor these businesses include the growth of financial asset worldwide, the globalization of investment activity, heightened demand for financial servicing outsourcing and continuing structural changes in financial markets.", Bank of New York, Annual Report 2002.

2.5 Family Office as the Organizational Solution for Family Business

The family office represents an organizational solution able to meet the requirements of family business. The unique needs of *Ultra-HNWIs* may require high levels of specialization and customization that justify the creation of dedicated structures, in particular if such needs are connected with family business management requirements.

The family office approach is the formalization of a task force aimed at the problems of one or more families (multi-family office). In the family office, in fact, a team of specialists with multidisciplinary competencies is dedicated to one or more family nuclei.

The family office shared by more families originates from the advantage of having a sufficient critical mass of assets to develop scale economies. In this respect, the trend shows an increase in the net worth well over US$ 100m[10]. In some cases, the indication given to client families is that when the net worth is between US$ 50m and US$ 500m, it is advisable to create multi-family office structures.

In the organization of the private or multi-family office, cases are quite varied. Three different matrices can be distinguished:

- family-originated family office;

- bank-originated family office;

- independent family office.

In the first case, one or more families decide to create a structure dedicated to their wealth management, using professional competencies already existing in the families or recruited in the market. At times the internal family office is managed by family members that are not involved in the core business or interested in preserving the family wealth after disinvestment of the family business. The goal lies in centralizing minimum competencies within the family nucleus to select the best external solutions in the areas of financial, tax, legal, estate management... In some cases the structures created to satisfy the needs of the original family nucleus be-

---

[10] A recent presentation by Family Office Exchange, a US association aiming at fostering the exchange of information and best practice in the sector of family office, points out the change in the definition of wealth from US$ 100 million to US$ 1 billion". Family Office Exchange processes the data of about 350 US Family Offices www.foxexchange.com.

come service providers also for other families in the logic of a Family-to-Family market.[11]

In the second case, the family office is organized by the bank and serves one or more families. The bank selects the competencies for the structure on behalf of the client. Best client solutions will be found within the bank or by resorting to third-party providers. The external family office allows the entrepreneur to concentrate on the family business and to entrust the bank with the selection of necessary competencies and organization modes.

As a matter of fact, also some bank-family offices originate in a Family-to-Family logic, as these structures are originally created to follow the wealth of the entrepreneur banker and bank owner. This is the case, for example, of *Julius Baer*, a private Swiss bank, present in sector of family business through *Julius Baer Family Office Ltd.* (Fig. 2.6).

The last is an independent company serving *Ultra-High Net Worth* families and entrepreneurs: *"As the size and diversity of your assets increase, so too does the complexity of the issues and challenges involved in managing them. To meet this special need, we have created Julius Baer Family Office Ltd., an independent company providing all-round services for wealthy families and entrepreneurs. In both cases, the Family Office is synonymous with first-class, comprehensive advice and services extending well beyond purely financial matters."*

---

[11] In Italy, Sicofind srl is an example of family office with family origins: it was set up to serve the interests of the Zanibon family and is now operating for more entrepreneurs according to the Family-to-Family logic; Francesco Aletti Montano & Co, from the name of the founder, is another example. For the different typologies of Family Offices with family origins see the analysis by M. Corbetta about the development of this sector.

Fig. 2.6 Julius Baer Family Office: an example of bank-originated family office

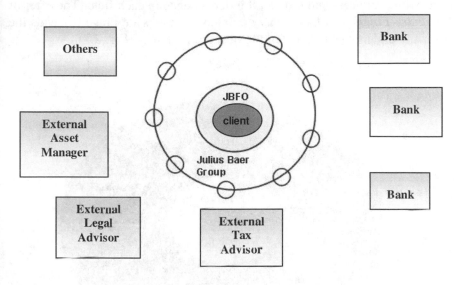

Source: www.juliusbaer.com, Julius Baer

Like *Bank of New York* for the service of family wealth management, *Julius Baer Family Office* underlines, on the one hand, the adoption of a multi-disciplinary approach to financial consulting and on the other the adoption of the principles of independence and openness. This is the logic of the open-architecture, where the structure is ready to find the solutions best suiting client interests in the outside market whenever no or simply unsuitable responses are provided by the Group: *"Julius Baer Family Office takes an <u>interdisciplinary approach</u> to financial counseling. We consult external specialists whenever necessary and adhere rigorously to the <u>principles of openness and independence</u> because we believe them to be in our clients' best interests. We coordinate services specially tailored to our clients' requirements for all aspects of asset management and consulting, estate and tax planning as well as a broad range of fiduciary and ancillary services. The experience, integrity and corporate culture you can expect from Julius Baer also form the basis of the professional client services offered by Julius Baer Family Office."*

In the third case, the family office is set up and managed by an independent firm of professionals with a background experience in legal, tax and financial matters,…The open architecture choice is intrinsic to these firms, whose vocation is all-round consulting based on financial planning.

These firms of independent financial advisors are specialized in the *Ultra-HNWI* segment and their strength is the complete absence of connections with producers and thus total independence in each field. The offer of *Signature Financial Management* emphasizes the wide range of needs the company undertakes to solve in the best possible way (Fig. 2.7).

Fig. 2.7 The independent family office

Source: www.sigfin.com - *Signature Financial Management, inc.*

As for outsourcing or insourcing choices, no general indications can be provided for the family-originated family offices as each family presents a different case. It would be misleading to make evaluations out of the specific context.

Irrespective of the matrix, the common features of family offices are:

- competencies integration;

- client focus;

- independence: in the case of bank-originated family offices, it is ensured by open architecture.

The first aspect is the "fundamental" element of the family office, i.e. the presence of a team of specialists capable of sharing their knowledge and expertise for solution optimization. The multi-disciplinary team of experts is the essential requisite for offering a broad range of solutions. The team of professionals represents an intrinsic restriction to segment development. Necessary competencies are found in senior professionals and necessary training processes are not too fast.

The design of these solutions is strongly focused on the client and each solution reflects unique needs. Extreme focus produces a business model where clients design their own "Client-to-Client" services, which in this particular case become the "Family-to-Family" model.

Independence refers to the identification of the best solution without any form of conditioning on the part of producers' sales policies. This implies the need for severe selection processes of providers and for the constant monitoring of performances after the choice has been made[12].

The production process that aims at the design, management and monitoring of unique solutions by expert professionals with multidisciplinary competencies is, by definition, scarcely routine, poorly standardized and, hence, a costly process.

IT supports for information research, management and monitoring contribute to rising costs of the production process. Fostering open-architecture structures without adequate IT equipment capable of internal/external information aggregation would mean accepting to lose client risk control.

The presence of excellent competencies and advanced technologies represents a barrier against the access into this market segment and imposes "restricted growth models".

According to the data of *Family Office Exchange*, in the USA over 3,500 families own a dedicated family office, about 50 institutions or families have set up a multi-family office. In Europe about 200 families have structured family offices and even more have informal structures.

On the basis of the evidence relating to the US experience, some trends can be identified in relation to the contents, in particular:

- growing integration of services and adoption of risk management approach to the family wealth;

- management of financial assets through "funds of funds" and growing attention to indexed funds or alternative investments;

- stress on family members education, family continuity and philanthropic purposes.

With reference to the first aspect, service integration results from the multidisciplinary competencies expressed by the team of specialists that make up the structure. Consulting is developed with the primary goal to keep risk under control, risk that is connected with investments, taxation,

---

[12] Cf. Musile Tanzi 2003.

business and family. The approach to risk management aims not only at measuring but also at managing the different typologies of risk.

Fig. 2.8 Multidisciplinary advice and risk management: two key elements in family office services

Source: www.foxexhange.com

As for asset management, strategies are aimed at keeping portfolio risks under control by means of funds. The process of asset allocation is based on the selection of the best funds in the market, without excluding passive funds and paying special attention to alternative investments, like hedge funds and private equity. There is high interest in the former, as shown by that today 70% of assets invested in hedge funds come from *High Net Worth* clients. At the end of 2002 there were 7,500 hedge funds[13], classifiable into a multitude of different management styles; this makes the selection, management and monitoring of the fund portfolio quite difficult. This activity represents the core business of most of the European family offices.

With reference to the training and educational process of family members, family continuity and pursuit of philanthropic actions, the tendency to include such activities into the family office is evident above all in the United States. There the external context encourages the comparison among alternative educational courses as well as the traditional private support to public interest activities. Moreover, in a proactive logic, the family office tends to design courses of action aimed not only at invest-

---

[13] www.vanhedge.com.

ment optimization but also at managing dynamics ensuring family continuity.

The propensity to grow the service value added in a multitude of interconnected fields, leads to reflect upon the cost of underlying production processes and service pricing. No doubt the wish to grow assets under management in a multi-family-office logic meets the need for lower fixed costs, though complying with the initial promise of unique solutions for family requirements.

Just as difficult is the concept of average pricing due to the diversity and uniqueness of provided services, the size of the assets under management and the already mentioned strong bargaining power of this client segment.

These reasons may explain the dispersion of replies revealed by *Family Office Exchange* to the question about the cost of pro-active wealth management of assets amounting to US$ 200m. The question is asked to family office managers (about 350) affiliated to the association (Fig. 2.9).

Fig. 2.9 How much should pro-active wealth management cost in the case of assets amounting to US$ 200m, excluding money management cost?

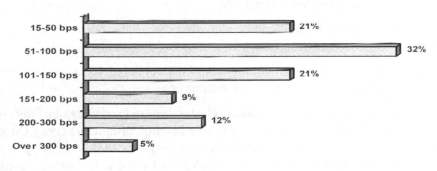

Source: www.foxexchange.com

Needless to underline that the question, not casually, refers to US$200m assets and that increasingly often feasible scale economies are considered also in this sector.

2.6 Private Banking, Wealth Management and Family Business: Critical Aspects

Over the past few years, the business area of private banking/wealth management has been subject to relevant pressures as a result of the slower pace of the world economy, the negative trend of stock markets and their high volatility, business scandals and the following restrictions by supervisory authorities.

These exogenous factors have not only limited or sometimes undermined the growth of wealth[14], but have also contributed to accentuating the perception of insecurity by clients who, on the one hand, are now feeling a stronger need to recuperate a consulting relation and, on the other, are more fragile and distrustful due to not always positive experiences.

Such experiences were also responsible for a kind of revival of more conservative attitudes in the field of investments, where now the prevailing goal is wealth preservation rather than the more aggressive wealth growth. In the meantime, there is a major need for bank customized services tailored to client requirements.

In front of this market, private banking operations present quite uncertain economic profiles. Private banking can no longer be considered a business area characterized by high and stable fees, low costs if compared with retail banking, limited risk and thus low necessity of invested assets. The present scenario features deeply different traits:

- income structure is subject to the pressure of reduced margins produced by growing competition;

- risk level has significantly increased due to the relevant operating risk; investments have grown and so has the allocated capital;

- cost structure has grown heavier in the course of years and in some cases become an element of weakness[15].

Economic conditions in this business area require careful evaluations on the profitability of the structure and on the level of sustainable costs. Once again, it is not significant to reason by average terms in this sector, given the variety of organization structures adopted by the different operating units. Then it is useful to observe that even in this case there is a dispersion of results regarding a benchmarking activity carried out by *Boston Consulting Group* in relation to a sample of about sixty international institutions[16].

With reference to income, the survey gives results per unit, i.e. income per relationship manager. This item is further divided into three factors:

---

[14] Cfr. Merrill Lynch-Cap Gemini Ernst&Young, *World Wealth Report 2003*.
[15] Musile Tanzi June 2003, n. 92/03 www.sdabocconi.it.
[16] The geographical distribution of the sample includes 21 participants in North-America, 21 in Europe and 19 in Asia, see "Prospering in Uncertain Time, Global wealth 2002", The Boston Consulting Group, www.bcg.com.

- number of clients per relationship manager;

- average volume of client assets and liabilities (CAL) under management;

- yield on managed volumes.

The US$411,000 average income per relationship manager results from a distribution where the maximum value is US$7m and the minimum value is under US$1m and the highest frequency of values is below the average.

Also the number of clients per manager seems scarcely significant. One explanation for the high dispersion of the average data can be the presence in the sample of very heterogeneous offering models that are positioned in different segments within the private market. The average of 131 clients per relationship manager is high and likely to be distorted by the presence of seven banks with over 250 clients per relationship manager, a case probably positioned in the *Affluent* market[17].

The average CAL volume is about US$4m and this integrated management logic of assets and liabilities results in an average income of 74 basis points for the bank.

Great variance is also revealed by the analysis of the cost structure. Indicative is the cost-to-income ratio per relationship manager: 54.55 per cent in the top quartile of leading companies as against 96.15 per cent in the bottom quartile of companies with the worst results (Fig. 2.10).

---

[17] Interesting is the aspect highlighted in the survey of productivity increase in the presence of an organization of wealth management based on teamworking. "To better manage their sales teams, companies should follow three measures: their yield on client assets and liabilities (CAL) managed, CAL per client and the number of clients per relationship manager. There are, of course, many different service models available to wealth management businesses. Some firms prefer their relationship managers to work separately and take an individual approach to managing clients. Others prefer a team approach, integrating several relationship managers and product specialist into a group that work together to serve clients. Each team member's skills should complement those of their team colleagues. Our experience is that team size is key to productivity and that complementary teams of about four to six relationship managers actually improve productivity". See "Prospering in Uncertain Time", Global wealth 2002, The Boston Consulting Group, www.bcg.com.

Fig. 2.10 Income and costs per relationship manager versus cost-to-income ratio (2001)

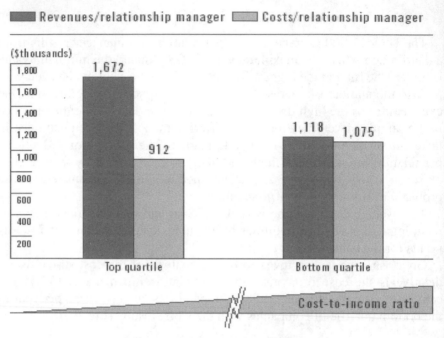

Source: The Boston Consulting Group, Global Wealth 2002

In this climate of uncertainty it is essential, in the first place, to pursue stability of incomes that are subject to high pressures and have become flexible because of the open architecture toward external service providers and, in the second place, to reduce structure costs that are high because of the need for high-standard competencies and suitable IT supports.

Profit and loss stability can be achieved by means of diversifying income sources, which can reduce the risk of concentration in only one compartment, whereas cost reduction may result from rationalizing production processes and exploiting corporate synergies.

The key word is "integration":

- integration of solutions provided to clients;

- integration of competencies serving clients needs;

- integration of outside (clients) and inside (corporate processes) communication.

Integration logic matches the requirements of the family business market, where it is the essential element to join family and business perspectives.

It is clear, however, that also in family business the level of complexity of the services provided varies depending on the size of the family business: different markets must be tackled with different offering models. The market of family business comprises client segments ranging from *Affluent* entrepreneurs or professionals to *Ultra-HNWIs* owning a family-controlled multi-national group. As a result, these opposite extremes cannot be faced with the same service models; organization solutions should instead be designed on a *continuum* basis in order to meet growing client complexity.

The result of these reflections cannot be univocal and should be adjusted to the multiplicity of contexts characterized by different vocations and his-torical-institutional matrices.

As for the Italian situation, the importance of small and medium enterprises and the family connotation of big industrial concerns grow the appeal of family business as strategic business area. This market space can be taken by either niche operators specialized and organized in professional firms or financial intermediaries owning adequate competencies to cover the entire range of requirements expressed by this client segment.

In this respect, in order to provide suitable solutions some considerations need making. In particular:

- access to this strategic business area requires strong coordination of central structures;

- synergies can be achieved only in the light of the characteristics of the parent company and of business areas involved;

- synergy development depends on the ability to create intangible interrelations, represented by the transfer of competencies among the different areas, and tangible interrelations resulting from sharing area resources.

As for the transfer of competencies and resource sharing, here follow some of the factors that may facilitate the process:

- collaboration-orientation of independent business areas;

- presence of top management members with integration functions;

- organization of committees, task forces and inter-function and/or division groups aimed at pursuing synergies among project-sharing business areas;

- creation of incentive schemes rewarding pursuit of synergies;

- incentive assignment to area managers in terms of overall performances[18];

- arrangement of training plans on interesting and involving issues
designed for the different areas;

- development of inside and outside joint communication among different areas.

The existence of these conditions depends once again on the characteristics and the capacity of coordination of the parent company. In family
business clear strategic approach and strong governance are the necessary
requisites to be perceived as reliable partners by the clients who every day
tackle exactly the same problems of management and ownership in the
context of their own enterprises.

2.7 Conclusions

The nature of recipients and contents in the area of private banking services reveals a sector serving family nuclei in a perspective of global financial planning that is aimed at the design and management of financial
and real assets, at optimizing liabilities, identifying solutions in the areas
of insurance, social security, taxation and succession planning.

The extended and complex structure of service supply characterizes also
the area of family wealth management, where the complexity of family requirements grows due to dynamics deriving from family business management.

The analysis of the typology of services provided to family business by
financial intermediaries operating in private banking induces to observe
the evolutionary path pursued by banks, which is characterized by the
growing complexity of the organization on the one hand and the gradual
specialization by segments or business areas on the other.

After specialization, the pursuit of integration among the different areas
is necessary to develop synergies within the company and to provide clients with comprehensive solutions. The benefits resulting from specialization may become a limit in tackling a sector like family business, which
requires strongly integrated competencies. The promise to analyze client
requirements by adopting an integrated vision of assets and liabilities implies the presence of organizational mechanisms that are able to share
competencies among the different business areas.

---

[18] See Mazzola 2003.

The creation of family offices for *Ultra-HNW* clients represents the extreme formalization of a supply model based on the integration of multidisciplinary competencies and on the creation of a task force of specialists dedicated to the requirements of one or more families.

The target market of family business services reveals to be extremely extended and differentiated due to the complexity of needs, the bargaining power of clients and the economic sustainability of demanded service customization. As a result, market segmentation prevents the organization from using a unique model of supply to satisfy the requirements of different segments.

Task specialization can be applied in the arrangement of global financial planning services for the *Affluent* segment, but it is hard to apply in the supply of unique services dedicated to *Ultra-HNW* entrepreneurial families and characterized by personal specialization.

The design of different strategic areas focused on different client segments for the purpose of exploiting company synergies must be based on the strong coordination of central structures and on the possibility of exchanging competencies, information and resources.

3 The Map of Family Business Financial Needs

Stefano Caselli

3.1 Introduction

The presence of a family group in the ownership of a firm characterizes the system of governance, the financing criteria and the typology of financial needs. This is not confined to profit and asset interactions between the family and the firm but involves the profile of requests made to the financial system as a whole. The resulting framework is quite complex: the entrepreneurial family as such, the firm governed by the family and the family business become independent actors who make requests and express needs which find different interlocutors, belonging to the sectors of corporate banking, private banking or to the area of consulting and professions (accountants, legal firms, notaries, advisors etc.).

The heterogeneity of the supply system is not to be attributed to market carelessness or lack of preparation, it is rather the clear reflection of the "particular" nature of family business so that the variety of competitors represents a structural condition of the relation between family business and financial system. Two needs or consequences result from this.

The first refers to the mapping of family business requirements. Independently from the individual characteristics of the financial intermediary or professional interacting with the family firm, the correct interpretation of the requirement system and the identification of a criterion for the relation between the individual requirement areas and the services provided are the necessary condition for permanence in the market and for the creation of a competitive advantage in the course of time. In other words, the issue of segmentation precedes that of identification of the competitive model to position the offer in the market of services designed for the family business.

The second refers to the identification of success critical aspects when using a segmentation model dedicated to family business. From this point of view, the specificity of intermediaries and professionals depend on their selection of product-need combinations consistently with their own general business model and with the elements of major interaction with family firms. This means that it is difficult to define a sole competitive model of family business banking but it is necessary to detect the diversity of possible models and the possible areas for overlapping and complementarity.

This chapter intends to tackle the issue of segmentation, whereas the issue of success critical factors for the appropriate positioning of family business financial services will be dealt with in the following chapter.

3.2 A Proactive Segmentation Model for Family Business

The creation of a proactive segmentation model requires a strong focus on the concept of services provided and market serviced. From this point of view, any process of segmentation starts by identifying the range of products provided and the possible firm categories representing the markets serviced by the bank. The crossing of the two variables (see Table 3.1) allows highlighting all the possible product-market combinations the bank must confront along with the existing competitive forces[1].

The poor-to-proactive evolution of segmentation models typology can be analyzed with reference to the contents gradually assumed by the product and the market[2]. From the point of view of the product variable, the dynamics qualifying the evolution of segmentation models regard the extension of the range of services, differentiation and aggregation into product critical areas: poor segmentation is characterized by a limited number of services, low differentiation and limited service areas; on the contrary, proactive segmentation is based on a wide range of products, which are differentiated and structured into homogeneous classes. From the point of view of the market variable, the poor-to-proactive segmentation progress means shifting from formal and subsequent firm classification criteria, which reflect neither financial product requirements nor behavior modes in the financial market, to classification criteria organized by categories of behaviors and product purchasing processes. Each category of firms represents a totally independent market, which is characterized by requisites of measurability, accessibility and importance.

---

[1] See Roach 1989.
[2] As for market segmentation issues in the area of financial services, see Caselli 2001.

Table 3.1 The "product-firm" matrix as seen by proactive segmentation

PRODUCT AREAS	FIRM SEGMENTS				
	Group a	Group b	...	...	Group z
Payment system services					
Corporate lending					
Financial risk management					
Insurance risk management					
Asset management					
Corporate finance					

The effective organization of a product-market system according to proactive segmentation requires the bank management to trigger the following processes:

- identify product categories provided by the bank;

- check discriminating elements conditioning firms' purchasing or non-purchasing product categories;

- select discriminating variables for identification of homogeneous firm categories;

- enrich behavioral models with qualitative describers;

- analyze competitive forces relating to firm category – product category

- combinations;

-    monitor steadiness of firm categories and structure of competitive
    forces in each product-market combination.

The above steps allow the bank to closely connect the segmentation
process with the supply function positioning process. This is because the
identification of product-market combinations is characterized by a functional correspondence with the firm requirement system and with the dynamics of the forces affecting the market in terms of information immedi-
ately translatable into the profile of the bank market behavior. Therefore,
the relevant information available enables the bank management to: select
target segments on the basis of available forms of competitive advantage;
identify relevant competitive actions to be undertaken against competitors;
position and differentiate supply according to characteristics of category
firms and to conditions made in the reference market; check results of actions undertaken; modify typology of strategic positioning on the basis of
comparisons between expected and achieved benefits.

3.2.1 Product System Analysis: the Product-Oriented Approach

The analysis of the bank product system can be carried out effectively by
distinguishing the following areas: payment system services, corporate
lending, financial risk management, insurance risk management, asset
management and corporate finance. Within each area further sub-areas can
be identified, such as payment system services in Italy and abroad, short-
term and long-term lending, securities management services and extraordinary corporate finance[3]. All the areas are sufficiently homogeneous inside
and sufficiently not homogeneous outside so that, on the one hand, each
area can be identified as an independent industry, characterized by specific
requisites as to production, supply process and pricing while, on the other,
the demand behavior can be classified by purchasing behavior, motivations, overall satisfaction and need relevance.

From a technical-methodological point of view, the analysis of the six
product industries includes two closely connected stages. In the first place
(i.e. the product-oriented stage) the bank needs to check for the entire
range of products the volume and the quantity sold, the resulting margins –
rather than the resulting profitability, if measurable – the purchasing discriminating elements, the reasons for non-purchasing, the degree of satis-

---

[3] This map of the bank product system, viewed as the most extended map of services that can be now provided to corporate customers, is widely accepted both
from the scientific and the terminological point of view. See Paternello 1995;
Cenni and Landi 1996; Caselli 2000; Caselli and Gatti 2003.

faction[4]. This allows re-aggregating the results achieved in each product industry and expressing a first level of qualitative and quantitative evaluations which can explain: the positioning of the bank product portfolio in relation to the market; buyers' behavior in connection with their distinctive features; the areas for potential growth. In the second place (i.e. the market-oriented stage), the bank needs to proceed and evaluate the competitive forces acting in the six product industries, by emphasizing their intensity and characteristics in relation to the specific attributes of the bank supply function. The bank can also evaluate any areas for potential growth in the product industries not yet controlled.

In the product-oriented stage the analysis of the purchasing behavior for the individual products and the study of the distinctive elements of the firms that develop similar behaviors offer a first high value added tool for the correct organization of a proactive segmentation model. From these elements it is possible to observe how the model strongly depends on the strategic and operating characteristics of the bank that decides to adopt market proactive segmentation; in fact firm behaviors, product satisfaction assessment and purchasing or non-purchasing motivations are largely connected with the way in which the bank supply function is formulated and organized.

In the light of some recent studies carried out on corporate financial be haviors in relation with the bank, a significant example of the application modes of this first stage of segmentation can be provided[5].

With reference to the industry of payment system services and, in particular, to the group of domestic commercial services, the purchasing discriminating element is the organization of information, accounting and treasury processes within the firm[6]. As a result, SMEs can be distinguished

---

[4] The use of the above parameters is subject to the kind of data available. The list provided is a sort of "optimal reference". This applies above all to the parameter of profitability and to that of satisfaction. The latter requires an ad hoc market research for the measurement of customer satisfaction by product industry.

[5] More specifically, reference is made to the main surveys carried out at the national and international level on the issue of SME specific purchasing behaviors in the different product industries. The above evaluations represent an effective benchmark to specify the critical aspects of the product-oriented stage with greater accuracy. For an exhaustive review of the mentioned studies, see Caselli 2001. As for payment system services and financial and insurance risk management, reference is made to the survey University of Bath, "Global Cash Europe 2001", Bath, 2002, which annually reports the results concerning the use of the above services by a sample of European SMEs.

[6] With reference to the diagnosis of the business system *of* service payments specifically relating to SMEs, see Mottura, Caselli, Gatti 2000.

into different segments which reflect the different degree of utilization of the services involved. At a first level, several SMEs are characterized by the purchase of just a few or no payment products: their common feature is a paper traditional information structure. Quite often entrepreneurs do not feel the need to innovate internal processes but they do not realize the presence of a coordinated and dedicated bank supply for this type of services. At a second level, a large number of SMEs show a sufficient degree of utilization of products. These SMEs tend to have already re-organized their accounting and information structures and are sensitive to the possible innovation of payment and cash services to align their position with system conditions. On the basis of their experience, some entrepreneurs are not totally convinced about the positive effect of the above services on the management of their information flows but declare they are on the average satisfied with the products they have used. At a third level there is an advanced category of SMEs. It is a restricted number of companies that purchase several cash and payment services and declare they are extremely satisfied with cost and time savings as to their internal administration procedures. The common feature is the entrepreneur's explicit and independent choice in favor of the organization of an integrated system for the management of information and accounting flows. Therefore the employment of innovative payment system services is coordinated by the use of interbank corporate banking and cash management. The use of foreign payment services is subordinate to the firm operating characteristics and therefore to the higher or lower propensity to develop commercial relations with foreign countries. A relevant element is the fact that quite often companies exclusively demand for services closely connected with the underlying operation and do not resort to high value added products because they are not effective and too expensive.

As for corporate lending, a relevant evaluation element is that the degree of utilization is affected by the dimensions of the purchasing firm. This relation is justified by the role the high-net worth company reputation plays in the relationship with banks. In this sense, biggest sized firms have a greater negotiating power and obtain open high-amount credit lines (e.g. stand-by lending and evergreen lending) as well as reduced rates and commissions. A general trend arises from the judgement of entrepreneurs, above all from SMEs, that is a demand for traditional rather than innovative lending services. This is due to the fact that real variables are more relevant than financial ones, in terms of knowledge, utilization criteria and management skills. As for purchasing discriminating features, great importance is assigned to the bank capacity to define the fiscal profile of the operation, by specifying benefits and drawbacks for the economic and financial profile of the company. The case of real-estate leasing is particularly significant[7].

As for financial risk management, utilization discriminating features are closely connected with either the firm ownership and management model or the entrepreneur's behavior qualitative components. In the first case two significant relations should be noticed: there is almost no causal relation between the firm industry and product utilization degree as firms in the manufacturing industry tend to use risk management services to the same degree as firms in the service industry; on the other hand, the fact the firm belongs to an Italian rather than foreign group strongly affects its demand for risk management services, which drops significantly. In the second case, entrepreneurs' attitudes are differentiated according to the different typologies of risk. In this connection, there is a widespread perception of exchange risk, which is managed with future contracts or swaps. The rate risk is almost totally unknown and just a marginal share of firms resort to risk management through derivative tools.

As for business risk management, SMEs' utilization seems to be absolutely exceptional and marginal. Exceptional because the purchasing process of risk management dedicated services in relation to both corporate structures and individuals does not seem to be planned within an organic reference picture on the basis of risk check-ups. Marginal, as the transaction volume shows considerable growth margins compared to the other service industries. Although demand side gaps seem to be prevailing, also supply side gaps should be highlighted above all for that the area of business risk management has not been completely focused as a relevant business area for banks.

As for asset management, SMEs' purchasing behavior should be distinguished on the basis of the complexity of the product supplied. At an elementary level, the purchase of asset management services aims at saving management, with criteria being similar to those of private banking. Therefore, no specific discriminating features for or against purchasing can be referred directly to the firm characteristics. At a complex level, asset management services regard the management of the company wealth. In this context, product specifications have a strong fiscal and legal content and purchasing dynamics are similar to those of corporate finance. Significant examples are startup services for holdings or trusts abroad.

As for corporate finance, despite the wide range of products in this industry, the development of the purchasing process is quite limited among SMEs. The concurrence of multiple factors justifies the quite limited num-

---

[7] For the "sale" of fiscal variables in the supply of lending services, see Caselli 1998.

ber of SMEs resorting to banks to satisfy their extraordinary finance needs. Such factors involve the closed ownership structure of firms that prevents acting on the liability mix; the enterprise perception of bank poor supply in terms of range and quality; the role played by holding firms in relation to controlled companies in terms of direct supply of security management services. Within this market area, as we shall see in the market-oriented analysis, there are intermediaries other than banks who, on the one hand, make the analysis of the competitive environment more complex and, on the other, tend to dilute transactions as banks lose the identity of exchange distribution and reference center[8].

3.2.2 Product System Analysis: the Market-Oriented Approach

In the market-oriented stage, product industries are analyzed under the profile of competitive forces and this represents the basis for a first indication regarding the positioning of the supply function of banks and, more generally, financial intermediaries. In this respect, big differences characterize the various product categories with reference to market forces structure and to competitive advantage creation for the operating subjects (see Table 3.2). The competitive diagnosis here offers a fairly flexible tool as it enables both production-specialized intermediaries and intermediaries with highly diversified supply to verify the nature and the frequency of competitive relations in the target market area.

In the industry of payment system services, competition is particularly keen in the domestic area on the entire range of products[9]. The bank competitive advantage consists in a cost leadership strategy carried out by extending the supply function and establishing agreements with service providers, taking into account that the market of corporate payment system services is bound to rely on three major vehicles that see information technology and the Web as the key elements of development: safety; management, control and concordance of standards; efficiency. Nowadays the structure of the market generally shows the characteristics of a commodity market where the low cost advantage results from suppliers' great power, demand's perception of non-differentiated products and quite limited margins. The presence of "product substitutes" referred to corporate treasury intragroup management accentuates such market characteristics. From this

---

[8] As for the "diluted" structure of the supply system of corporate finance services designed for SMEs, see: ABI – Prometeia 2000; Autorità Garante della Concorrenza e del Mercato – Banca d'Italia 1997; AIFI 2000.
[9] See evaluations by ABI 1994.

point of view, the supply of domestic payment system services should be managed as a value creating lever in the customer relation. This means customizing the consequences generated by payment services. Significant examples are the supply of consulting services regarding the design of corporate IT systems, the rationalization of accounting and treasury integrated management systems according to cash management criteria, the implementation of on-line connections with the bank. Here the poor cost leadership strategy becomes the tool serving a more complex differentiation strategy of the supply as a whole. On the contrary, with reference to foreign payment system services, the competitive structure is significantly different both for the limited competitive pressure inside the industry and the product characteristics[10]: on the one hand, corporate demand seems to be limited and not too varied in front of the supply of a wide range of services; on the other, the product typology cannot be easily standardized, above all in terms of implementation of integrated multi-currency cash management systems or of home banking services abroad. In this case, in fact, the overall positioning of the finance system does not seem sufficiently compact and precisely defined due to the following factors: safety systems are still insufficient above all in the area of international and non-EU transactions; cash flows transfer standards have not been given a final definition and are still overlapping (see, for example, SWIFT and EDIFACT); efficiency levels are not homogeneous and, on the average, pretty low[11].

---

[10] See Mottura, Caselli, Gatti 2000.
[11] See Generale Bank & MeesPierson 1999; Hagopian and Horrel 1998.

Table 3.2 The market-oriented stage: the structure of competitive forces and bank strategy for value production

Product Industries	Internal competition	Corporate customer power	Threats from substitute products	Threats from new entries	Supplier power	Competitive advantage
1. Payment system services	Strong in domestic market. Weaker in the foreign market area.	Generally strong due to standard format of domestic product. Weaker in the foreign area.	Weak due to primary need for payment services. Possible competitive pressure from group centralized treasuries.	Weak due to primary need for payment services. Growing relevance of technology providers as payment system providers.	Limited range of suppliers. Generally strong power of technology providers.	Poor cost leadership. Chances of service enrichment in most complex areas (e.g. cash management).
2. Corporate lending	Very strong over the entire range of corporate lending services. Weaker in the area of subsidized loans.	Power tends to be function of assets growing amount and stability.	Generally weak and regarding only equity, in relation to degree of fiscal advantage.	The industry is glutted. Exit risk for current market operators.	Category not present apart from segment of subsidized loans. Here, generally strong power of providers.	Poor cost leadership.
3. Financial risk management	Weak due to substantial growth market areas.	Weak, mainly due to product lack of knowledge.	Strong pressure from inside compensation criteria and intragroup compensation forms.	Limited number of banks in this industry. Enter good chances for banks not operating in the industry.	Strong power of suppliers when distributing banks outsource to producing banks.	Differentiation leadership connected with product innovation capacity and management flexibility in matching corporate needs.
4. Business risk management	Weak due to substantial growth market areas.	Weak, mainly due to product lack of knowledge.	Limited use of intragroup compensation forms.	Limited number of intermediaries in the industry. Enter good chances for intermediaries not operating in the industry.	Strong power of suppliers when distributing intermediaries outsource to producing intermediaries.	Differentiation leadership connected with product innovation capacity and management flexibility in matching corporate needs.

Table 3.2 Continued

Product Industries	Internal competition	Corporate customer power	Threats from substitute products	Threats from new entries	Supplier power	Competitive advantage
6. Corporate finance	Competition structure tends to have oligopolistic profile due to market limited extension and restricted number of operators.	Extremely weak due to great complexity of product and competence gap.	Referred to corporate lending products as long as they help to meet the need for financial resources.	Strong due to variety of subjects potentially interested in market area (banks, close-end funds, venture capitalists, merchant banks, professional agencies, mutuals). High barriers against enter in terms of relational network access competencies.	Strong power of suppliers when distributing intermediaries outsource producing intermedia ries. Very strong power of suppliers as to legal, fiscal and strategic financial services.	Differentiation leadership.
5. Asset management	Strong in saving management. Weaker in legal and fiscal services for corporate asset management.	Generally strong in saving management due to standard content of products. Weaker in more complex asset management services.	Possible use of in-house asset management with the support of professionals	Market shows no barriers against access to saving management area. Strong competition makes industry hardly accessible. Enter good chances for foreign intermediaries and professionals in the area of asset management.	Strong power of suppliers when distributing intermediaries outsource to producing intermediaries. Very strong power of suppliers as to legal and fiscal services.	Complex cost leadership in saving management. Differentiation leadership in asset management.

Within the industry of corporate lending, the system historical diffusion of multi credit lines and short-term loans has somehow displaced the segment of long-term lending and of, partially, subsidized loans. This has entailed a strong levelling of products pricing and a substantial reduction in profit margins, thus confirming a competitive model relying on cost leadership in a narrow sense. However, the development of actually corporate dedicated services and the supply of lending products actually consistent with the financial structure of corporate customers will lead to a different subdivision of lending services according to functional correspondence principles of tools, prices and risks with the length of the operation and user requirements. According to this logic, the cost leadership formula remains a necessary condition in the segment of short and long term lending, but it will grow more complex as long as the credit is no longer identified by its being a commodity but a high value added specialty[12].

Nevertheless, in front of this scenario of development, we should also underline that loan approval, which represents an essential instrument of development for corporate customers in the presence of an unlikely substitution with equity, risks becoming a mature and scarcely profitable activity for financial intermediaries. This is due to the structural interest rate reduction which makes loan underwriting less appealing as well as to the high stock of actual and potential credit losses which destabilize intermediaries' overall profitability. In this case, there are strong and actual threats of exiting the corporate lending industry for the intermediaries whose activity is either mainly focused on asset management or aimed at large corporates and not consistent with the local dimension of credit exchange, which is typical of smaller sized companies.

A differentiated evaluation should be made on the basis of corporate characteristics in the area of subsidized loans. Not only do these products extend the bank supply but they allow banks to position their action after the subsidizing process and to differentiate their supply by supporting the company in the selection of low-cost sources. The value added provided by the bank can be created thanks to the interface function carried out between the individual local territory and the overall market circuit of subsidized lending. This function is developed by encouraging information ex-

---

[12] This change is seen by Forestieri G., "Il sistema bancario italiano verso un modello di corporate banking: mito o realtà?", in Baravelli M., "Le strategie competitive nel corporate banking", Egea, Milano, 1997, as a necessary condition for the transformation of the competitive model of Italian banks, which have developed a poor lending supply where credit is considered a raw material rather than a finished product. For further information, see evaluations developed in the course of the second chapter in this volume..

change and by supporting companies in their approaching the market. In this sense, the effectiveness of the bank role will be evaluated in relation to the evolution of two different lines of intervention respectively positioned within the reference territorial area (horizontal information) and within the relation between the local territory and the national market (vertical information). In the first case, a strong activity of horizontal information may develop as long as banks, supported by competent local institutions, on the one hand perform a screening action of the local economic structure in order to identify and promote among enterprises available tools for subsidized lending and, on the other, assist companies interested in specific interventions. Such actions may end up with providing increasingly growing services, such as direct consulting or planning local marketing actions to stimulate and educate entrepreneurs to access a wider range of differentiated financing sources. In the second case, vertical information activity allows reducing asymmetries between the local scale of minor firms and the national scale of subsidized loans. This is the necessary requisite for the consolidation of connections between the demand for financial resources, which is locally distributed, and the structure of the supply referred to the State, re-financing institutions and specialized intermediaries.

In the industry of financial risk management, competitive forces seem to be structurally different from previous industries. This may be the result of that the product has a strong connotation of technical specialization and thus requires a high interaction between the intermediary and the corporate customer. In this sense, purchasers' power is on the whole weak, as a result of their lack of knowledge and limited management capacity. The bank competitive advantage prevailingly proves to be differentiation leadership, which derives from the supply of an integrated package of lending, exchange risk management and rate risk management tools rather than exchange regulating and rate risk management tools[13]. If not, the bank will succeed in acquiring no defensible competitive advantage and the volume of risk management market will not grow. Quite different is the competitive dynamics regarding large corporates but also company groups where the financial know-how and the possibility of internal risk management with intragroup netting logics identify corporate customers as purchasers with great negotiating skills and excluding the bank from the market. In this respect, the bank possible competitive positioning is clearly connected with the bank capacity to propose treasury supervision advisory and management of group net credit lines. If not so, the bank is quite likely to be

---

[13] For the mapping of intervention criteria and of product contents of financial risk management services designed for corporate customers, see Lazzari 2000.

subject to the negotiating power of the counterpart according to a transactional logic and of price reduction.

With reference to the industry of business risk management, competitive forces tend to replicate the characteristics described for financial risk management. Again, apart from the products relating to life insurance and characterized by a low financial content, the services provided bear strong elements of technical specialization and thus require an equally strong interaction between the intermediary and the corporate customer. As a result, the purchaser's power, above all of the small enterprise, is quite limited due to product lack of knowledge. The competitive advantage of financial intermediaries prevailingly proves to be differentiation leadership, which derives from the supply of social security plan management or individual insurance management services which are provided after mapping and screening the risks present in the company. This seems to be significantly complex as risk analysis requires technical, engineering, legal and financial competencies. In addition, due to the highly technical specificity of the product and to a larger extent than in the industry of financial risk management, the construction of the competitive advantage requires the intermediary to take a stand as to choices of service origination, brokerage and assembly. If this affects the creation logic of costs and revenues, the financial intermediary must be highly skillful at risk screening and problem solving focused on meeting customer requirements.

As for asset management services, the distinction between saving management and asset management is of crucial importance (see Table 3.3). In the first case, the enterprise demand becomes marginal as requirements concern individuals somehow connected with the enterprise as owners, members of owner-families or of the staff. Therefore, asset management activity is part of a more general process of expansion of business opportunities, according to a logic of overall cross selling and of customer relationship upgrading. In this industry, the competitive dynamics follows the typical profile of investment services provided to private customers. In the second case, the enterprise demand is specifically "industrial" as asset management requirements originate from the enterprise need to protect and develop its assets and wealth. As a result, the system supply may concentrate both on financial instruments in a narrow sense which, by means of a joint intervention on company financial structure and governance, protect corporate assets above all during the critical phases of discontinuity of the corporate development process, as well as on legal and fiscal instruments that may affect the company structure[14]. In the first group there are share-holding interventions, family buy outs or listing admissions, which represent the management instruments for the generational turnover process. This area, due to the characteristics of the individual products, falls within the product industry of *corporate finance*[15]. Vice versa, in the second group there are company law instruments, such as the set-up of a holding, the change of the company structure into a group, the need of a foundation rather than a trust. Despite the technical and legal diversity of the above instruments, the common feature is the intervention on the company design in the attempt to protect and manage their wealth against , even in this case, critical phases of discontinuity of the development process or the necessity to rationalize the company structure so as to increase the efficiency of production processes and wealth transfer.

Table 3.3 Asset management and family business

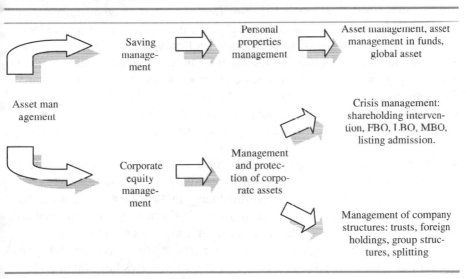

In this industry the competitive scenario is characterized by a competitive advantage based on the model of differentiation leadership, as a result of the value added and the low standardization in the services provided. Another two elements distinguish the competitive dynamics. The first is the substantial contamination between service financial specifications on

---

[14] For this distinction see Iovenitti 1998. Reference should be made to Iovenitti's work for an accurate analysis of technical contents in the instruments of company law mentioned in this book.

[15] See evaluations by Perrini 1998.

one side and technical-legal specifications on the other. This implies the presence of financial intermediaries and professional agencies, whose activity (origination, brokerage and assembly) is not established *a priori* and whose market relations can be either co-operational or conflictual. The second element is connected with demand minimum access thresholds. Like for all of the services requiring high standards of knowledge for the purchase - due to their technical contents and their impact on company financial structures - as well as high purchasing costs, corporate customers tend to pay for a knowledge and economic gap whose extent may prevent the purchasing process from even starting. As a result, the competitive choice for the financial intermediaries is focused on the establishment of an economic model balancing the number with the average cut of operations. This choice may be followed by the exit from the market of the enterprises positioned below the threshold.

With reference to the industry of corporate finance, the market size still seems quite limited, above all if specifically related to enterprises exclusively. If this, on the one hand, indicates the presence of a largely exploitable area for the supply of new products and growing profits, on the other it underlines the existence of structural gaps in terms of firms' financial requirements as well as of financial intermediaries' production capacity. The reasons for such phenomenon are to be attributed to the characteristics of the company ownership structure and to the relations between enterprises and financial system, which have already been examined in the second chapter of this volume. The preservation of the company ownership structure is faced with a fragmented credit supply system which, in fact, develops the function of equity without having equity control rights and price-risk correspondence. If several changing factors move toward the gradual financing of choices relating to the definition of company control structures and corporate funding, banks must position their supply correctly in a hostile though still developing competitive environment. This can be observed in relation to the fact that: i) enterprises have favorable information asymmetries about the actual knowledge of their industrial projects, the risks they actually run in some operations, the real and financial goals they pursue, the balances and relations among partners; ii) a relevant share of financial, fiscal and advisory requirements are managed by the network of professional agencies which establish relations with the enterprise; iii) foreign merchant banks tend to act more consistently in the Italian market, proposing themselves as interlocutors with consolidated experience in the management of specific products and operations. Consequently, the strategic positioning of, above all, Italian banks, must solve the problem of information and management gaps, which place the bank in a position of weakness in comparison to industrial interlocutors.

This is particularly outstanding in an industry where competition is largely played on service differentiation and thus on competence, knowledge and relation which produce value in the course of time. In addition there are the evaluations already described for asset management in relation to enterprise wealth management so that knowledge and economic gap may start a vicious circle where the economic thresholds established by financial intermediaries are bound to exclude a relevant number of enterprises from accessing corporate finance services[16].

3.3 Family Business Financial Behaviors: Toward a Combined Family-Firm Evaluation

The second line of analysis for the preparation of a proactive segmentation model consists in defining the firm segments that represent the "markets" for which the bank must formulate different competitive strategies and implement different systems of supply. Market identification stimulates a strong projectional activity before and after the process of segmentation. The *ex ante* identification of the method that allows distinguishing homogeneous groups of enterprises is not a neutral and objective choice. Segmentation criteria, in fact, can be developed on different operating levels and with different approach criteria, whose function is to create an initial connection with the characteristics of the organization structure and the roles of the bank. The *ex post* results of the segmentation process must be first gathered and shared within the organization and secondly engineered into processes and solutions of supply with clearly defined borders. On the whole, the *ex ante* stage accomplishes and concludes the process of proactive mapping of corporate customers, whereas the *ex post* stage involves positioning and organizational choices concerning the competitive supply strategy designed for SMEs. For the interpretation of segments from the point of view of supply competitive positioning, reference should be made to the seventh chapter of this volume, where the issue of strategies is the object of study and discussion.

The identification of SME homogeneous groups consists in defining the different models of financial behavior. To this aim, the process input uses both quantitative data taken directly from market actions performed by enterprises and quali-quantitative data collectable from bank information systems. The former refer to the number and type of financial products acquired at the bank, the number of existing credit relations, the frequency of

---

[16] See the evaluations by 1997.

utilization of the individual products, the historical evolution of the above behaviors. The latter include information about the ownership structure (shares distributions, partners' age, possibility of succession), the organization of company functions (number, tasks, staff per function), the tasks assigned to personnel in charge of financial management, about turnover distribution over the different business areas and so on. As for the process output, SME behavioral models are defined according to the structure of empirical relations identified among the characteristics of the ownership-management structure, the frequency of utilization of financial products, the kind of business developed and the type of relations established with financial intermediaries.

The process of segmentation must rely on a reliable criterion for the interpretation of SME financial behaviors. In the previous chapter we have observed that prevailingly evolutionary interpretation criteria fail to provide a reliable and effective frame of reference. On the contrary, despite the more extended areas of analysis and evaluation, multi-polar interpretation schemes allow widening the frame from a simple correlation between time and turnover growth rate to a complex system of relations among enterprise characteristics, its financial choices, its organizational processes and its ownership and management structure. From this point of view, however, the variety of multi-polar models requires less complex homogeneous categories, with a view to achieving factual economic and operational solutions from the enterprise's point of view.

There are two possible solutions: the former is based on a sole market interpretation parameter; the latter is based on two distinct interpretation parameters of the market (see Table 3.4).

The one-parameter solution focuses the attention on the SME as the only center producing specific financial requirements the financial intermediary can satisfy through its supply process. Then the complexity of relations within family, property and enterprise is channeled into the unity of a sole interpretation scheme.

The two-parameter solution focuses the attention distinctively on the enterprise and on the family, thus accepting the different behavioral and financial characteristics of the two subjects. In this case, the market interpretation becomes more analytical and enables the intermediary to exploit the relations within family, property and enterprise to formulate its supply. Yet, the identification of a twofold segmentation parameter exposes the bank to possible conflicts of organizational assignments and to possible lack of consistency in the supply process. This results from the fact that if the family is identified as the pole expressing financial needs, this is very likely to drag typologies of needs falling into the private area, thus forcing the bank to find organizational solutions balancing the conflicts of roles governing either corporate or private customers. In addition the multiplicity of interpretation schemes, though making the market mapping more complete, may actually displace the bank supply if, due to economic factors or lack of competencies, the bank is not able to generate a high number of differentiated processes in the area of both production and supply.

Table 3.4 Identification of family business behavioral models: possible implementation criteria

Segmentation typology	Characteristics	Advantages	Disadvantages
Based on a sole analysis parameter: the enterprise	The enterprise is the sole center formulating and expressing financial requirements the bank can satisfy through its supply process	The complexity of enterprise/family/property relations resulting from multi-polar interpretation schemes is channeled into the unity of the enterprise financial behavior. The bank has a sole market interpretation criterion to make its choices of supply positioning. This may facilitate implementation and actual utilization.	The use of a sole market interpretation criterion may reduce effectiveness of supply composition as the complexity of enterprise/family/property relations is not revealed by segmentation process.
Based on two analysis parameters: the enterprise and the family	The enterprise and the family are two distinct centers formulating and expressing financial requirements the bank can satisfy through its supply process.	The complexity of enterprise/family/property relations resulting from multi-polar interpretation schemes is further enriched through distinction between enterprise/family specific segments. The bank has a more complete and deeper market interpretation criterion to make its choices of supply positioning.	The multiplicity of interpretation schemes may reduce effectiveness of supply composition due to conflicts of organizational assignments (corporate roles versus private or retail roles) and to excessive number of identified targets.

The market segmentation system based on the twofold parameter drives the attention on the multi-polar interpretation scheme of SME financial behavior, by distinguishing the corporate profile from that of the individuals who hold the property of the enterprise. In this sense, the nature of SMEs imposes the overcoming of the approach to the enterprise as a sole subject, which is clearly identified and provided with its own consistent financial needs. Therefore the interpretation frame becomes more complex and better organized as it evaluates the elements of diversity and interdependence existing within the enterprise managerial system, which includes corporate variables and those concerning the relations between the enterprise and its owners and among the owners themselves, considering the importance of family links and dynamics.

The separate evaluation of the two contexts forces the bank to make specific operating choices. Critical aspects might be the following:

- distinction and articulation of product categories according to enterprise and family point of view;

- identification of "contextual situations" both for the enterprise and the family, which characterize the origination of homogeneous financial needs.

With reference to the first point, the bank product system must be designed in relation to the different purchasing profile indicated by the enterprise and the individuals connected by family relations (see Table 3.5). This represents a more refined interpretation of the product system developed in the product and market-oriented approach. Analytically, all the products belonging to the different product industries should be accurately mapped by measuring the frequency of the needs satisfied and their distinctive features in relation to origins, enterprise or family.

In the industry of payment system services, the prevailing affinity is related to the enterprise. Family requirements, in fact, are to be referred to the retail area of credit and debit cards. Cross-selling between the family and the firm and risk of conflicts seem limited. Quite similar is the context of the lending area, where the development of various forms of loans may be retail-oriented with reference to the logic of private loans. Unlike payment services, loan approvals may represent an important tool to acquire family members' fidelity. The situation is different for medium and long term loans, where the bank may partially finance family members' real estate operations or support the acquisition of shareholdings. If in the first case, cross-selling and firm fidelity acquisition through family members become more important, in the second case the bank operations fall directly in the industry of corporate finance services. Here, the fact that such operations belong to the category of corporate finance services avoids any conflict of task assignment and competencies between corporate and retail customers in favor of the first. More delicate and complex is the balance to be established in the context of medium and long term lending, for example for real-estate purchases, where the assignment to the corporate area would increase fidelity acquisition synergies but might dilute the bank's ability to seize private purchasing criteria.

The industry of risk management is totally different. As for financial risk management, the value of application in relation to the family is only exceptional and cannot be structured in a pre-established scheme of supply. This does not exclude the possibility of purchases by the family members for speculating purposes, though these activities fall within the industry of asset management services. With reference to business risk management, products specifically designed for individuals range from risk management, to wealth transfer management and development of social security plans.

Life and death insurance policies, enriched with financial contents of different degrees, represent a crucial instrument for the operating connections they can create with the areas of asset management and corporate finance. Apart from creating new spaces for deeper asset allocation of family members' wealth, the management of "death risk" allows designing a plan of action in the case of death of critical roles in the SME, thus allowing both the enterprise and the bank to manage *ex ante* a possible and sudden growth in the business risk which, in some instances, may coincide with the risk of failure for the business itself[17]. Yet, the focus on the supply of an effective action plan meets two obstacles. The first results from the physiologic difficulty – given the object of the service - to actually implement a plan for the development and promotion of the services connected with "death risk " management". The second obstacle regards the need for strong co-ordination among the bank different areas, which include not only insurance risk management, but also corporate finance, asset management and, because of the consequences on credit risk, that of lending[18]. The co-ordination effort may in fact preclude the unfolding of an effective and above all repeated and extended action aimed at SME customers. Less complex is the development of services regarding social security plans, where the focus on individuals is more significant and the approach logic is based on cross selling and mutual fidelity acquisition between firm and family.

The service area of asset management has a typically retail value and, at the same time, is quite close to corporate finance. This is because the se-

---

[17] The risk factor connected with the non-planning of the "death" event is absolutely relevant, above all in the case of enterprises relying on the capacities of a restricted number of people; the lack of suitable solutions may undermine the continuity of the business activity and heavily downgrade the creditworthiness profile, thus exposing financiers to hardly manageable situations. See Corbetta 2001.

[18] As for the co-ordination of competencies with reference to the management of the "death risk" impact, see Beckard and Dyer 1988. More generally, see evaluations by Manzone and Trento 1993.

lection of products, as already explained in the evaluation of product industries, shows a range of quite remarkable technical and financial contents and monetary sizes. If in the first case, the management of trading or of smaller sized personal properties involve only individual family members, in the second case the distinction between business and family logic becomes far vaguer as the financial requirements expressed by the two entities and the specific consequences in the course of time are subject to mutual conditioning. Above all in the case of corporate governance services, the maintenance and development of personal properties, the management of fiscal flows and the creation of company structures dedicated to the management of family business continuity have a different impact on the overall life-cycle of the family/firm wealth. If this mix represents a positive factor for financial intermediaries as it creates a quite extended potential market area, measured under the profile of cross selling opportunities and of customer relationship, some delicate questions need to be answered. This is because distribution and assignment of responsibilities within the bank must lead to the identification of "mixed" corporate and private teamworking solutions rather than "one-way" solutions where production specialization of the corporate or private area, on the one hand, simplifies the customer relational process but, on the other, exposes the bank to dangerous deviations in terms of problem solving and competencies for the management of requirements.

The area of *corporate finance* obviously presents a specific focus on the enterprise requirements. Like the area of asset management for the services relating to the management of corporate assets as well as of corporate governance, the supply of corporate services generates consequences and new requirements on the part of the family (see Table 3.6). This can be observed in terms of:

- corporate governance;

- enter and exit processes;

- increase in financial resources critical mass.

Table 3.5 Distinction of product typologies in relation to family and firm requirements

	Product typology	Firm	Family
Payment system services	Electronic funds transfer (Riba, Rid and Mav)	XXX	
	Credit and debit cards	XXX	XXX
	CBI standard	XXX	
	CBI advanced	XXX	
	Cash Management	XXX	
	Overseas	XXX	
Lending	Consumer credit loans	OOO	XXX
	Short-term lending	XXX	
	Medium and long term lending	XXX	OOO
	Subsidized loans	XXX	
Financial risk management	Exchange risk management	OOO	
	Interest-rate risk management	OOO	
	Price risk management	OOO	
	Asset/liability management	OOO	
Business risk management	Corporate insurance risk	XXX	
	Individual insurance risk		XXX
	Wealth transfer management	XXX	XXX
	Social security plan management	XXX	XXX
Asset management	Trading	OOO	XXX
	Personal properties management	OOO	XXX
	Corporate asset management	XXX	
	Corporate governance services	XXX	XXX
Corporate finance	Advisory on securities management	XXX	
	Strategic consulting – legal and fiscal	XXX	XXX
	M&A, LBO, MBO	XXX	OOO
	Private equity and venture capital	XXX	OOO
	Listing admission	XXX	OOO
	Company restructuring and crisis management	XXX	OOO
Relevant requirements	XXX		
Partial requirements	OOO		
No requirements			

In the first case, most of corporate finance products are intrinsically designed to intervene on the structure of corporate capital and property: operations involving extra-ordinary finance, venture capital and private equity, listing admissions and company restructuring modify the balance among the owners to a different degree and with different goals. This has an impact on family internal balance, above all in terms of current assets allocation and possible shareholding in future profits. The management of this kind of balance is concurrently a critical factor for the successful continuity of the family business and a business area for the financial intermediary, who may act as a legal and strategic advisor or as a financing subject. Given the nature of the intervention, the contiguousness with the field of action of professional agencies is high, above all when the advisory activity has less technical and legal contents and aims at more relational and social aspects.[19].

In the second case, changes in corporate governance may lead partners to enter or exit from the property structure. This process is functional to the re-distribution of equity by selling shares and transferring wealth from individuals' to corporate assets. In this context, the bank has three possible ways of action: it may act as designer, financier or facilitator. The designer role is connected with legal, fiscal and relational advisory, which is often the cementing but also detonating element of the whole transaction. The financier role instead involves the bank ability to provide financial resources with the constraint of debt capital in favor of individuals who intend to develop enter processes. Finally the facilitator role involves the bank ability to act as broker in the quest of counterparts potentially interested in purchasing company shares. In this sense, this role supports exit processes of partners who intend to sell their shares.

In the third case, the critical mass increase of financial resources marks the bank field of action in favor of the overall wealth supporting business growth. This is quite important in some critical phases in the life-cycle of the enterprise such as the shift from small to medium size, acquisitions, access to international markets, listing admissions. The element common to all of these phases is the inadequacy of family resources in terms of volume, reference time horizon and risk for the correct and effective development of corporate plans. The bank therefore bridges the gap between necessary and available resources by either entering the capital directly or by financing the property under the form of debt. The first solution seems to be more reasonable as the critical nature of the phase brings about not only the need for financial support but above all for managerial support. In other words the firm needs balance and solidity to be maintained in its decision-making process and overall asset structure.

The presence of the family and the firm as two different entities along with the resulting differentiation of the services provided consistently with the requirements expressed by the former and the latter requires the identi-

---

[19] The contiguousness of financial intermediaries' and professional agencies' fields of action grows more marked when the external subject plays the "third actor's" role, that is of the subject outside the property who acts as if belonging to it due to the trustworthy relations established with the owners and to the highly relational, human and social content of the intervention. As for the profile of the "third actor", see evaluations by Corbetta 1995 and De Cecco 1994 which reflect the issue from the point of view of the firm and the financial system.

fication of a different market segmentation criterion going beyond the "traditional", "transitory" and "complex" firm distinction, which is typical of the one-parameter logic, according to which the firm status conditions that of the family and vice-versa, within a sole reference context.

Table 3.6 Needs overlapping in corporate finance operations: corporate and private joint action field

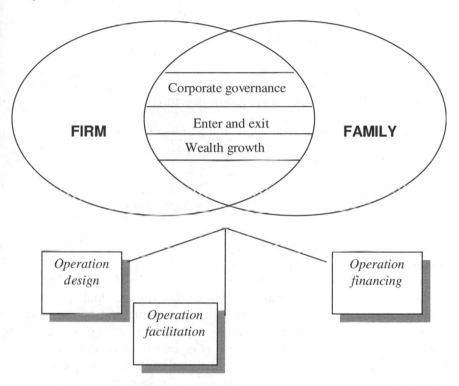

The path leading to a market framework able to provide banks with a set of guidelines for their commercial action consists in finding the distinctive aspects or the "contextual situations" that characterize the corporate and the family business, thus identifying different categories of requirements for financial services[20]. Such categories must contain some pre-requisites to be functional and effective not only in view of the their formal definition but also for their implementation upon supply positioning. In this respect the necessary and sufficient pre-requisites are the recurrence of requirement categories, their importance, their frequency in the market

---

[20] For this market interpretation and segmentation logic see Caselli and Gatti now being published.

operational practice and their conceptual clarity as to the relation between requirements and corporate or family "status". This leads to merging rather than fragmenting categories in a relevant number of situations whose closeness increases management overlapping.

With reference to the firm, relevant contextual situations can be summarized as follows:

- startup;

- business development;

- growth consolidation via acquisitions;

- growth consolidation via group structure;

- growth consolidation via listing admission;

- internationalization;

- restructuring

- crisis.

The above mentioned contextual situations are important because they pragmatically join some typical prescriptions of the development model of the business life-cycle where the origination profile of financial requirements is sufficiently clear and well outlined – for example, the case of business startup is characterized by some managerial and not necessarily sequential phases, which naturally require quite well-defined financial services. A relevant example in this sense is given by the process of acquisition or internationalization in which, irrespective of the stage of development achieved by the company, the reference operational context, the investment dynamic and the typology of business risks tend to take up a typical structure from the business and the financial point of view.

The approach of relevant contextual situations must be replicated for the family, whose origination profile of requirements can be summarized into the following categories:

- wealth protection and management;

- family members' protection and management;

- property restructuring;

- succession;

-    business transfer.

Again, the different contextual situations define the different "stages" in the development process of wealth and human life-cycle which characterizes the family entity into its different components. This means that the above situations do not reflect a necessary time sequencing, but seize the variety of the situations which are objectively critical for the maintenance and the development of family financial and human resources in the course of time

Wealth protection and management here refers to the set of strategic and operational decisions the family is called to make to preserve and develop its net worth in the course of time. This may involve general aspects for the definition of company structures according to the objective – for example trusts or holdings located abroad – as well as the development of management policies for family members' assets. Quite different is the case of the protection and management of family members, where the prevailing origination profile of financial requirements is concentrated on the creation of a defense shield against risks that may undermine the stability and the composition of the family nucleus and is therefore directed toward the area of insurance and social security services. The stages of property restructuring, succession and transfer are more complex as a result of the tightly interweaving relations between asset-management requirements and corporate finance requirements. This is due to the fact that the above situations tend to involve issues regarding corporate governance and wealth transfer.

On the whole, the bank capacity to join the profiles of the different stages, for the family and the firm, with the specific features of product industries represents the critical aspect for the definition of an effective positioning in the market and for the development of effective supply policies in terms of satisfaction of SME requirements. If this is true from the logical point of view, in economic terms the actual implementation of the indications resulting from the complex framework of family-firm relations/contextual situations must be contextually introduced in organizational structures and production processes which impose obligations and restrictions on the management. In this sense it is necessary to join the different options left open by the diagnosis of segmentation criteria with consistent and profitable supply models.

3.4 From Mapping Requirements to Market Positioning as to Family Business

Market positioning choices in the corporate area are closely connected with the selected segmentation process and the diagnosis produced by the bank under the analysis profile of product industry-SME customer segment combinations. This means that segmentation methodologies initially chosen by the management have a decisive impact on the prescriptions the bank obtains from market mapping and comprehension. The identification of bank product industries and firm homogeneous segments provides the bank with a reliable operating support to define market strategies that must be adopted for the different product-market mixes as well as to more generally define the necessary resources and competencies to support supply processes. From this point of view, the more sensitive the segmentation criteria to the market dynamic structure and the more proactive toward the environment as it is able to interpret and advance exchange behaviors, the more the bank can gradually consolidate a consistent policy of differentiation not only in terms of services but also of organizational functions.

In addition, the identification of the characteristics of the competitive system which defines product industries and the choice of the aggregation mode of SME segments may lead the bank to different kinds of utilization, as the concept of positioning contains itself a multiplicity of actions with quite different significance and level of application. Analytically, utilization modes can be summarized as follows:

- mapping of product-market mixes for the identification of bank strategic business areas and for the arrangement of the most suitable organizational structures and production processes to satisfy customer needs;

- implementation of an effective methodology for the dynamic comprehension of the market, in view of the creation of a *tableau de bord* for the corporate division in order to organize overall market strategies as well as those for individual client managers;

- definition of an effective methodology for the dynamic comprehension of the market in order to focus the attention on the adequacy of a bank specific product division positioning;

- creation of an effective market monitoring methodology in order to allow individual client managers to trigger operational marketing actions or to adjust more general market policies to customers being served.

The first utilization mode seems to be wider since it places the segmentation process at the top of the bank strategic planning process, so that not only the identification of the market target is an independent variable but also the organizational structure is considered modifiable and adjustable as per the composition and the aggregation of strategic business areas[21]. On the contrary, the three remaining utilization modes interiorize the constraint of the organizational structure and, according to the utilization level, join market interpretation with the operating processes best suiting goal achievement. As a result, when the bank starts divisionalization by defining market areas as large corporate & institutions, corporate, retail and small business for the purpose of credit risk organic management, the segmentation process is necessarily a subsequent stage and inside the market areas thus identified.

For this reason, the segmentation process is more widely applied in the corporate area, so that the importance of the market area, the variety of SME models and the need for the client manager's strong grip lead to a more attentive analysis of customer behaviors. On the contrary, in the retail area, the lower complexity and the smaller size of enterprises strongly reduce the possibilities of forming homogeneous reference segments. This means that the resulting positioning logic prevailingly relies on product strategies as the market analysis of product industries prevails over that of enterprises.

Two-parameter segmentation models consider the family and the enterprise as two connected but distinct production centers of specific financial requirements the bank can satisfy through its supply process. Compared with the segmentation logic based exclusively on the enterprise profile, here the detail and the analysis is more accurate and better suiting the operative specificity of a family-owned SME. In addition, this requires better tuning from production and commercial processes as well as from client managers who govern corporate portfolios. In the case of less flexible and less reactive organization structures as to their adjusting to demand changes, the use of two-parameter segmentation models can therefore be-

---

[21] This hypothesis is the least frequent although it is the most effective as the segmentation process is here followed by a consistent alteration of the organization and production structures. This situation, however, might occur in the case of radical startup of corporate banking undertakings or when a new intermediary is entering the market. Elsewhere, the organization structure is generally defined ex ante and followed by a market diagnosis process which should confirm and implement the operating activity.

come too complex and quite likely lead to paralysis[22]. If this is true in principle, the bank that has identified the development of the corporate area as its priority goal can hardly elude in the medium term the need to understand the complexity of the corporate behavior through the joint analysis of the corporate and the family system.

With reference to the corporate system, it is possible to identify homogeneous firm categories based on the contextual situations experienced by the enterprise, as shown in the fourth chapter of this volume. The identification of the different situations highlights the specific nature of each category in relation to the specific features of the product (see Table 3.7). The high degree of detail and the complexity of the resulting mapping obviously do not lead to a punctual differentiation of the outcomes for each product-firm pair, but to verifying the presence of sufficiently extended areas of invariance of purchasing behaviors, so that the bank and client managers can develop aggregate market actions.

Firms falling into startup category show a strongly differentiated profile due to the specificity of the contextual situation, both from the strategic and the financial point of view. As a result, all of the six product industries are highly sensitive to this category by clearly identifying the market areas where the bank can take action. This is particularly evident in lending and corporate finance, where high external financial requirements, the uncertain time of investment return and the uncertain development cycle of the

---

[22] The choice of the segmentation model does not consist in a merely commercial choice but, as already and repeatedly stated in the course of this research, it involves the most complex issues of consistency between the organization structure, production processes and market positioning choices. In this sense, the characteristics of the segmentation model must be joined with the degree of reactivity of commercial policies and, more generally, of bank strategies. As stated by Henry Mintzberg, this occurs because the presence of an action model – in this case segmentation – represents a "model within a decision flow". As a result, faced with analytical and complex models, the bank should be able to exalt and exploit the component of "emergent strategy" rather than that of "deliberate strategy" which, on the basis of the complexity of the segmentation model, would risk generating dangerous deviations from demand specifications. On the contrary, in the presence of less complex and less detailed segmentation models, the component of "deliberate strategy" tends to be more effective due to the generic nature and the extended size of identified segments. This means, for example, that in the retail segment, where product industries segmentation prevails on that by firm categories, the definition of product strategies planned ex ante is rewarding compared with the possibility to free emerging strategies in the course of the exchange activity between the bank and the firm. For further information on this subject, see Mintzberg 1985 and Mintzberg 1978.

segment require bank intervention on equity and on medium and long term liabilities.Asset management intervention can be significant as long as startup relies on dedicated company architectures[23].

Firms falling into the development category are distinguished on the basis of their diversified need for lending instruments: they may need to establish a correct plan for terms and amounts or to utilize fiscal leverage to reduce the taxable sum total. As for liability planning, the firm involved by development may need corporate finance services, above all for private equity operations, and both financial and insurance risk management services should non-managed risk undermine the physiological and organic process of development.

Table 3.7 Bank positioning as to market segmentation based on a two-parameter analysis: the firm vision

FIRM STATES	PRODUCT INDUSTRIES					
	Payment system services	**Lending**	**Financial risk management**	**Insurance risk mgt**	**Asset management**	**Corporate finance**
Start-up	Availability of payment and cash management tools is not relevant variable.	Only medium and long term lending, though lending supply is residual compared to that of equity. Supply can be concentrated on subsidized loans.	Availability of financial risk management tools is not relevant variable.	Availability of insurance risk management tools can be referred to firm risk insurance if this is important for accomplishment of start up. Upon corporate charter insurance and social security plans can be considered for directors.	Availability of asset management tools is not relevant variable. Relevant if start up provides for design of corporate complex structures (e.g. foreign holding).	Corporate finance services designed for venture capital, pure advisory and strategic advisory.

---

[23] See Cressy R.C., "Commitment Lending under Asymmetric Information: Theory and Tests on UK Startup Data", in "Small Business Economics", n. 5, 1996.

Table 3.7 Continued

Development	Firm larger extension urges for supply of basic payment services (Riba, Rid, Mav) and verification of CBI standard. Use of company credit cards can be checked in relation to staff number.	Firm larger extension urges for supply of services diversified over entire time range of operations. Strong fiscal value of medium-term operations must be exploited. Effective also for mezzanine finance tools as they allow pegging investor returns to growth prospects.	Management phases do not allow identifying demand specific differentiation. Attention on exchange, price and interest rate risk depends on firm business. Only in case of group structure, bank must prevent and anyway manage strong impact of risk internal compensation. In this case, asset and liability integrated management services can be relevant if coordinated with cash pooling and cash management services.	Firm development justifies utilization of staff social security plans.	Availability of asset management tools is not immediately correlated with firm evolutionary phases. Relevant if development phase provides for design of a complex company structure (e.g. foreign holding); if staff number justifies supply of trading and saving management services.	If company growth goes along with important development prospects, private equity services may be of interest.
Growth consolidation: acquisitions		Firm larger extension urges for supply of services diversified over the entire time range of operations. Strong fiscal value of medium term operations must be exploited. Acquisition logic must lead to dedicated leveraged tools.		Firm larger extension allows and justifies organization of insurance risk check up to verify nature and frequency of pure risks in the company.	Presence of complex real assets may require integrated management service (purchase, sale, transfer from property to leasing). Supply of trading and financial management services for enterprise securities portfolio seems irrelevant if firm remains in SME segment.	Presence of M&A, MBO and LBO operations requires overall control of entire operation chain value (mere advisory, strategic advisory, financing, private equity if necessary).

Table 3.7 Continued

Growth consolidation: group structure	Group structure allows verifying whether each firm has set of basic payment tools and whether purchase of company credit card can be defined. Group connections largely justify supply of cash pooling and cash management services.	Group structure requires check up of aggregate financing forms.		Group structure requires strategic advisory services.
Growth consolidation: listing admissions	Firm final structuring urges for supply of basic payment services (Riba, Rid, Mav) and verification of CBI standard and possibly CBI advanced. Use of company credit cards can be checked in relation to staff number.	Firm larger extension urges for lending ser vices diversified over entire time range of operations. Strong fiscal value of medium term operations must be exploited. Listing admission process leads bank to check whether debt entire structure is consistent with evaluation profile relative to equity and market expectations.		Presence of listing admissions requires overall control on entire operation chain value (mere advisory, strategic advisory, financing, direct equity interest, if necessary).

Table 3.7 Continued

				Firm international presence justifies upgrade of insurance risk check up to develop non-domestic risk management, also by means of international risk management services (e.g. International Finance Corporation)		Firm international presence may require complex M&A and Project Finance operations that must be entirely managed by bank.
Internationalization	International value of firm cash flows urges for supply of CBI advanced services and of international payment services, also according to group logic.	Firm international presence urges for: diversification of lending services; import and export lending tools, also in relation to leasing, integrated with insurance risk management; support of international investment by exploiting local control of the area; international subsidized loans.	Firm international presence justifies potentially stronger pressure on exchange and interest rate risk.			
Restructuring	Availability of payment and cash management tools is not relevant variable.	Debt lever must be consistent with overall management goal and aim at changing cost-length mix through long and mezzanine term tools.	Availability of financial risk management tools is relevant variable only if risk management is important element of financial restructuring plan.	Availability of insurance risk management tools is relevant variable only if risk management is important element of financial restructuring plan.		Firm restructuring and above all crisis represent specific areas for corporate finance. Once again, critical element for bank success is capacity to manage operation entire chain value, with special stress on strategic advisory

Firms involved in a process of growth consolidation may present different aspects, sometimes regarding acquisitions, group structures or listing admissions in a regulated market. The three contextual situations are characterized by significantly differentiated financial requirements in relation to the specific attributes of the real context. In the case of acquisition policies, the critical areas for bank successful access are those of corporate finance and asset management as they have a stronger impact on the context of property relations and equity modifications resulting from acquisition processes. In the case of group structuring, apart from the bank focus on problems concerning equity management, in terms of corporate finance and asset management, the major specific features are in the system of payment services and in that of financial and insurance risk management. This is due to the pooling dynamic of financial flows within the group which, on the one hand, reduces the areas for bank action because of the firm possible exploitation of the physiologic matching effect and, on the other, multiplies the bank chances of access thanks to the larger field of action resulting from the presence of the group and by the latent need for an overall supervision of the aggregate cash and risk management. In the case of listing admissions, the area of prevailing interest is corporate finance due to the need for the overall management of the value chain and of the different businesses the firm is due to manage as it approaches a regulated market for the positioning of its shares.

Firms involved in an internationalization process based on export or even on a foreign investment strategy are characterized by a transversal requisite since their international presence may appear in a number of different contextual situations. Internationalization, however, draws the bank attention as it generates important changes on the structure of SME financial requirements due to the currency definition of flows, the qualitative and quantitative change in external financial needs and the presence of risks connected with the fact the firm is operating in new markets. As for product industries, the area of payment system services and that of financial risk management play a significant role considering the support required by the presence of one or more currencies differing from the domestic one in cash and payment flows and by risk management. In addition, depending on the complexity of the adopted internationalization process and selected market segment, also the areas of insurance risk management and corporate finance show a weight and relevant differentiation. In particular, this occurs when export flows are substituted by production displacement and direct investments.

Firms involved in restructuring or experiencing a phase of crisis, despite the deep difference between the two situations from the economic and real point of view, show common elements for the bank that must position the supply process. Apart from the opportunity and the restrictions of a customer relation characterized by a difficult and more or less reversible situation of either of the counterparts, supply strategies are concentrated in the areas of lending and corporate finance. In this sense, above all in the area of corporate finance, the bank capacity to manage wide-ranging advisory activities on the entire portfolio of financial services provided to the enterprise is a crucial and decisive element.

With reference to the family vision, contextual situations for market mapping refer to macro-areas of requirements which condition to a different degree the family life-cycle as well as the relational and exchange profiles with the firm (see Table 3.8). As outlined in the fourth chapter of this volume, the presence of these requirement areas not only polarizes the specific attributes of requirements, but also provides a complete frame of analysis which, combined with the distinctive features of product industries, helps client managers to further improve their strong grip and relationship with the enterprise.

Table 3.8 Bank positioning as to market segmentation based on a two-parameter analysis: the family vision

FAMILY STATES	PRODUCT INDUSTRIES					
	Payment system services	**Lending**	**Financial risk management**	**Insurance risk management**	**Asset management**	**Corporate finance**
Wealth protection and management	Supply of payment system and cash management services seems disconnected from phase of family life-cycle. Services supplied must focus on credit and debit cards, also connected with company system. Other services seem not to be relevant, except for home banking which is closely connected with trading services in asset management area.	Supply of lending services can have strong fiscal value with reference to real property leasing: high fiscal advantages allow developing demobilization, buy back and acquisition operations aimed at increasing family wealth.	Supply of financial risk management services has very limited application usually with reference to high net worth assets exposed to above risks. Financial risk management tools seem to be disconnected from family management phases.	Supply of insurance and social security risk management tools finds wide application in connection with insurance policies on family "assets".	Asset management services may become much or more complex depending on bank overall strategies: asset management, asset management in investment funds, trading. The presence of an entrepreneurial family leads to dedicated high profile asset management solutions (private banking). This does not prevent management of real assets (art objects, real estates, etc....).	Supply of corporate finance services finds application in the different forms of legal and fiscal advisory. This is closely integrated with supply of asset management and insurance risk management services in any family management phase.

Table 3.8 Continued

Family members' protection and management	Lending operations can be applied in relation to consumer and personal loans for family members' specific activities. Relevance of medium-term operations, above all for real estate acquisitions.	Risk management refers to family members' life and other risk policies. In addition there are social security plans or long term investment plans of financial resources.	Asset management services provide corporate governance solutions to protect family members (trusts and fiduciaries).
Property restructuring	Lending operations have limited application to support buy in operations in the company.	Insurance and social security risk management do not find distinctive specificity in this phase.	Asset management services provide dedicated corporate governance solutions (trusts and fiduciaries), along with mixed financial-insurance solutions relating to wealth transfer.
Family members' protection and management	Lending operations can be applied in relation to consumer and personal loans for family members' specific activities. Relevance of medium-term operations, above all for real estate acquisitions.	Risk management refers to family members' life and other risk policies. In addition there are social security plans or long term investment plans of financial resources.	Asset management services provide corporate governance solutions to protect family members (trusts and fiduciaries).

Table 3.8 Continued

Property re-structuring	Lending operations have limited application to support buy in operations in the company.	Insurance and social security risk management do not find distinctive specificity in this phase.	Asset management services provide dedicated corporate governance solutions (trusts and fiduciaries),
Succesion	Lending operations have very limited utilization, usually to support buy-in operations in the company.	Supply of insurance products is effective if it allows better ex ante planning and ex post management of succession compared to schemes provided for by the law.	along with mixed financial-insurance solutions relating to wealth transfer.
Business transfer	Lending operations are not relevant in this phase.	Supply of insurance products is effective as long as it allows better ex ante planning and ex post management of transfer compared to schemes provided for by the law.	Asset management services concentrate on investment and management of resources after transfer. Again, given the relevance of amounts, the activity is bound to be high profile.

Whenever the family needs its wealth to be protected and managed, the firm demands for services prevailingly focused in the areas of asset management and insurance risk management. This is due to the fundamental goal which is connected with the growth of the available assets, in the different forms of financial net worth, real assets and artistic-cultural goods[24]. This statement should not confine the bank field of action to private banking, thus provoking dangerous role overlapping and dangerous internal conflicts, as the process of wealth management drags and involves more specifically corporate interest areas. There are two relevant areas for bank action. In the first place, within lending activities, the fiscal employment of such instruments as leasing allows wealth investment operations with significant performances above all in the real estate segment.[25]; this goes with

---

[24] See Musile Tanzi 2001.
[25] See Caselli 1998.

leveraged operations for acquisition of company shares. In the second place, within the area of corporate finance, the family quest of profitable investments needs the bank intervention in the segments of M&A operations as well as for the purchase of shares in closed-end funds with a strong support in terms of legal and fiscal advisory.

Whenever family members need to be protected and managed, the bank is called to design solutions dedicated to the individual. This prevailingly involves the areas of asset management and insurance risk management, although important spaces can be found also in the area of personal loans. As for asset management, apart from the various forms that can be supplied, a crucial element is the definition of the structures which allow the individual to define the typology of relation between personal and corporate assets. Therefore, trusts and fiduciaries are particularly important in this context. As for insurance risk management, instead, family requirements are associated to the need for protection against the risk of death and accidents as well as for the arrangement of social security plans. Upon these bases, it is possible to co-ordinate the "personal" risk system with events and situations involving the enterprise, so as to obtain an integrated vision of the corporate system that is also able to reduce the bank business risk.

Property re-structuring is a typical phase for the family, when the balance of shares held by the partners is altered due to the exit of some partners, the entry of new partners – members of the family or strangers – or to the re-distribution of control within the family.[26] The core demand here consists in the need for a reliable reference partner, able to provide advice and supervision in legal, fiscal and strategic matters for the purpose of guaranteeing a compact control group and the balance between the family and the firm. This means that the bank should concentrate on areas of interest and fields of action that typically belong to professional agencies, above all for the requisites of the "third actor" and "confidentiality" which are of fundamental importance[27]. On the basis of this assumption, the product industries able to differentiate the bank action are corporate finance and asset management because an intervention seems to be necessary in the field of personal properties management and on that of corporate equity structure.

Requirements resulting from the phase of succession do not differ from those previously described. In fact, apart from the psychological and sub-

---

[26] See Danco 1982.

[27] For this aspect reference should be made to evaluations and assessments included in the second chapter, in relation to the description of the profile of professional agencies in the Italian market.

stantial relevance of its consequences, succession is an element of property restructuring. As a result, the need for a global advisor becomes essential and of crucial importance for the correct development of succession from the fiscal, legal and strategic point of view. Apart from the obvious relevance of corporate finance and asset management products, another two elements should be considered in view of the successful positioning of the supply.[28]. The first element consists in planning succession *ex ante* by means of insurance and financial products and in managing succession *ex post*, either in the case of previous careful planning or of a sudden and unexpected traumatic event. The second element consists in a managerial action which may be requested when no valid alternatives are available within the family or the unexpected character of the event does not allow the family to make arrangements for an effective solution among its members. In this case, the bank action may proceed along the path of capital shareholding in pursuit of counterparts – as partners or managers – or that of defining solutions of temporary management or tutorship for the younger members of the family[29].

Business transfer represents the exit of the family from the owned enterprise. This means the system of financial requirements will involve operational advisory services and post-operational asset management services. In the first case, the bank will undertake to find counterparts and to carry out the deal from the economic and legal point of view. This implies the availability of a wide network of market relations in the entrepreneurial sector and high skills in assessing counterparts in managerial and financial terms. In the second case, wealth management becomes necessary when the operation has been concluded and the sale of the company shares have produced remarkable returns which must be suitably invested according to family goals. This may bring about complex and extreme solutions such as the entry into another company or the creation of a closed-end fund[30].

---

[28] See Gibb and Davis 1995; Kets de Vries 1988; Kets de Vries 1993; Reid 1993.
[29] For further considerations on succession and bank field of action see Corbetta, Bolelli, Caselli, Lassini 2001.
[30] See Cressy and Olofsson 1997.

4 Synergies Between Corporate and Private Banking

Stefano Caselli

4.1 Introduction

The research developed in the previous chapters has examined the complex nature of the distinctive and structural features of the family owning one or more businesses as well as the map of the financial requirements emerging from the combined evaluation of the enterprise and the owner family. In particular, the last study has allowed us to outline a logical reference framework in order to proceed with the verification and the correspondence between the system of requirements and that of the financial services. From this point of view, the explanatory scope of the above approach develops irrespective of the strategic and organizational choices made by financial intermediaries as it appears only subsequently as a general criterion for product positioning. This results in the further necessity to understand the mechanisms and the logics which enable financial intermediaries to define their own positioning by considering the specificity of the family/firm relationship as well as to organically exploit the business opportunity resulting from the family/firm connection.

This overall necessity leads to tackle two different issues that are connected and sequential.

The first issue regards the financial and the assets connections between the family and the firm. This allows us not only to clearly analyze the target functions of the two actors and to re-connect the different areas of requirements to quantitative parameters but also to establish whether the distinctive features of the same financial and assets connections represent an element of interaction potentially useful for the financial intermediary.

The second issue regards the financial operations which, due to their own nature or their being consistent with financial and assets connections, are bound to trigger important synergies between the systems of products typically designed for the corporate and the private area. In other words, the critical aspect of the intermediary's positioning choice is solved as long as the scope and the nature of the operations are synergetic and comprehensive of the corporate and the private area.

4.2 The Relationship Between the Owner Family and the Owned Firm: General Prescriptions

The financial structure of family business, which has been analyzed in the first chapter of the research, presents a distinctive character that reflects both size-specific and country-specific factors. If the former are intrinsic in the concept of small and medium size, the latter depend on the financial and industrial organization of the respective country. This means that the structure of corporate liabilities is characterized by an aspect common to any economic system, though showing some differences from country to country which can be gathered into a homogeneous reference path.

From the analytical point of view, the high volume of bank debts characterizing average corporate liabilities - above all for SMEs - finds a reference in the prescriptive logic of corporate finance so that the ratio between debt and equity is established on the basis of the compared evaluation between failure costs and the fiscal advantages deriving from opening different financing channels. If this applies to any typology of firms, in the specific instance of small and medium-sized enterprises both the notion of failure costs and that of fiscal advantages may be broadened so that on the one hand their strictly economic meaning is even strengthened and on the other the value of mutual interdependency connections between the owner family and the owned firm can be included.

Failure costs resulting from the direct relation between the financial leverage increase and the funding average rate increase applied by lenders - once the "market" acceptability threshold of the business risk has been exceeded[1] - must include also the costs deriving from the owner's loss of business control. Despite the difficult measurement of such costs, the notion of family failure assumes a strong operating value as the change in the family-firm direct relation may generate drawbacks not only in terms of future missing profits but above all in terms of explicit and social costs resulting from the failure or from breaking the existing relationships within the family. The above costs are referred, for example, to forms of dramatic and unexpected subdivisions of the family wealth due to the exit of one or

---

[1] The growth of the firm debt relation may lead to exceed a psychological and functional threshold, beyond which the firm stakeholder system judges risk intolerable. This step does not necessarily lead the firm to failure, but it may generate additional costs due to the exit of some financiers, to the growth of the cost of money applied by other lenders, to possible reactions on the part of suppliers and customers. On this issue see Bradley, Jarrel and Kim 1984; Kane, Marcus and Mc Donald 1984.

more family members as a result of the changed ownership and the entry of external partners.

As for fiscal advantages, the distribution of the tax shield established by the policy maker affects directly the net rate of financing sources and the cash-flow distribution upon tax payment. This means that the firm's allocation of liabilities and its mid-term financial planning are strongly conditioned by the rules on deductible expenses and the fixing of incentives or selective criteria. The differentiation of rules is not limited to the distinction between debt and equity, but also to debt distinctions as to the origins of the debt or to contractual forms[2].Moreover the incidence of the fiscal advantage can be rated in relation to the bank debt, the market debt and the different forms of fund raising among partners as well as to the length of financing and the distinction between leasing and debt. In any case the distribution of the tax shield does not exhaust the comprehension of fiscal advantages as the analysis should be extended to the performance of the family assets and thus to the relative impact of fiscal variables. This is necessary as family members allocate their financial resources according to whether they aim at the capital, at financing the firm or at investing their assets. Therefore the comprehensive review of tax variables requires a process of joint maximization of the fiscal advantage for both the firm and the family.

The general relation which opposes failure costs and fiscal advantages can be formally expressed, considering the above mentioned interactions between the family and the firm. Hence we can write

$$Kf_{firm} - Kf_{family} >=< \Delta taxshield (Debt - Equity) \qquad (4.1)$$

where Kf_{firm} indicates the firm's failure costs and Kf_{family} those of the family. The above relation can be expressed more correctly by describing a series of elements. In the first place, the concept of tax shield should be suitably analyzed on the basis of quantitative and time parameters in order to have it effectively quantified. This can be obtained by means of the concept of debt weighted average cost and equity cost after taxes. So doing, not only can the tax shield be financially evaluated but the same variable relating to the pricing of financial resources as expressed by the capital market is thus included in the evaluation of the allocation of corporate liabilities. In addition the identification of the above parameters is not sufficient when we turn from financing to the investment of resources which

---

[2] For a description and exhaustive evaluation of the different forms of impact of fiscal variables on the structure of firm liabilities see Dessy 2001.

becomes binding when the firm and the family dimensions are joint. Here, the debt after tax weighted average cost must be bound to the after tax average return lenders would obtain if they decided to invest in debt but in a different form [3]. Equally, the equity after tax cost must be bound to the after tax return lenders would obtain if they made another investment in equity. The bound must be interpreted as the enter and exit condition of the owner family on both equity and debt. In the first case, if the owners expect higher returns from investing in debt not related to the owned firm but to the market as a whole, debt fund raising will develop outside the family. In the second case, if the owners expect higher returns from investing in equity not related to the owned firm but to the market as a whole, equity fund raising will tend to develop theoretically outside the family on condition that the cost of fund raising is lower than the cost of debt.

In the second place, family failure costs must be analyzed by considering the different components characterizing their nature. Then the three identified components have a development dynamic that is a dependent variable of the variations in the firm's equity.

The first component is the expected loss of returns due to the owner family's non-participation in the business capital. This loss is considered both in strictly monetary terms, (i.e. loss of future dividends) and in broader terms (i.e. loss of possible influence on the distribution of the same)[4]. This means that the above variable is directly correlated to the growth of equity in the presence of the family more profitable investments in other bonds. In this case, the absence of profitable investments in the firm deters any further re-investment of resources and the growth of equity can be guaranteed only by subjects outside the ownership. Therefore, the

---

[3] A significant example in this respect can be the comparison between the cost of capital obtained through the form of shareholders' financing and the return on the investment in bonds. In both instances, the legal form consists in investing and raising debt funds, but due to the presence of different fiscal rules, the investor's profitability may turn out to be different at a parity of conditions. See Tagliavini 1999.

[4] It is worth noticing that if family failure costs include expected losses due to non-participation to business capital, by symmetry firm failure costs must also include the firm missing profits due to the investment of debt rather than equity. This happens when the presence of ambitious development plans requires a massive employment of "patient" capital so as to guarantee the risk of the same plans and the uncertainty of cash-flows dedicated to the repayment of lenders. Although this approach is theoretically correct, in the practice it is difficult to identify in advance the category of "ambitious plans" and its formalization in terms of non-profits.

renunciation to the equity growth is the only means to reduce the expected losses due to the non-participation in the business capital.

The second component regards the costs of portfolio re-allocation as a result of the changes in the firm ownership. The different weights and balances within the family resulting from the changes in the assets invested in the firm or from the entry of new partners may produce transaction costs because of the necessity to re-establish the lost balances. Anyway, the definition of new balances produces both explicit costs and losses due to the unexpected disinvestment of assets.

The third component regards the "social" costs that may have a direct or indirect monetary impact. This component is an extension and somehow a completion of the second one as it emphasizes the expenses borne by the family as a result of the changed social relations among the various members of the family. The growth of equity generates imbalances which have not only immediate monetary but also relational consequences, which may reveal different economic effects in the course of time. Quite often such effects are lower profits for the firm due to the non exploitation of business opportunities because of the presence of latent or actual conflicts within the family. Yet, the amount of social costs is a direct function of the complexity of the family, that is of the number of generations and the number of people directly involved in the business management system. The presence of multiple family nuclei does in fact extend the size of potential conflicts and the amount of transaction costs to be faced to solve the same.

As a result of the three variables, the previously mentioned formula changes as follows:

$$Kf_{firm} - (EL + K_p + K_s) >=< r_d - r_e \tag{4.2}$$

where Kf_{firm} indicates the amount of the firm's failure costs, EL the expected loss due to non-participation in business capital, K_p the amount of portfolio re-allocation costs, K_s the amount of "social" costs, r_d the after tax cost of debt and r_e the after tax cost of equity.

The relation reveals the arbitrary nature of the choices regarding the structure of the business capital in the presence of family ownership. This leads to the fact that the growth of capitalization can be justified either by system fiscal policy factors so that the second part of the relation generates a differential that is favorable to equity and higher than that of the first part of the relation or by family corporate governance factors, which significantly reduce the cost component Kf_{family} relative to the first part of the relation. In addition, SMEs' size profile makes the presence of any governance capacity unlikely both in terms of business and social relations between the family and the firm as well as within the family itself, so that family failure costs are considerably reduced. Moreover, the absolutely low capitalization, which is produced by the presence of family failure costs and at parity of differential between r_d and r_e, makes EL, K_p and K_s components more sensitive to the changes in equity. As a result, a sort of vicious circle is likely to be activated so that the limited amount of equity tends to direct the choices regarding the structure of business capital toward the area of debt.

The relevance of debt, which is characterized by size-specific and family-specific factors, is nevertheless further strengthened in Italy by a fiscal policy structurally favorable to debt with reference to the second part of the relation. From the functional point of view of the system, this is consistent with the remarkable development of bank financing circuits as reference structures for the support of corporate investment choices.

The consistency between firms' selection criteria of financing sources and the development path of the financial system produces a series of important drawbacks in the approach modes adopted by financial intermediaries in the attempt to meet the requirements of small and medium-sized enterprises. In this context there are a number of prescriptions which enable us to understand and compare positioning choices as lending represents the corporate reference product – which is strengthened by the action of a non-neutral fiscal policy – as long as it feeds the process of fund raising and guarantees the achievement of a dynamic balance between capital structure and ownership relations. Prescriptions can be summarized as follows:

- the importance of the credit function makes credit underwriting the financial intermediary's access key to firm financial requirements and family-firm relations;

- the importance for the firm to have financing sources available makes credit underwriting the tool leading to the firm's "contractual capture", thus leaving some areas for cross selling and origination in relation to non-credit products;

- credit becomes the "balance beam" of family corporate governance and gives the financial intermediary the possibility to develop a deep knowledge of the corporate system and therefore of its risks.

The specificity of the three components described above points out that within the financial system banks have a competitive advantage with corporate customers which makes them different from the other subjects as their own organizational and structural characteristics guarantee *ex ante* a stronger control of the credit function. This can be observed under three different aspects. First of all, irrespective of the counter-position and of the choice between the specialized and the generalized model of supply, the institutional specialization of the credit function gives the bank stronger incisiveness in corporate financing as a result of the monetary value of the services provided. The financing monetary profile not only allows the bank to play *a priori* the insider role of corporate financial flows, but it also becomes SMEs' instrument for reducing the complexity – in terms of knowledge and costs – and the information asymmetries of the financial system. Secondly, the monetary function potentially allows conveying cross-selling policies which multiply the areas for the identification of more and more complex requirements. The ability to understand these areas is of major importance for financial intermediaries to extend their range of services. The control of the monetary function gives banks a potential asset that gives them the chance to increase their volumes and margins on a constant basis in the course of time. Thirdly, the actual geographical distribution of banks allows them to better penetrate local economies and better monitor local enterprises. If this aspect is less relevant for big firms, for small and medium-sized enterprises the bank's "local distribution" represents a key factor for the creation and the development of market relations. The local nature of the divided bank contains the latent power of originating the entire range of financial operations. This can be exploited by the bank as the element triggering an all finance supply process which is typical of the "pure" universal bank or it can be exchanged with external economies in terms of creation and development of a network of specialists who, according to their product competencies, re-compose the internal complexity of the all finance supply in the market.

4.3 The Relationship Between the Owner Family and the Owned Firm: the Nature of Assets and Financial Connections

4.3.1 Distinctive Aspects

The system of assets and financial connections which develops between the owner family and the owned firm moves from a substantially simple reference frame (see Table 4.1): the matching of the firm/s assets statement/s and that of the family shows that if, on the one hand, the firm represents one of the financial assets in the family portfolio, on the other hand the firm liabilities need to be backed in the fund raising process and the family can meet this requirement by using its own financial resources in the form of debt or equity.[5]. This means that if in the first case the family-firm connection is on the level of assets and thus assumes the value of maximum aggregation, in the second case the family-firm connection is financial and thus assumes the value of family individual investment operations.

Table 4.1 The family-firm connection system: the assets and the financial perspectives

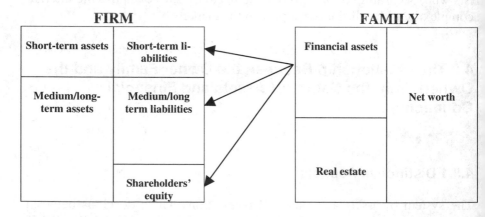

---

[5] As a matter of fact, for the purpose of a more accurate and exhaustive review of cases, the allocation of real assets in the form of capital increase should be included among the various financial operations characterized by the allocation of resources to the firm.

The reference to the financial and assets perspectives obviously serves to clearly identify the different criteria which connect the corporate and the family system. Yet, two important elements should be focused in order to better explain this mode of interpretation.

In the first place, the financial and assets perspectives tend to interweave, as the firm's financing choices affect its value at a parity of risk. This means that a specific financing strategy developed by the family for the firm necessarily generates an induced effect consisting in the growth of the firm value and therefore of the family net worth. This is true irrespective of the returns profile of the specific financing choice and of its contribution to the development of the family financial assets.

In the second place, within the financial perspective, the possible forms of lending financial resources to the firm are highly differentiated. This depends on the different destination of financial resources (short-term liabilities versus consolidated liabilities) and on the different contractual forms which, in that specific time and legislative context, can be actually used[6]. This means there is a direct correspondence between the firm requirement areas and the family allocation criteria of financial resources, whose joint profitability will need evaluating in the course of time (Table 4.2).

Table 4.2 The family allocation criteria of financial resources

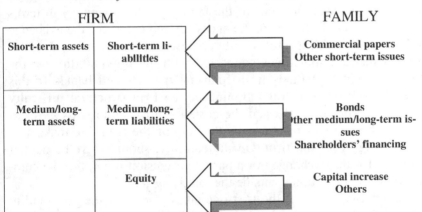

---

[6] It should be noted that, irrespective of the specificity of the family different direct financing tools, it is possible to employ indirect or triangular forms of financing, where the family provides its own guarantees to a third party financing the firm. This scheme can be used with any contractual form of financing

Taking for granted the natural overlapping of financing processes and wealth creation processes in general terms, the specificity of the assets and financial profiles requires a deeper analysis of the internal rules which characterize, on the one hand, the family selection of financing operations within the firm financing process and, on the other, the investment of the value produced within the family assets portfolio.

4.3.2 The Relationship Between the Owner Family and the Owned Firm: the Financial Perspective

The financial connection between the owner family and the owned firm can be fully understood by analyzing two distinguished and sequential elements:

- the modes of development of the firm external financial requirements;

- the impact of fiscal variables on the economic area in relation to the firm-family exchange of financial resources.

The actual development of the family financing operation implies the verification of two different conditions.

The first is that the firm financial profile should be, at that specific time, consistent with the specifications of the family portfolio strategy in terms of size, length and risk. If not so, the necessary requisites for the exchange would be missing, except for the hypotheses of necessity and extraordinariness that are sometimes connected with the impossibility for the firm to raise additional funds from financial markets and banks. In this case, the phenomena of credit rationing or the firm structural difficulty would increase both the risks and the costs of "firm failure" (Kf_{firm}) – as identified in the previous paragraph –, thus urging the family to make a financial exchange with the firm. On the contrary, should there be neither the requisites for the exchange nor a particular tension for Kf_{firm}, the company would try to raise funds outside the family system.

The second condition – if the first one takes place – is the profitability of the exchange for the firm and the family. This means that the more asymmetrical the impact of fiscal variables on the borrower and lender's profiles the larger the optimization areas for the family-firm exchange in terms of after tax return on the investment as well as of after tax cost of financing. Therefore an ideal continuum could be traced: at one end the maximum economic area for the exchange and on the opposite end the absolute absence of economic area. The maximization of the economic area is characterized by the presence of a fiscal system according to which any financing operation is able to produce a fiscal advantage equal to the expenses incurred and, correspondingly, no taxes on the lender returns. Vice-versa the economic area is absent when no financing operation is able to produce any firm fiscal advantages and, at the same time, produces taxes on the lender returns. It is evident that the reality of facts falls somewhere in between the two ends in a different way, in the course of time, from country to country, depending on the financial means and the fiscal strategies followed by policy makers.

The specific analysis of the modes of development of external financial requirement (FFE) moves from the traditional interpretation model, according to which the dynamics of the firm internal sources and investments can be connected effectively with its development path in the course of time. This is according to the analytical relation referred to the t - t-1 time interval:

$$FFE_t = V_t \left[\left(\frac{CI}{V_{t-1}} * \frac{\Delta V}{V_{t-1}} \right) - \frac{CF_t}{V_{t-1}} \right] \qquad (4.3)$$

where FFE indicates the firm external financial requirements referred to the time interval t and t-1, CI is the capital utilized to produce the turnover and CF is the cash flow produced by the firm in the same time interval. The study of this relation allows us to identify the firm different stages of development (start up, introduction, development, maturity, saturation, decline or recovery) and to outline the corresponding trend of the formula variables so as to find the size and the trend of the firm FFE[7]. Such stages of development fall within the mapping of requirements by firm "contextual situations", which have already been examined in the previous chapter.

Although the approach is correct, and often utilized in corporate valuation practices above all at start up and introduction stages, in order to understand the financial profile of the family-firm relationship, two additional complexity elements must be introduced. In the first place, the owner family – except for small scope situations – confronts itself with not just one but a portfolio of firms and corporate projects, sometimes branched by groups according to different criteria. In the second place, the logical criteria of "start up" and "introduction" must be suitably analyzed

---

[7] For a deep analysis of the relations between FFE dynamics, the variables included in the formula for determining FFE and the trend of the firm development cycle, see relative literature (Mottura 1987; Caselli and Gatti 2003).

on the basis of the concepts of sector or undertaking, considering the owner's degree of knowledge of the same.

With reference to the first critical aspect, the presence of more FFEs generated by different firms and by individual projects within the firms is likely to produce a logical unbalance between the aggregate FFE and the family ability to meet a relevant portion of such requirements. If this is true in statistical and absolute terms, at a dynamic level the phenomena characterizing the management of the different FFEs lead to a partial internal compensation. This develops through market transfer policies or organizational and partnership solutions which, by exploiting the centralized treasury, the pool or of the group structure, lead to the re-distribution of credits and debits among the owned firms. As a result, the aggregate FFE becomes a net rather than gross total and allows the family to measure more effectively the scope of its commitment as well as to better design the relationship between the set of firms and that of external lenders. In addition, the determination of a net FFE must not lead to neglect the causes of the financial phenomena, that is the asynchrony, the size and the risk of the different stages of development achieved by the different firms being considered since these phenomena establish the profile of actual repayment of financing sources.

With reference to the second critical aspect, the different stages of development experienced by the family-owned firm or firms represent the indispensable support for the analysis and interpretation of the risk generated by any choice of FFE financing and, as a result, of financing choice in general. A specific evaluation in this direction requires the introduction of additional parameters, which make the valuation of the different stages more accurate as they are related to the typology of the firm sector and to the relationship between the firm and the sector itself (Table 4.3).

More specifically, at start up and initial stage of development, the risk profile of the undertaking and the resulting verification of compatibility with the family portfolio of financial assets is closely connected with the different hypotheses of entry into the competitive arena. In this sense, the three different hypotheses illustrated in Table 4.3 correspond to decreasing risk profiles at parity of conditions. In the first hypothesis, the family may decide to undertake a sector start up with one of its enterprises, thus tackling high risk levels. This requires the massive investment of family resources, which can be sided by the presence of other investors if the interest in the start up is considerable and if the entrepreneur's reputation is capital-capturing. The strong unbalance of the family portfolio on the risk-side requires a careful re-allocation of not only financial but also real asset classes, if the size of the investment is liable to affect the family asset-side to a remarkable extent. In the second hypothesis, the family may decide to enter an already existing but not known sector, with a new enterprises. In this case, the risk profile of the undertaking is more closely connected with the lack of experience in the sector and only partially with the sector dynamics. As a result, financial resources do not come necessarily from the family, but also from the financial system, in the form of traditional debt. In the third hypothesis the family may decide to enter an already existing and known sector with a new enterprise. This usually results in a substantial risk reduction – at a parity of sector profile – and may encourage the family to make radically different financing choices, which range from the full exploitation of the financial leverage to the massive investment – in debt or equity – in an undertaking where the characteristics and the rules of the competitive dynamics are well known.

Table 4.3 The relationship between the firm different stages of development, external financial requirements and the impact of family investment choices

Firm development stages	Possible relations between firm and sector			FFE profile	Risk profile	Compatibility with family financial portfolio
	Hypothesis A:	Hypothesis B	Hypothesis C:			
	new firm and new sector	new firm in unknown sector	new firm in known sector			
Start up	Entrepreneur enters sector start up with one of his firms.	Entrepreneur enters an already existing sector for the first time.	Entrepreneur enters a known sector.	Always positive depending on intensity of capital required by sector commodity.	Potentially high, depending on size and length of positive FFE area. Risk degree decreases when moving from hypothesis A to hypothesis C.	The risk return combination is usually set at high risks and high expected returns. Such relation tends to moderate when moving from hypothesis A to hypothesis C.
Development	Firm and sector start up produces first positive results, depending on revenue growth.	Firm through phase of revenue increase in an unknown sector.	Firm through phase of revenue increase in a known sector.	Positive but decreasing. The size of operating FFE depending on revenue increase speed.	Potentially decreasing depending on positive FFE reduction and on firm capacity of cashflow creation. Risk profiles of three hypotheses are closer.	Gradual risk level decrease may push the family to introduce additional capital.

Table 4.3 Continued

Firm development stages	Possible relations between firm and sector			FFE profile	Risk profile	Compatibility with family financial portfolio
	Hypothesis A:	Hypothesis B	Hypothesis C:			
	new firm and new sector	new firm in unknown sector	new firm in known sector			
Consolidation and maturity	Differences among three hypotheses are less marked. Consolidation choices may push the firm to make acquisitions, develop holding structure, internationalize or to establish final and physiological dimension.			FFE becomes negative in relations to current activity. New financial requirements may result from consolidation choices.	Risk is no longer connected with financial structure and expected fund repayment but with industrial management and consolidation choices.	If necessary, family receives flows of repayment and/or return on invested resources. Participation is highly compatible with management of financial portfolio. Possible additional investments depending on consolidation choices.
Restructuring	Firm activity is no longer aligned with sector dynamics or sector shows signs of saturation or potential decline.			FFE may become positive again.	Risk increase depending on reasons for restructuring..	Restructuring stage urges family to invest new resources also as virtuous signal to financial system..
Decline and crisis	Firm is no longer able to compete in the sector or the sector is facing crisis or structural decline.			FFE is positive.	Risk is high and drives to radical choices, such as market exit or firm liquidation.	Crisis may need the family to employ new resources and a to make definite choice on participation role.

The analysis of the economic area is instead focused, at a parity of evaluation, on the size and the risk of FFE financing choice, on the family-firm profitability profile in making a financial transaction. In this sense, the criterion of the economic area must be considered a general guide for making choices, with the physiological and recurrent possibility of making sub-optimal choices in front of necessities and obligations resulting from the firm financing requirements and from the family investment choices. The determination of the economic area must be based on the analysis of the body of fiscal rules locally enforced regarding the criteria of cost deductibility for the borrower and the taxation of returns for the lender. In Italy, the above regulations show a quite steady and well outlined configuration (Table 4.4).

With reference to the borrower, the fiscal policy maker distinguishes three forms of financing sources, i.e. debt, leasing and equity[8]. The debt component benefits from a net fiscal effect equal to 29.75% (that is 34% of IRPEG after 4.25% of IRAP) whereas leasing shows a fiscal structure that cannot be defined *a priori* but is dependent on different factors such as the typology of asset, the borrower's VAT profile and the maturity month of the operation. As a result, according to the different cases, the fiscal profile of leasing is definitely better or definitely worse than the debt. Finally, equity scarcely and partially benefits from the effects resulting from the DIT in the 1996-2001 period. This means that, up to now, the investment of equity does not produce any fiscal advantages for the firm and thus, at parity of conditions, it represents the most costly strategy.

In this connection, it should be underlined that although the reference context of the fiscal variables is characterized in the Italian system by high volatility, regulations governing the deductibility of interest rates for financing sources and the three categories of "debt, leasing and shareholders' equity" have remained quite stable in the course of time. In addition, it is necessary to verify the possible introduction, starting from 2004, of a mechanism of thin capitalization aimed at, on the one hand, reducing debt relative profitability starting from a given level of the financial leverage employed by the firm and, on the other, at re-directing the investment of financial resources from the debt logic to that of equity.

---

[8] For an accurate and exhaustive review of fiscal effects on corporate lending choices, see Caselli and Gatti 2003.

Table 4.4 The borrower's and lender's tax profiles in the Italian tax system as of 30.06.2003.

The borrower's fiscal profile

Financing sources	Reference taxes		
	IRPEG or IRPEF[9]	IRAP	VAT
Debt	Interest rates and charges fully deductible.	Interest rates fully non-deductible. Charges fully deductible.	Not applicable.
Leasing	"Average rental" and charges fully deductible if lease maturity is at least equal to half the period of ordinary depreciation allowance of the asset. Real estate is an exception as leasing maturity is at least 8 years.	Only value of the asset and charges fully deductible if leasing maturity is at keast equal to half the period of ordinary depreciation allowance of the asset. Real estate is an exception as leasing maturity is at least 8 years.	All the contract components are VAT taxable.
Equity	The fiscal effect is established according to equity variations occurred between 30.9.1996 and 30.06.2001, through the DIT mechanism.	No effect.	Not applicable.

The lender's fiscal profile

Investment modes	Recipient's legal status for purposes of IRPEG or IRPEF taxation on financial profits	
	Individual person	Corporate body
Debt	12.50% final tax rate or 27% if annual return is 2/3 higher than BOT annual average return.	Taxation upon income tax return.
Equity	12.50% final tax rate or taxation upon income tax return and use of tax credit .	Taxation upon income tax return and use of tax credit.

The combined analysis of the lender's and borrower's profiles enables us to draw a map of possible exchange behaviors between the firm and the

---

[9] The indistinctive reference to IRPEG and IRPEF intends to show that tax deductibility rules relating to the three areas of financing sources, for which a different fiscal treatment is provided, are identical. As a result, however, the impact on the fiscal income statement will be different depending on IRPEF average rate for partnerships.

family, by taking into account the fiscal asymmetries developing in each profile.

The first consideration regards exclusively the asset borrower. The presence of three reference categories – four in perspective with thin capitalization – produces interesting areas for investment changes and financial planning, above all as to the confrontation between medium-term debt and leasing. Vice versa, such areas do not appear in the short term and once again the lack of profitability is confirmed for equity investment as it is connected with no kind of fiscal advantages.

The second consideration regards instead the asset lender. The possibility to finally tax debt returns on the basis of two rates, which are largely lower that the maximum IRPEF rate, actually creates a kind of "profitability aisle" in the investment of resources. However, it is necessary to check whether these profits can be effectively spent for the purpose of making an exchange with the owned firm, by moving the reference context from the short to the medium term.

In terms of short-term financing choices, the family source is in competition with any other financing source in the market. This means that the objective functions of the firm and of the family are radically different, as the firm aims at the lowest rate and the family at the highest within the monetary system. It is therefore difficult to match the different requirements, apart from the case where carry out strategies, that is when the family utilizes the debt lever to obtain dividends at a lower rate. In this instance, the allocation of resources in the form of debt becomes a tool of family financial strategy rather than a corporate financing tool as capital allocations and withdrawals are a kind of "vehicle" to produce profits which represent deductible costs for the firm – differently from dividends – as well as income taxed at a fixed rate for the percipients. Therefore, the intensity and the usage of the criterion described must take into account the more general restriction of a risk of elusion which can potentially occur if the amount of profits is not on line with the "reasonability" of the market rates[10].

In terms of medium-term financing choices, although the family source is always in competition with the other financing sources in the market, the nature and the different degree of the commitment as against a short-term operation can reduce the interest conflict of the rate. This means that the family may well diminish the pressure on the return target if a short-term debt represents a tool for creating corporate value. Finally, the profitability

---

[10] The use of thin capitalization aims at preventing partners' non-physiological and non-reasonable use of debt.

of the family-firm exchange may vanish if leasing can actually produce remarkably higher fiscal advantages in comparison to those of debt.

The third consideration is finally more general. The comparison between the structure of financing sources and the investments modes from the fiscal point of view acquires the described profile only if exchange criteria are referred to the domestic context. This means that the quest of fiscal asymmetries can extend the exchange reference context by creating dedicated vehicles which, from the part of either the borrower or the lender or of both, allow carrying our asset transfers characterized by lower profit taxation and higher expense deductibility. The design of a structured operation must obviously produce advantages that are steadily higher than transaction costs, by taking into account risks connected with the volatility of the relative fiscal provisions.

4.3.3 The Relationship Between the Owner Family and the Owned Firm: the Assets Perspective

The understanding of the family-firm relationship is based on the simple observation that shareholding is one of the family's portfolio components, where all its financial and real assets are allocated[11]. This means that, irrespective of the different degree of "affection" and "commitment", shareholding has the same value as any asset class from the point of view of risk and return as well as of its capacity to contribute to the growth of the wealth in the course of time. If this is absolutely true from the point of view of the form, from that of the substance the position of shareholding within the wider context of family assets is based on a prior analysis of its distinctive and differentiating elements in comparison with other forms of alternative investment.

The understanding and the precise collocation of shareholding within the family portfolio is based on four fundamental rules which characterize its dynamics in the course of time:

- the controlled enterprise/s is/are characterized by a specific risk profile and above all by a specific trend which is related to the

---

[11] Reference is obviously made to shareholdings that require the family direct commitment from the operating, affective and ethical point of view. Vice versa, shareholding without such characteristics are just investments in financial assets. This distinction is clear in the presence of a quite limited number of firms. If the family assets are of quite relevant dimensions and the shareholding system has international and branching features, this distinction becomes more confused and more arbitrary.

trend of its/their own sector cycle. As a result, correct asset allocation must act on the other components of the family portfolio by carefully checking (or removing) any possible cycle synchronies with shareholding. This is carried out to reduce dangerous synergies in terms of risk and, in a broader financial and assets planning, to establish which parts of the financial portfolio might be specifically dedicated to meeting the firm FFE;

- shareholding creates a powerful induced effect which is connected, on the one hand, with the possibility to invest other portfolio components in order to proceed to financial transactions for the enterprise in the form of debt or equity (portfolio expansion effect) and, on the other, with the possible investment/commitment of financial or real assets in the form of a guarantee backing the growth of corporate lending (portfolio compression effect);

- shareholding tends to produce a strong "hostage effect" because of which a large part of family energies and attentions are prevailingly directed to corporate management rather than to the management of financial or assets portfolio;

- shareholding is nevertheless aimed at producing value in the course of time and at increasing family wealth.

The combined analysis of the above aspects is decisive to assess the scope of the assets connection between the family and the firm and to evaluate the structural diversity of shareholding in comparison to the other classes of investment. From this point of view, two main points should be underlined.

In the first place, the family-firm connection with the development cycle highlighted in the context of the financial perspective must be extended to the assets variables relating to the firm corporate value and guarantees. This is because FFE trend and the relative financing choices directly condition the corporate value in the same way as the relative support to the debt strategy stimulates the investment of a share of assets to support the settlement of the relative obligations. Therefore, rather than establish strict relations between the above measures, it is necessary to verify constantly and case by case how relations develop between the family and the firm dynamics in relation to the different development stages of the firm itself (Table 4.5).

Table 4.5 The relation between the firm different development stages and the assets perspective of the family-firm relationship

DEVELOPMENT STAGES	FIRM		FAMILY	
	FFEs	DEBT/EQUITY	VALUE	GUARANTEES
Start up (hypotheses A, B, C)				
Development (hypotheses A, B, C)				
Consolidation and maturity				
Restructuring				
Decline and crisis				

In the second place, the shareholding value increase must be properly analyzed on the basis of the family objectives. This means that, differently from the other classes of investment, the meaning of the shareholding value changes in relation to the utilization function required by the family. In other words, the meaning of value and wealth is provided with usability according to the targets of the family assets management. Therefore, two macro-situations are to be distinguished: the former regards the meaning of value in a narrow sense, the latter regards the meaning of value in a broad sense.

In the first case, the concept of value refers to the measurement of the present value of future income flows, in the typical logic of a market oriented evaluation. Although the above approach is correct and can always be used to control portfolio assets evolution, it does not bear a specific meaning of usability in the "continuity" life stages of the family and the firm. Vice versa in the "discontinuity" life stages of the family and the firm, the meaning of value mentioned above has a clear and specific aspect of usability and necessity. In particular, in the context of family "discontinuity", the meaning of value in a narrow sense becomes necessary as the firm must be evaluated. This occurs in situations relating to succession, turn-around and transfer of property. In these instances, wealth must necessarily have a marketable meaning as it may be exchanged and utilized. Obviously, the criteria for value measurement will be conditioned by and take into account all the different contextual situations urging for such evaluation. In the case of firm discontinuity, the meaning of value in a narrow sense is that of a signaling instrument for the financial system. In the stages of start up, strong development, consolidation through acquisitions or of re-structuring and crisis, the need to involve external lenders – in the perspective of lending and equity – requires the profile of the firm to be completely and organically evaluated. This means that the value measurement in a narrow sense represents the typical and necessary means.

In the second case, the concept of value refers to the spendability and utilization of the assets produced by the firm. Here the condition of continuity in the development stage of the firm and the family moves the meaning of usability onto the firm capacity of producing assets that can be used by the family in the course of time for the most different purposes: consumption, expenses, investment in financial assets, investment in real assets. Obviously, this is true if the firm is able to produce additional income and the family is interested in withdrawing the same income. The utilization process of firm assets can occur in quite different ways, partially influenced once again by the relative fiscal variables.

The first mode is based on the *carry out* logic in the form of interest receivables or dividends, according to the size and the characteristics of the economic area emerging from the firm and the family. The second mode is based, instead, on the transfer of typically family expenses into the firm, so as to benefit from cost deductibility. This obviously depends on the type of expenses and on the type of business purpose characterizing the family firm/s. The third mode is finally based on the transfer of family investments into the firm, so as to benefit from the tax advantage resulting from the depreciation of investments that have been carried out. The second and the third modes share the aspect of the *carry in* logic, that is the utilization of the corporate vehicle to benefit from the fiscal leverage as a supporting instrument in the family expense and investment processes.

4.4 Synergy Producing Operations Between Corporate and Private Banking

The identification of the typology of relationships developing between the family and the firm in the financial and assets perspectives represents an important scheme of analysis to establish the necessary conditions for the implementation of the supply on the part of financial intermediaries. In other words, the understanding of the mechanisms governing the financial transfers between the firm and the family as well as the firm's contribution to the growth of the family wealth are the necessary conditions for the supply of dedicated services to the family business.

The logic link separating the available financial and assets perspectives from positioning financial requirements in the map consists in the identification of the financial operations and situations which are characterized by remarkable synergies and overlapping between corporate banking and private banking designed services, irrespective of the positioning choice and the nature of the financial intermediary willing to approach the family business.

The research of synergies and overlapping areas requires a direct link between the specific aspects of financial and assets connections and the specific aspects of both the family and firm financial requirements. This is necessary to clearly identify the "playing ground", that is the map of business areas the financial intermediary can successfully enter. The map can be classified on the basis of two different parameters (Table 4.6):

- the typology of investment in the overall family portfolio (asset class);

- the typology of the subject interested in the investment (owner class).

As for the asset class parameter, the observations made in the previous paragraph about the "diversity" characterizing firm investment lead us to distinguish family assets into two macro-areas: one regards the firm as such and the other the portfolio after investments in the controlled firm/s. The portfolio must be then divided into sub-areas according to the following:

- investment in financial assets;

- investments in real estate;

- investments in other profit business (arts, precious metals, commodities, jewels);

- investments in instrumental goods (cars, airplanes, ships, other transports);

- investments in non-profit business (charity, social services, etc...).

With reference to the owner class, the identification of the family as the generic, but correct, holder of property interests and rights must be divided into two different categories: on the one hand the family, that is as a coalition of individuals headed by one leader or by a restricted number of members with acknowledged charisma, and on the other the individual members of the family, that is the holders of specific rights and interests, irrespective of the assets structure of the family as a whole. It is apparent that such distinction becomes more important as the number of family members and generations increase.

Table 4.6 Reference scheme for the identification of synergies between corporate banking and private banking

		OWNER CLASS	
		FAMILY COALITION	**FAMILY MEMBERS**
	FIRM	Family wealth invested in firm, in the various possible forms	Wealth of family individual members invested in one member's owned firm, in the various possible forms
ASSET CLASS	**PORTFOLIO**	Family wealth invested and collectively utilized in financial assets, real estate, instrumental goods and in profit and non-profit business	Wealth of family individual members invested and individually utilized in financial assets, real estate, instrumental goods and in profit and non-profit business.

The analysis of the asset class/owner class matrix offers not only a comprehensive perspective of the internal aspects of the family-firm relationship but above all allows specifying that the nature of synergic operations relies on the capacity of wealth transfer inside the four sections of the matrix, with the final goal to increase the overall wealth or to achieve its more effective internal allocation. This is apart from *technicalities,* which are specific of the single partial aspects of the overall portfolio (financial asset management, real estate management, advisory on art investments, etc.). From this point of view, strongly synergic operations can be grouped into three main categories:

- leasing on real estate and instrumental goods;

- advisory on family discontinuity management;

- corporate finance operations connected with assets transfer requirements.

The specificity of leasing operations, as the synergy-creating tool in wealth transfer, is its fiscal asymmetry in the depreciation process[12]. This means that, at a parity of conditions, the passage from the status of owner to that of lessee reduces costs significantly. The lower the asset depreciation rate, the stronger the effect. As for real estate, apart from the lowest depreciation rate in the Italian fiscal system (13%), there is the lease eight-year minimum life. If the potential lessee's income allows him to pay leasing rentals, for example by renting the same real estate, or he has a sufficient critical mass under the profile of taxable income, the transfer of the family real property into the firm represents a powerful wealth creating

---

[12] For an exhaustive review of leasing operations see 1998.

tool[13]. In this respect, the situation proposed in Fig. 4.1 is a useful exemplification as it shows how real estate leasing allows the owner-family to increase the returns of the real assets owned by individual persons.

The reference to advisory for the management of family "discontinuity" cannot be directly associated to just one contract and one operation. It rather indicates the capacity of the financial intermediary to grasp and gather all the different and deep effects that may result from the occurrence of a relevant event in the life of the owner family. Succession, turnaround and transfer of property are the emblematic situations in this respect. Apart from the individual financial operations that may be employed on the part of both the family and the firm – as outlined in the mapping of requirements in the previous chapter – the distinctive element for synergy-creation is the counterpart's commitment, that is his ability to propose himself as the partner who, at the same time, is the "transaction third party", the "confidential reference" and "privacy guarantor". This allows the advisor to have a central role among the actors and the financial, legal and fiscal operations that are performed in relation to the customer' needs.

The functions characterizing the advisor's role are multiple and cannot be listed in an exhaustive manner. Yet, some specific tasks certainly stand out and are more recurrent : write the "family agreement", which defines social and property relationships within the family in order to preserve its prosperity and identity; establish corporate governance connected with the event of discontinuity; establish fiscal governance connected with the event of discontinuity; identify counterparts in the event of business transfer and entrance of new partners; identify the management in case the structure is opened to members outside the family; develop mentoring and tutoring for younger family members who are about to enter the firm.

Corporate finance operations show a hybrid nature in multiple operations: they involve exclusively corporate financial aspects as well as family assets management and governance profiles. This has already been focused in the previous chapter, where several requirements areas of the family and the firm have highlighted the need to resort to corporate finance operations. Owing to the great variety of cases and technicalities of single operations, the next chapter will be dedicated to a more specific and exhaustive review. Here it is worth remembering that also in this case the synergy element is given by the presence of wealth transfer flows within the "asset class-owner class" matrix.

---

[13] For a more detailed analysis of the various organization hypotheses of real-estate leasing operations, see Caselli and Gatti now edited.

Fig. 4.1 Real estate leasing for value creation within the family-firm relationship: an example

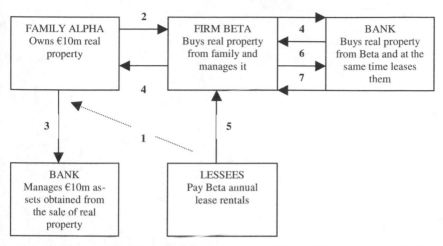

Family Alpha owns a large real estate (about €10m). The estate includes housing and office premises, which are leased to third parties. The rentals flow is equal to €600,000 per year (1). The family pays IRPEF on this flow at the highest marginal rate and has no chances to deduct various expenses resulting from the management of the real estate. Therefore, the investment net return is about 2.40%/year, without considering risks and charges resulting from possible extraordinary maintenance. A leasing operation becomes possible as one of the family businesses has real estate management included in its business purpose. Family Alpha transfers its real estate to firm Beta (2) for a value of €10m. Family Alpha has reached its first goal, that is have a financial mass to be allocated in more profitable investments compared to the initial 2.40% (3). To face capital outflow, firm BETA sells the acquired real estate to a bank (4) and at the same time stipulates an eight-year leasing contract for a total amount of 10m. The resulting effect on Beta is particularly interesting: in the first place lease rentals collected by Beta (5) are channeled to the bank and thus employed to pay a relevant share of leasing rentals (6); in the second place, the high acceleration of the leasing contract produces a relevant mass of deductible expenses, thus reducing significantly Beta's fiscal drag; thirdly , Beta's real estate management costs become deductible. At the end of the leasing contract, Beta becomes the owner of the property (7) and continues to collect leasing rentals (5). Family Alpha achieves a second goal: real estate management costs are now deductible and Beta value increases as a result of the fiscal drag reduction and of the purchase of the real estate. The overall financial evaluation of the operation leads us to observe that in the course of the leasing contract, family Alpha has at least doubled its assets as it has financial assets available (€10m) and the ownership of real estate for an overall value of €10m.

5 Corporate Finance and Financial Advisory for Family Business

Stefano Gatti

5.1 Introduction

Wealth management services for clients who are entrepreneurs or hold quotas or shares in family-owned firms (private companies) have some very particular features as regards *investment* or *asset management*. As a matter of fact, wealth management providers have to take into consideration two aspects of this type of clientele. On the one hand, an entrepreneur and his/her family or an entrepreneurial family are considered to be individuals with their own assets and annual income flows which must be optimized according to the established principles of asset management. On the other hand, however, the source of the income flows is closely linked to the management of the company and a large part of the entrepreneur's wealth is invested in the company itself. These characteristics raise particular problems in terms of optimizing the client's wealth.

This particular aspect has always had and continues to have considerable influence on those providing advisory services to entrepreneurs and entrepreneurial families. When financial intermediaries realized that this type of clientele presented some rather unusual features they began to gradually change their private banking activities. Although these activities initially focused mainly on managing the financial assets of high or very high net worth individuals, irrespective of the source of their wealth, they gradually turned into highly personalized services. This involved switching from an approach based on "financial" private banking to a broader one based on the management of the client's overall assets i.e. "wealth management". The search for a new role also meant segmenting the high or very high net worth clients even more and identifying groups of clients – including entrepreneurs and their respective families – with diversified needs due to the different source of their income or assets portfolio.

Moreover, the entrepreneur clientele often requires services involving deal planning, deal structuring and funding special transactions for companies in which the entrepreneur or his/her family hold equity stakes. Therefore, in the competitive arena, it is common to find not only operators traditionally associated with finance (mainly banks and private bankers) but also those associated with management or financial consulting.

This chapter focuses on the relationship between personal and company asset management. Since a considerable part of the family assets are tied up in running the company, it is necessary to examine how corporate finance and corporate financial advisory services are integrated within the overall personalized management services. It is also necessary to precisely define what kinds of services can be offered, when they can be offered and who can provide these types of services and the kinds of business models they have developed.

The chapter is divided in the following way. Paragraph 2 describes the position of corporate finance in the more general framework of the management of the entrepreneur's wealth. Paragraph 3 evaluates the consequences in terms of the services requested to optimize the personal wealth of the entrepreneur and his family. This paragraph aims to describe, in a prescriptive way, the services that an operator should provide in order to be considered a credible partner in the wealth management business. Based on the different kinds of services required, paragraph 4 describes the effects on the offering and the prevailing business models. As regards the first point, we explain the links between *private banking, corporate finance* and the advisory services offered to entrepreneurs or entrepreneurial families; as regards the second point, we illustrate the business models adopted by large integrated banking groups and consulting firms traditionally associated with management consulting and corporate finance. We also describe developing trends in wealth management services for family businesses that are empirically observable at the international level.

5.2 Corporate Finance Operations and Wealth Management Services for the Entrepreneur and His/Her Family

Corporate finance and corporate finance advisory services in the area of family business – often referred to as M&A services – have one thing in common: what changes hands in a transaction is represented by a firm or part of a firm. Corporate finance advisory usually deals with shares or quotas representing companies or company divisions. If physical assets are to be bought or sold, they are usually incorporated separately from the original firm (parent company) by means of an equity carve-out or a spin-off before the sale takes place.

As regards integrated wealth management services for entrepreneurs, there are two kinds of operations, depending on the owner's objective:

1. entry and exit business operations;

2. operations aiming at the organizational and managerial rationalization of the existing businesses or the reorganization of the existing ownership structure.

The first group of operations involves the acquisition of assets or company equity stakes (even by resorting to highly leveraged financial structures) and those involving the sale of an entire business or business divisions to industrial partners, financial operators (*private equity*) or through listings on the Stock Exchange.[1]

The second group involves a different approach. In the first place, it can involve modifying the company assets so that the organization and management structure best suits the company profile and the separation between company wealth and personal wealth is sharper.[2] A company is likely to request these services when it has reached a more mature stage in its life cycle. By that time, its turnover is so high and management structure so complex that major changes in management have to be introduced. In this connection, particularly useful operations include equity carve-outs of firm divisions, creating group structures or even going offshore to set up holding companies in tax havens. This group of operations also includes reorganizing the company ownership structure in order to resolve succession issues through donations, acquisitions/intrafamily sale of shares, spin-offs or mergers.

This is shown in Fig 5.1. The matrix is made up of two dimensions.

The first, shown on the horizontal axis, indicates the presence of equity stakes in the entrepreneur's assets. When the company is small, the legal form of the firm is likely to be an individual firm (a firm entirely owned by a single person) or a partnership. However, it has been empirically demonstrated that when companies become larger, there is a tendency to make a

---

[1] Berger and Udell 1998 point out that during their life cycle, small family-owned firms are characterized by very different financial structures. The role of private equity is statistically more important when the business is at a more advanced stage of development and when the company is rather large. See also Fenn and Liang 1998. As regards exit from the business through IPOs, Bitler, Moskowitz and Vissing-Jorgensen 2001 empirically demonstrate that the percentage sold by the entrepreneurs has a negative impact on the subsequent valuation of the firm. This confirms the literature on market signaling (the sale of a small quota should indicate that the entrepreneur has a good opinion of the company and values it highly).

[2] Ang, Wuh Lin and Tyler 1995.

sharper separation between personal/family wealth and company wealth by creating independent legal structures and concentrating equity stakes in the hands of the entrepreneur. However, transforming physical assets (the firm) into financial activities (equity stakes) affects both asset management – the acquision or sale of companies takes place through the acquisition or sale of equity stakes – and the tax system. As a matter of fact, in many tax systems, the gains derived from the acquisition or sale of a company are liable to taxation just like corporate income. However, the capital gains derived from the sale of equity stakes by a physical person (the entrepreneur) are subject to a tax regime which is different from ordinary income taxes.[3]

Fig. 5.1 Corporate finance operations in the management of family assets

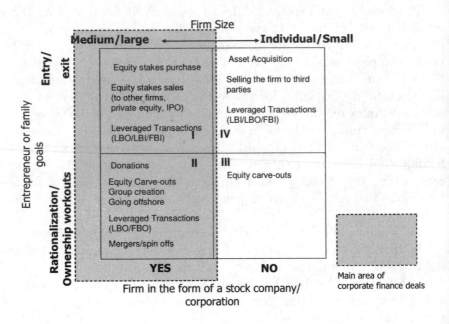

---

[3] The organizational variables are important in separating private wealth from corporate wealth. Avery, Bostic and Samolyk 1998 demonstrate that the organizational structure (corporate vs non-corporate) directly affects the wealth of the entrepreneur since, in the case of unincorporated structures, he/she has to commit a larger share of his/her personal wealth in order to obtain credit (and therefore to expand the business). As Lel and Udell 2002 also empirically demonstrate, personal wealth is involved when starting up a small business. Bento, White 2001 also consider the importance of the organizational structure of small businesses.

As we can see, corporate finance operations are more commonly found on the left of the matrix. In fact, operations regarding the management and rationalization of family assets invested in entrepreneurial activities become more rapid, efficient and less costly when the assets themselves are represented by equity stakes. When this is not the case, it is preferable to first carry out carve-outs or spinoffs and subsequently corporate finance operations on equity stakes representing companies or company divisions.

The second dimension of the matrix – the vertical one – focuses on the objectives pursued by the entrepreneur through corporate finance operations in the area of family business. These objectives include the entry into a new business, the total or partial exit from a business or the rationalization of the corporate structure and reorganization of the positions of the family members. It should be pointed out that it is sometimes impossible to distinguish between these two objectives. For example, there might be a single company with one or more business divisions from which the entrepreneur wants to withdraw by selling to third parties. In this case, simply selling the individual company (Box IV) is unfeasible since the business area or areas for sale must first be separated through spin-off/carve-out (Box III) and the equity stakes corresponding to these areas subsequently sold (Box I). A similar procedure is followed when the entrepreneur assigns business areas to family members in order to prevent them from participating in the same company (Box II).

If the two dimensions cross, we obtain four boxes illustrating the different kinds of corporate finance operations.

Box I includes corporate finance operations regarding equity stakes on the entry or exit from a business. These operations involve the acquisition of equity stakes by third parties or the sale of equity stakes to non-family members. The acquisitions can also involve a considerable use of debt (leveraged transactions in the form of LBO/LBI or FBI). As regards the type of sale, the difference lies in the party making the acquisition: if the negotiations are private, the sale might be made to another entrepreneur/family or to a financial partner through private equity operations (with or without an agreement to buy back at a certain date). The second possibility is going public through an offer for sale of the company shares.[4]

---

[4] In Box I, we only include the possibility of sale through IPO even if the Italian OPVS (offer for sale of already issued shares accompanied by the issuance of new shares to be underwritten by new shareholders) represents a feasible model. In this case, exit is certainly not definitive: in these cases, the entrepreneur might convert part of the equity stake into cash, thus reducing his/her financial commitment to the company by diluting the control quota determined by the underwritten tranche. Morcover, in these cases, the entrepreneur continues to maintain his/her ties with

Box II includes corporate operations regarding equity stakes aiming at rationalizing the assets used by the company or reorganizing the positions of the family members. This box differs from Box I in that the entrepreneur invests/disinvests by acquiring/selling more or less considerable parts of assets from/to third parties who are not family members. Instead, in Box II, investments or disinvestments are absent or limited to family members only. Box II includes:

- donations to ensure family succession;
- mergers and spin-offs: the first might be necessary to simplify the group structure and the subsequent chain of command, the second might be useful to separate company areas/physical assets and the respective equity stakes to assign to the different family members or to the successors of the business (especially if the company spin off is not proportional);
- equity carve-outs and creation of groups: this involves first reorganizing the company assets so as to separate the operational activities (usually in the hands of professional managers) from those involving the management of the equity portfolio concentrated in a holding controlled by the entrepreneur. Moreover, creating group structures can be accompanied by the entry of new members in minority positions (with the aim of enlarging the group dimensions with no need for the controller to invest more money) or locating holdings in countries with a low rate of taxation on dividends;
- leveraged transactions: this also involves LBO/FBO operations which, from the standpoint of the individual seller (acquirer), fall in Box I but from the standpoint of the extended family, can represent a way of reallocating the wealth and liquidity among the different family members. Take the case of two siblings who agree to carry out an LBO operation in which one acquires the shares of the other by creating a highly leveraged company.

Boxes III e IV have many of the same operations carried out in Box I and II. The difference lies in the fact that in these cases the companies are not corporations with issued shares and they are not usually large. This leads us to make the following important observations:

- the number of corporate finance operations that can be carried out are considerably reduced and limited to raising cash through the

---

the company subject to IPO since he/she remains a member of the Board of Directors.

sale or acquisition of firms and (much more rarely) the realization of leveraged acquisitions/buyouts;

- when corporate finance operations have to be carried out to reorganize corporate assets, it is necessary to resort to the activities in Box III (as a preventive measure, companies or business areas are separately incorporated in ad hoc legal entities) and then proceed to carry out the operations in Box II or I.

5.3 Corporate Finance Operations: Links With Entrepreneurial Assets and Consequences in Terms of Required Services

The above-mentioned corporate finance operations obviously affect the personal wealth of the entrepreneur and his/her family and provide important information in terms of the services required by entrepreneurs to satisfy their personal needs.

Keeping in mind that the company is only one of the assets included in the entrepreneur's portfolio, an integrated approach to wealth management has to provide assistance in the following areas:

1. succession planning services;

2. legal and taxation services;

3. asset management services or retirement planning services;

4. *company valuation and corporate finance services.*

These services will now be described in detail.

5.3.1 Succession Planning Services

When an entrepreneur decides to definitely leave the business or wants to reorganize his/her equity holdings and still continue to participate in the company, it is necessary to obtain advisory assistance in devising a suitable succession plan.

Wealth managers usually develop relationships with entrepreneurs in this area of activity when unusual events occur in the life of an entrepreneur: events in the entrepreneur's personal life (children ready to enter the firm, the death of key collaborators, accidents leading to disability or injuries) or external circumstances seriously affecting the firm (reorganizing the business due to a sharp increase in turnover or business decline, a change in the tax system etc.).[5]

When these events occur, entrepreneurs need assistance to help them identify the objectives they want to reach when planning their succession. In fact, these objectives can be very different and include maintaining their economic independence after leaving the business completely or in part, ensuring the firm and his successors long-term success even at the cost of personal sacrifice in terms of proceeds from the sale, minimizing tax on disinvestment capital gains, fair treatment of all the family members.

These different objectives can significantly affect the kind of corporate financial advisory services offered.

5.3.2 Legal and Tax Advisory Services

Corporate financial advisory always require specialized legal and taxation services. Assisting the entrepreneur during negotiations, evaluating the extent to which taxes affect the value of the company and the entrepreneur's wealth are very important elements that always recur in exit and disinvestments operations as well as in intra-family shares deals or reorganization of business, particularly in the case of organizing family holdings abroad.[6]

In this sense, deal structuring has the dual objective of minimizing the tax on the company and on family wealth or income. Wealth management must therefore possess specialized technical expertise in order to provide the client with the most effective solutions.

---

[5] Rutherford and Oswald 1999 indicate that successful companies resort to strategic planning to deal with problems instead of ignoring them or facing them when they occur. In these cases of excellence, the presence of a highly-trained entrepreneur with considerable professional experience is a constant factor highlighted by empirical evidence.

[6] Cavalluzzo and Geczy 2002 draw particular attention to the influence of the tax variable when choosing a particular organizational structure.With reference to the United States, empirical data show that taxation together with the problems of separating personal and corporate assets, the increased complexity of the ownership structure and specific sector factors clearly explain the decision to opt for a proprietorship (the firm is owned by a single physical person), partnership (limited partnership), S-Corporation or C-Corporation (joint-stock company). Moreover, organizing business activities in the form of a Corporation is advantageous in terms of capital cost with respect to the alternatives represented by the individual business and limited partnership.

5.3.3 Asset Management and Retirement Planning Services

Corporate divestitures or equity transactions have an immediate impact on the personal wealth of the entrepreneur. The sale of an entire company or business division, the transfer of shares, a listing on the Stock Exchange obviously require strategic support and advice on the best way to invest the proceeds of disinvestment which are often quite high. Moreover, in the case of a definitive sale, these sums should ensure the seller and his/her family a suitable living standard in the medium-long term.

However, these services are also requested by entrepreneurs who, although not undertaking major divestitures, operate in mature businesses characterized by a strong cash flow generation potential. The flow of periodic returns and the various compensations received from the company might require an asset management or retirement plan that can guarantee an adequate return for the entrepreneur himself/herself.[7]

In this type of activity, wealth managers can suggest different strategies depending on their background.

In the case of wealth management developed in private banking, the services can cover the entire spectrum of the entrepreneur's needs:

- defining the desired risk-return profile;

- devising an investment plan;

- allocating savings in the asset class proposed.

However, in the case of wealth managers with a management consulting or financial advisory background, the allocation of the sums based on the suggested investment plan is not directly feasible since these managers are not financial intermediaries. In these cases, the service includes the search for a suitable asset manager for the entrepreneur and also the continuous monitoring of the performances obtained.

---

[7] As regards the compensation methods of the owner-managers of a family-owned firm see Cavalluzzo and Sankaraguruswamy 2002. Although the context analysed is the U.S., the results also apply to Europe and Italy. In fact, the authors argue that the remuneration methods of the owner-manager of a small business derive not only from the profits but also from the compensation received as member of the Board of Directors or CEO and from the interest payments if the business is financed by the owner himself. The different compensation methods aim to optimize the entrepreneur's personal tax burden.

5.3.4 Valuation and Corporate Finance Services

The principal market actors providing these services include established operators in corporate and investment banking and financial advisory services.

Each M&A deal involving the whole or part of a firm is finalized after a detailed analysis and assessment is made. In fact, it is necessary to examine sector trends, evaluate a company's past and future strategy, determine the value of the firm/business division and the relative equity stakes, define the most suitable deal structuring and finally, in the case of an acquisition, find the necessary funding.

Even for these types of services the different background of the competitors has important consequences in terms of the services supplied. Financial advisors (but not always in the case of managers with a management consulting background) can provide these services directly. However, in the case of financial wealth managers (mainly banks and financial intermediaries), they might request some form of support from their own corporate finance or corporate and investment banking staffs or from external partners linked through network relations (accountants, business lawyers, financial consultants). The first option is actually very uncommon and limited mainly to large-size transactions.

5.3.5 A Summary of the Services Offered According to the Different Types of M&A Deals

By crossing the services analyzed in the preceding paragraph with the indications obtained from the matrix shown in Fig. 5.1, we can see the different types of services related to M&A operations designed to manage the entrepreneur's family assets (see Fig. 5.2).

The matrix is made up of columns – representing the different types of corporate finance operations provided for entrepreneurial families and corresponding to the different objectives of the entrepreneur/family – and rows representing the services required by the single operation or overall wealth management.

The boxes which are shaded indicate they are not active. However, the absence of services in these boxes does not mean that the entrepreneur does not require advisory services.

Fig. 5.2. Corporate finance operations in the management of family assets

	Type of operation							
	Entry/Exit			Rationalization/Family Issues/Firm's or Group's Organisation Structure				
Type of service	Acquisition	Divestiture	Leveraged Transactions	Donations	Split Offs	Merger Spin Offs	Leveraged Intrafamily Transactions	Going Offshore
Succession Planning Services								
Legal and Tax Services								
Investment Mgmt								
Retirement Planning Services								
Company Valuation								
Corporate Finance								

As a matter of fact, in the case of acquisitions and investment management/retirement planning services, if an entrepreneur acquires equity stakes, the problem of investing the proceeds does not arise; however disinvestment of part of his/her personal assets might be necessary as a preliminary measure before making an acquisition. In this case, the investment management service is provided before the M&A deal and is not directly linked to the realization of the operation. The same reasoning obviously holds true in the particular case of leveraged acquisitions.

If we cross donations with *investment management/retirement planning services*, donating shares or equity stakes can have serious repercussions on the donor's remaining assets. Therefore, it is necessary to evaluate whether the remaining assets ensure the entrepreneur a good standard of living. Therefore, investment management service is provided as a preventive measure before deciding to make a donation (often in connection with succession planning services which – as shown in the matrix in Fig. 5.3 – are not shaded).

The remaining shaded boxes concern M&A deals carried out through mergers, spin-offs or offshore family holding incorporation. For these boxes, the same observations hold true as in the case of donations. In fact, the wealth of the entrepreneur is not affected by these operations except in the case of donations following spin-off operations which benefit other family members.

The other boxes of the matrix represent other services which can be offered by those administrating the entrepreneur's personal wealth. More precisely, succession planning services represent a common element underlying all the operations indicated in the column. Legal and tax services are necessary in order to minimize the tax burden (at the corporate and personal level) of corporate financial operations. Finally, company valuation and corporate finance services are requested for each deal which, as pointed out earlier, is based on the valuation of the company which is the object of the transaction.

Investment management services are instead required for disinvestments and leveraged intrafamily operations when the entrepreneur is selling his/her assets. In these cases, the cash flows derived from the disinvestment have to be suitably allocated in securities, real estate or pension fund investments

5.4 Corporate Finance Services in the Wealth Management of Entrepreneurs: Effects on the Offer and Prevailing Business Models

The preceding paragraphs show that entrepreneurs and their families are very special clients in the panorama of services offered to *high or very high net worth individuals.*

Since they are individuals possessing an income and assets they require advisory services which help them identify the most efficient asset allocations in order to reach their desired objectives. Generally, from the standpoint of the entrepreneur as an individual, the objectives are often centered on security, protection of the family members and discretion.

As entrepreneurs, the clients participate in the management of the company and the success of the company is a prerequisite for the achievement of family objectives. These objectives depend all the more on company success the greater the family's financial commitment, the less the firm is mature and the greater the investments required to reinforce the firm's market position.[8]

---

[8] The close connection between the business risk and personal risk of the entrepreneur and his/her family was the subject of an empirical study carried out in the United States. In this connection, see the sample of 692 businesses analysed by Ang, Wuh Lin and Tyler 1995 and the findings of Haynes and Avery 1996 based on the NSSBF (National Survey on Small Business Finance). The holding of a considerable equity stake by the entrepreneur or family members (and therefore the dependence of personal wealth on the success of the business) is also documented by Bitler, Moskowitz and Vissing-Jorgensen 2001. According to these authors, a considerable financial commitment by the entrepreneur and his/her par-

Optimizing the investment in the firm and consequently even the cash flows benefitting the entrepreneur and his/her family require services and expertise that – as shown in Fig. 5.2 – are not usually found in traditional investment management which usually deals with the administration of assets made up of activities different from the entrepreneurial ones. The expertise required to perform the services described in the preceding paragraph are more similar to those of strategic consulting, management consulting as well as corporate finance and financial advisory services. From the standpoint of a bank, the services are provided by the corporate and investment banking division rather than the private banking or asset management one.

Therefore, wealth management of a family business requires a multidisciplinary approach comprising at least three types of services:

1. *consultancy*: as shown in the following paragraphs, consultancy concerns the personal or family profile of the entrepreneur (for example, succession planning, optimizing the tax structure, allocating the wealth derived from corporate assets) as well as his/her role as head of the firm (for example, strategic planning, management consultancy regarding the organization of the company or group).

2. *investment management*: the principles of allocating the available wealth and income of the entrepreneur and his/her family require expertise in finding the best risk-return combinations compatible with the client's investment profile. This concerns investments in both securities and real estate. These services are likely to be of crucial importance to those entrepreneurs whose firms have a steady free cash flow profile and low growth rates of the invested capital (cash cow firms).

3. *corporate finance and investment banking*: the management of an entrepreneur's wealth might entail adopting an integrated approach to the efficient management of part of the wealth represented by the company and the part invested in other assets. In this connection, structuring, funding as well as taxation and legal services are requested when carrying out corporate finance operations.

---

ticipation in the firm increase corporate performance even considering the heterogeneity of the sample analysed.

In short, satisfying the needs of the client in the area of family business depends on a *"client-centric vision"*[9] in which the three above-mentioned services aim to provide an integrated wealth management solution.

5.4.1 Competitors Offering Wealth Management Services to Entrepreneurs and Entrepreneurial Families

The possibility of providing integrated *investment management*, consultancy and *corporate finance* services to a highly segmented clientele has made this market niche extremely competitive and selective.

This paragraph presents some models of service providers chosen among those examined at the international level. Based on empirical evidence, two types of potential competitors emerge:

- large, integrated banking groups

- consulting firms, especially those oriented towards corporate financial services

5.4.1.1 Large, Integrated Banking Groups

In the case of large, international banking groups, the situation is not completely homogeneous in the approach to *wealth management services*. This applies to large European and American financial intermediaries.[10]

A common feature of these groups is that wealth management services are well established in the private banking divisions or in group-controlled companies providing private banking services. In fact, historically, all the large banks began by assaulting the private high income segment of their clientele and adopted a relatively undifferentiated approach, regardless of the specific needs of this clientele, and focused on asset management services (often management of securities portfolios).

In the end, however, this approach turned out to be quite inefficient both in commercial and strictly economic terms.[11] This led to a second stage in

---

[9] As will be shown, UBS uses this term to describe its approach to wealth management services.

[10] Since the business of wealth management is almost exclusively represented by large banking groups, the intermediaries we chose to analyse were taken from the available League Tables. The European intermediaries (Source R&S – Mediobanca) and the American ones (Source: The Banker) rank among the top 10 by volume of revenues and total assets.

the development of private banking services in which asset management was accompanied each time by services focusing on the specific needs of the high or very high net worth segments of the clientele. In short, the strategies of the most trustworthy competitors began to shift towards the philosophy of the "global management" of the client's assets or wealth management and not just "financial" private banking.[12]

These services are offered by many foreign banks.

Deutsche Bank is the leading European banking group in terms of revenues and total assets. In October 2002, it began restructuring its PCAM (Private Clients and Asset Management) division in order to set up a special division devoted to *Private Wealth Management* closely integrated with SBB (*Small Business Banking*) activities. This integration is designed to enable the bank to provide an integrated offer in which the core services of private banking are heightened by those closer to *corporate and invest- ment banking*: in addition to active advisory, portfolio management, alternative investment services (centered on hedge and real estate funds), "*Special Services*" include family office, financial planning and fiduciary services.

Since this integrated service is still in its early stages, the focus still tends to be on private banking services (see Fig. 5.3).

Services similar to those provided by Deutsche Bank are also provided by BNP Paribas to a high or very high net worth clientele through its Private Banking (Banque Privée) division. Even in this case, there is a tendency to integrate management and *personal financial planning* with corporate financial consulting services[13]. However, the latter are still handled at the local level by the Corporate and Investment Banking division

---

[11] "Unlike competitor banks, some of which reported losses ranging from 30 to 50% last year, the Citigroup Private Bank had earnings growth of 45% over the last two years". See Citigroup (2002).

[12] A more personalized approach was naturally accompanied by an increase in the access threshold to integrated wealth management services. The family office offered by Deutsche Bank, besides being available to only German or US-residents, has a minimum threshold of 30 million US dollars; those offered by Credit Suisse Trus, 50 million euros.

[13] In addition to the traditional asset management consulting services and the investment funds and securities services, BNP Paribas Private Bank also offers the so-called "Personalized services" in the areas of art advisory, real estate management, prestige land and country estates, luxury properties transactions (the last 2 managed directly by the Paris headquarters), trust and family holdings. It is obvious that, except for the last consulting service for the group structure, the BNP approach still tends to be mainly oriented towards private banking and personal financial planning services .

through external partnerships with professionals and consultants specialized in corporate taxation and corporate finance.

Fig. 5.3. The approach of Deutsche Bank to wealth management

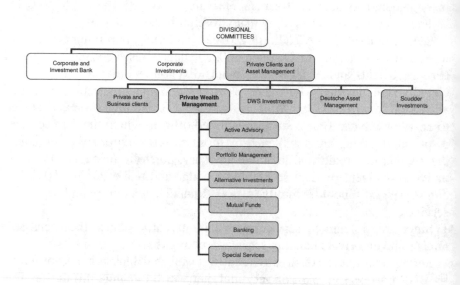

Source: Deutsche Bank, Company Information, 2003.

The approach of UBS, focuses more on the small business and entrepreneur clientele segment. In fact, for some time, the Wealth Management and Business Banking division has adopted a very segmented approach to its private clients: in addition to the "Sports and Entertainment Group", there is also a "Family Business Group" division devoted to entrepreneurs and entrepreneurial families. UBS PaineWebber (see Fig. 5.4) also tends to offer personalized wealth services.

Credit Suisse is also trying to focus more on the entrepreneur clientele by introducing its Credit Suisse Trust in its Private Banking Division in order to offer integrated wealth management services for *very high net worth individuals*. The fact that the bank is also planning to create a family office is a clear indication of the Group's strategy (Fig. 5.5).

Fig. 5.4 UBS: the "client centric solution" approach to family business

Source: UBS, UBS Family Business Group, 2003.

Fig. 5.5 The approach to wealth management of the Credit Suisse Group

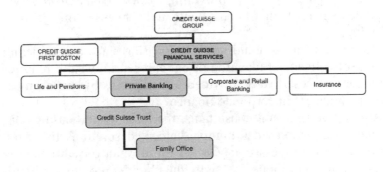

Source: Credit Suisse Group, Company information, 2003.

As regards the American banks, following the wave of mergers between commercial and investment banks which characterized the late '90s, banks have recently begun to change their approach to private wealth management services. Due to their strong position at the international level and the expertise they acquired by integrating investment banking structures, the large American banks are adopting a very aggressive strategy of highly personalized services.

Citigroup, for example, the leading American bank in terms of total assets, opened a specialized Citigroup Private Bank division in May 2002. This division has become the commercial vehicle offering private clients all the bank services including the traditional private banking services and – in the case of entrepreneurs and entrepreneurial families – corporate and investment banking. The underlying idea is to demonstrate that Citigroup is not a private banker but a "private partner".[14]

The model represented by JP Morgan-Chase and Bank of America are quite similar since they have concentrated their wealth management services in their respective Private Bank divisions. In addition to asset management these divisions offer the following services:

- tax planning

- charitable planning

- estate planning

- private company advisory services.

5.4.1.2 Consultants

The second group of actors providing *wealth management* services to entrepreneurs is made up of consultants in the areas of strategic and financial planning.

The phenomenon should not be surprising since a considerable part of the personal financial planning of entrepreneurial wealth requires the professional services already provided to companies by management consultants or by experts in corporate finance.

Among the financial consultants, the Price Waterhouse Coopers Small Business Centre provides highly segmented solutions to entrepreneurial families. This business unit was set up to replace traditional "corporate" services with "corporate and individual" or "corporate and family" based services (see Fig. 5.6).

---

[14] "The Citigroup Private Bank quickly began to transform itself from the classic private banking model into a new paradigm: It evolved to become an entry point to the breadth of financial and investment resources of Citigroup for its ultra-affluent clients around the world...The Private Bank works with the wealthiest families in the world. As a result, we are always leveraging the best investment opportunities of Citigroup in order to increase our share of their portfolios". See Citigroup 2002.

Fig. 5.6 The approach to wealth management in Price Waterhouse Coopers Small Business Centre

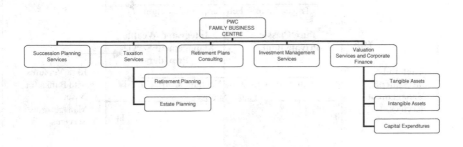

Source: Price Waterhouse Small Business Centre, Company Information, 2003.

The approach of Grant Thornton and its People and Relationship Isssues in Management (PRIMA) Service is similar to the approach of Price Waterhouse Coopers. The strategic consulting services focus on the relationship between the individuals who manage the business and the consulting services offered to the company :

"As well as dealing with the business needs in terms of audit, tax compliance and other services traditionally associated with business and financial advisers, we have been working with business owners for many years and recognise the unique challenge they face [...] (We) are able to provide a valuable insight into the crucial relationship issues surrounding business management, and the financial and commercial options that are available to help resolve internal conflict".[15]

5.4.1.3 A Summary of the Market Trends of Wealth Management Services

The current situation of the offer of wealth management services is summarized in the following matrix (see Fig. 5.7).

The market trend shows a gradual shift towards Box IV in which the strategic grouping of integrated wealth management service providers is prevalent with respect to specialized operators.

---

[15] See Grant Thornton 2001.

Fig. 5.7 Strategic groupings and forecast trends in the wealth management of entrepreneurial families and entrepreneurs.

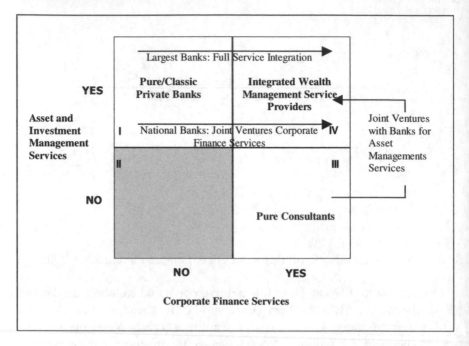

With the rare exceptions of some European and American banks, the cases empirically found to be more numerous are concentrated in Box I and III. The first is made up of banks still oriented towards an undifferentiated private banking service and the third is made up of management and corportate financial consultants who are organizing special groups or centres to provide services to entrepreneus or their families.

It is likely that in the future a completely integrated wealth management service will be provided only by the large multinational intermediaries since only they can provide independent commercial banking, investment banking and consulting services regarding asset management and corporate finance issues.

Smaller, national banks and consultants will tend to make outside alliances and partnerships to deliver the services they cannot provide because of operative and regulatory constraints (for example, in Europe, asset management services are by law the domain of investment companies) or constraints regarding the available human and financial resources. The banks will look for legal, tax and, in part, corporate financial consulting services abroad, as is now the case. The consultants will tend to directly carry out the activities of wealth management, legal and tax optimization and corporate finance by stipulating "portage" agreements with the banks in order to offer their clients asset management services or finance services for entrepreneurial families.

6 Family Office: Which Role in Europe?

Daniela Ventrone

6.1 Introduction

The sector of private banking is undergoing growing changes and family office has now become an interesting and highly potential reality. Customer requirements increase and grow diversified and the deeper awareness of risk/return profiles provoke migration from one bank to another, in pursuit of reliability and professionality. In Western countries families show a more critical attitude versus financial intermediaries: the relevant losses experienced by asset management, often higher than expected, have led a lot of private customers to reconsider the trustworthy relation with their advisor. The phenomenon has been undoubtedly accentuated by the deeper awareness of possible conflicts of interest within the financial intermediary, a problem that has involved not only great international merchant banks, the protagonists of several legal proceedings in the past few months, but also national banking groups[1]. In this respect, a recent study by Price Waterhouse Coopers Consulting[2] has shown how some of the change fundamental motivations that up to some years ago had only a minor relevance (e.g. product and service pricing, lower performances, dissatisfaction with services and new regulations, etc.) are now growing more important and will become of crucial importance in the forthcoming futfirom the point of view of family business, the demand often goes beyond mere asset management to embrace the management of the complex relation between the family and the enterprise. As we have seen in the previous chapters, the effort made by several financial intermediaries aims at successfully managing the evolution from private banking to wealth management logic, for the purpose of coordinating the set of variables making up the firm and the family wealth. If the set of services provided by the intermediary can be easily listed, from asset management to corporate finance – here including for example fiscal, legal and real estate advisory – it seems much harder to establish, in the first place, whether skills and re-

---

[1] See contributions by Corbetta G. and Marchisio G. in this research.
[2] The study has been carried out in Europe, USA, Australia, Canada, Switzerland, Japan and Hong Kong. See PWC Consulting," Global Trends in Performance Measurements", 2001.

sources required by such strategic and organizational changes are actually available in Italian banks and, in the second place, which change implementation modes might be applied by executing processes designed to integrate customer-oriented services.

It is of primary importance to tackle the issue of wealth management for HNWIs, who now in Italy account for about 1% of clients with a net worth equal to 14% of the total wealth[3]: the growth rate for the next few years is expected to be about 8% despite the current financial downturn. Competition for market share increase should become even keener, especially when considering that this segment presents the bank with a 28% average contribution margin[4]. As a result, the segment is quite important for trade banks and for all of the institutions interested in operating in wealth management. In addition, Italy is still a fragmented market, subdivided into global players and small operators: no bank exceeds the 6% market share; development potentialities are striking and the industry is facing a period of constant evolution and consolidation.

As the competitive scenario is undergoing remarkable changes, a lot of banking groups are deciding which model of corporate governance they intend to develop and which market segment or niche they are about to focus on. Each bank must consider a lot of aspects with consistency and determination: the business strategy to be adopted, the organization model, the service to be provided, the development of human resources and IT systems. According to the different path pursued, there will be multiple possible solutions. Within this context, the family office is one of the possible models available.

The chapter is structured as follows: paragraph 2 outlines the phenomenon of the family office within wealth management by illustrating strengths and competitive advantages; paragraph 3 distinguishes the prevailing business models in the family office according to demand-supply combinations: the analysis is focused on the fundamental requisites the family office must comply with in order to provide an excellent service in the market of wealth management; paragraph 4, on the contrary, focuses the attention on the costs of the family office structure; paragraph 5 will try to clarify whether the family office is an effective operative solution for Italian banks and which organization structure it should adopt within the group.

---

[3] See Cap Gemini and Ernst & Young, "World Wealth Report", 2003.
[4] The affluent segment accounts for 9% of retail clients and generates 42% of margins; mass clients account for the remaining 91% and generate only 30% of profits. Data are taken from an analysis by Delia-Russell and Di Masci 2002.

6.2. The Family Office Distinctive Features

The family office may represent the most complex and sophisticated solution for the new orientation of wealth management for family business: it deals with the integrated management of the assets of affluent families and organically tackles the different issues characterizing the family-firm relationship. Its origins are to be found in the traditional figure of the trustworthy banker or the family lawyer[5], able to follow all the different phases of the family business life-cycle.

The main goal of the family office consists in its being considered as the sole family interlocutor. It is generally composed by a team of people[6] who are ready to solve any problem or request and to interact with all of the other professionals possibly involved in wealth management.

As shown in Fig. 6.1, the family office can be defined as the evolution of the market of independent financial planners (IFP). IFPs tackle market challenges by acting as intermediaries between the client and the providers of the individual services so as to coordinate the different activities, by looking for the counterpart best suiting client requirements, negotiating costs and monitoring service quality. The family office supplies all this, by expanding its range of services, limiting the degree of service outsourcing and thus trying to supply several in-house products. In this way, the family minimum access threshold is higher and the company investment in human resources is high. Moreover, as the capacity to provide integrated reporting of all the aspects of management and to be constantly innovative should not be neglected, another factor able to produce competitive advantage is technology: software constant updating and complex IT systems are necessary in order to manage the numerous positions, check financial risks, increase transparency and available information and reduce human error margins upon accounting phases[7].

---

[5] According to Pictet, Swiss private bank, "very wealthy families are looking for a solution which provides them with a comprehensive and integrated approach to wealth management. They are looking to the Family Office concept as the solution to their need for a sophisticated, integrated and objective approach to managing their wealth. The Family Office acts as a focal point for the family's wealth management programme in the fullest sense. It provides the family with a multi-disciplined team of advisers, able to look at the big picture of the family's wealth. This option allows the families to have access to a high-quality, integrated service which it would find difficult and expensive to put in place itself". See Pictet public information, www.pictet.it.

[6] See Delia-Russell and Di Mascio 2002.

[7] Technology, in fact, has become a strong presence in the client-bank or client-family office relationship. In the first case, it often replaces the direct relation of

Fig. 6.1 The family office positioning in the market of wealth management

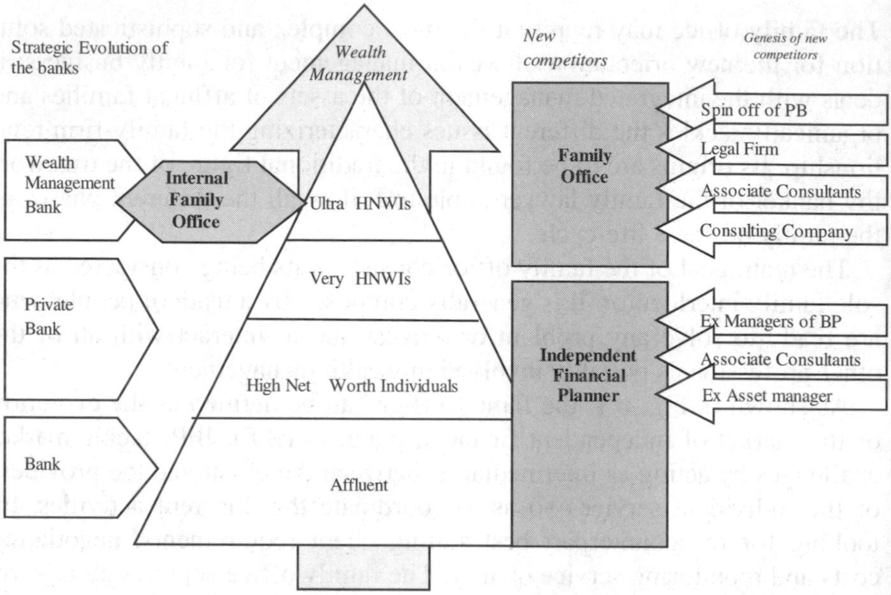

Source: Delia-Russell and Di Mascio 2002.

On the other hand, utmost care is dedicated to satisfying customer interests and the relational factor acquires great importance. Moreover, thanks to the fundamental centralization of a part of the activities, quite often the family office can reduce outsourcing to exclusively low value added services. Finally, it acts as intermediary with other specialized professional figures, such as private equity or hedge funds managers and art consultants.

---

meeting and discussing the client financial position; in the second case customization is so high that communication with the specialist team is irreplaceable and software is only a useful support and a stimulus toward relation transparency. Moreover, some of the particularly simple products can be managed directly from home by the family, thus reducing family office back-office costs. The virtual channel is the tool that by means of aggregate applications allows a synthetic representation of the value and the evolution of family assets. The possibility to visualize a global picture and to rapidly supply a complete report of the family office activity allows coordinating short-term strategic choices as well as strategies regarding financial, property and real estate matters more easily. Moreover, it allows remote online interaction between the family members and the different professionals, thus overcoming often considerable geographical barriers. See 2002.

Therefore, one of the strengths characterizing the family office is its independence and the almost total lack of conflicts of interest. The fundamental requisite lies in that the team should be free from any kind of commercial pressures and thus be able to concentrate on advisory in the family interest as they are not due to achieve exogenously defined budget levels in a strict or prescribing way. In the same way, when the family office outsources services, the choice of partners has to be ideally motivated by rationality and the professional profile of the counterpart rather than by an advantageous fee structure. To conclude, it is very important for the family office to safeguard its reputation by avoiding or at least reducing, whenever it is possible, opportunistic behaviors: though raising margins in the short term, they might reveal to be dangerously detrimental in the medium term.

The strictly family-centric approach provides a global view of the family assets so that the main success factors can be identified, pursued, protected and developed. This aspect is particularly important when, apart from liquid assets, the family holds shares in leading listed or not listed companies, which must be strategically managed for their strong impact on the managerial and financial balance of the business. A critical aspect is the ability to segment clients according to their position in a matrix composed by different factors, such as nature, members and cohesion of the family; family and business financial and qualitative life-cycle[8]; current and prospective life-style; company competitive market and necessity of extraordinary finance and, more generally, corporate finance operations. This methodology allows raising a new ad-hoc effective frontier for the client, a fundamental support for designing effective and consistent operating solutions. It is clear, in fact, that the entrepreneur's family who is about to manage company succession[9] and whose business has been consolidated

---

[8] In the case of the family, relevant discriminating elements are the age and the health conditions of the entrepreneur and the family members, which strongly affect the management of financial flows.

[9] As for succession management methodologies, it is absolutely important to understand that the change occurred within the family context in the past decades has an important impact on the supply. In the case of traditional businesses, for example, when a member of the family intends to continue the family business and the other does not, it is necessary to divide the family wealth into fair quotas among the heirs. If sons are not full-aged, solutions must be designed and agreed upon in order to solve the possible conflicts that might emerge among family members, such as giving a kind of monthly lump sum salary until financial independence is achieved. See Corbetta 2001 and, as for private equity operators' attention dedicated to succession planning, Testa, Huwitz & Thibeault, LLP, "Successful succession planning: Thinking about tomorrow today", in www.altassets.net.

for several generations shows a completely different profile in comparison to the young successful actor who has decided to invest his assets not only in financial but also real assets. In the first case, in fact, it is important for the succession to occur without provoking serious traumas for the family and the business: in terms of assets it might be necessary to change diversification policy and transform some assets into monetary assets to liquidate the sons who do not want to work in the family business. Moreover, the requirements and the life-style of the head of the family are likely to vary quite deeply due to the exit from the firm. If we take instead the case of the young actor, requirements will be totally different: the "celebrity" status drives him toward a very expensive life-style and the relatively recent assets necessitate the creation of a "brand-new" management strategy considering that the financial cycle, except for a few cases, is generally concentrated in the first twenty years of activity.

The last example clearly shows that differences between new money and old money families are extremely deep in wealth management and they are responsible for the great heterogeneity of service demand[10]. The former generally tackle wealth management with great seriousness and care, they do not accept to outsource this task passively and require a constant flow of information about investments. More and more often these individuals became rich when they were under forty and created their wealth independently, in a short time and by subjecting their wealth to noticeable risks. Moreover, they employ considerable resources in process checking and monitoring and play an active role in negotiating and proposing new solutions. Finally, they consider their privacy very important and prefer not to delegate the management of their extras (e.g. bill payments and travelling organization) to an external agency. On the other hand, old money families very often prefer to delegate a large part of their tasks, without worrying too much about checking and monitoring the performances or the reports provided by the family office. These clients are not interested in pursuing ever-innovating services or the new opportunities offered by the most advanced technological platforms. The major consequence of this split between the requirements and the demands expressed by the two categories of families lies in the different approach implemented by the family office: more labor-intensive in the case of portfolios created in the course of several generations; more innovation and dialogue-oriented in the case of a more recent wealth.

---

[10] See interview to Mr. Longo effected by Bloomberg in 2003; Mr Longo is director at Accredited Investors and wealth manager with great experience in family office. The source is www.wealth.bloomberg.com.

One of the major advantages of accentuated customization is undoubtedly the possibility of establishing a long-term relationship, where the family is followed through its evolutionary process, so as to solve critical stages and requirements emerging in the course of the family's financial and biological life-cycle. The goal is the increase and not just the mere preservation of the family wealth. It is worth noticing, in fact, that the reference time horizon usually refers to the cycle of more generations and the main goal is wealth preservation but also new value creation[11].

The need to be aware of particularly reserved matters, whose public knowledge might have highly negative consequences on the family business (e.g. the launch of a new product or a company re-structuring operation) or on the family (e.g. harsh conflicts among family members or a disease), underlines the major importance of the trust factor. The management of customer relations has an important role to overcome the initial diffidence of the first contacts with the family office in a relationship based upon transparency and clarity.

In close connection with these factors is the necessity to ensure continuity and steadiness in the relationship: the client is followed by a team of specialists who, through teamworking, discuss the most important decisions and the possible impact on the different aspects of wealth management, constantly supported by sophisticated back office work. Each decision that is bound to change the family profile (e.g. the set-up of an offshore company, the management of company succession or the re-allocation of financial assets) must be first discussed and agreed upon among the team members, by solving possible dissents and avoiding useless delays or costly strategic changes. As a matter of fact, quite often families who have decided to resort to the family office indicate among their main motivations the elimination of the inconveniences resulting from following and coordinating legal and fiscal advisors on a separate basis, which would lead to a non-optimal overall situation. In this context, the family office is no longer perceived as a luxury product for the few, but a necessity for those HNWIs who believe that not delegating the complex management of the financial and family life-cycle to a trustworthy office is too complicated, demanding and high-cost.

The following figure has been extracted from a study carried out by PWC Consulting[12] in 2001 about the changes in the European market of private banking over a ten-year period: wealth management and, in particular, the family office seem to be an increasingly interesting solution for

---

[11] See Datamonitor, "European High Net Worth Customers", London, 2001.
[12] See PWC Consulting, "Global Trends in Performance Measurements", 2001. Percentages in Fig. 6.2 refer to customer use of the service.

private clients thanks to the great flexibility of the service.[13]. The two areas, in fact, reveal the most significant increase as to the number of respondents utilizing them compared with 10 years earlier.

Fig. 6.2 The evolution of client needs from 1990 to 2001.

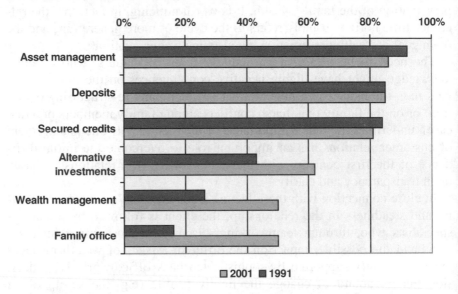

Source: PWC Consulting, "Global Trends in Performance Measurements", 2001.

For particularly wealthy families, the family office great flexibility represents the best solution: their extremely customized services and the great attention toward changes provide an unquestionable advantage for establishing a relation based on mutual trust and collaboration. Due to the extremely complex supply, only the most affluent segment of U-HNWIs requires the intervention of the family office. Nevertheless, establishing a service access threshold is quite an intricate task[14]; the analysis of the major family offices worldwide shows significant differences among the vari-

---

[13] Generally, as indicated by Fox Exchange, the professional association acting as clearinghouse for the best practice and the new developments of the market of wealth management, the family office is trying to meet all of the family requirements. The wide range of the service demand and the great flexibility of the supply do not allow us to provide an accurate description of each of them.

[14] The review Trust & Estates (www.trustandestates.com) published an article (The Multi-Family Office Mania, November 2002) illustrating that only individuals with liquid assets amounting to a minimum of $100m can access lifestyle management, charity management and to extraordinary finance services.

ous banks: for example, Whittier Trust Co fixes the minimum threshold at US$10m, Credit Suisse Family Office at €50m, Hamilton and U.S.Trust Corporation at US$100m and Pictet at US$150m.

Withers is one of the major operators in this segment, with Italian clients ranging from Benetton to Max Mara. Apart from business areas like finance, fiscal and legal advisory, etc., Withers provides solutions for particularly complex situations, such as cohabitation, pre-marriage agreements and divorce. Quite important for the US market are lifestyle management services, that is the set of activities aimed at simplifying the daily management of family life by providing services relating, for example, to bill payment, management of houses, yachts and air-crafts, children's education, travelling and leisure time, concierge services and recruitment of household staff.

One of the emerging issues is the complex management of children's education: private universities, masters, specialization courses and stages abroad must be accurately chosen and organized and the advice of specialists is often required to facilitate the student's career profile. Not to mention all the issues emerging in case of disease and, in the past few years, a new segment connected with alternative social security plans seems to have grown increasingly interesting. The highest incidence of divorces, separations, cohabitations and professional mobility and flexibility further complicate an already intricate scenario.

6.3 The Family Office Legal and Organization Structure

The legal structure of the family office results from the combination of a number of different factors due to the wide flexibility of services. To obtain a more complete picture it will be advisable to carry out our analysis by strategic groups.

A first distinction should be made between the dedicated family office (or private family office), which aims at managing only one family, and the multi-family office, which provides its services to a group of families:

- dedicated family office: its primary principle is absolute discretion about the family and the services provided. It is often hard to get to know about its existence as it does not belong to official statistics and no reliable data can be thus obtained. Generally, it is a non-profit organization and, being set up by the family itself, it sponsors no activity and develops no marketing policies;

- multi-family office: it generally results from the spin-off of private banks, legal firms or consulting firms or from the expansion of the business area of previously dedicated family offices. As it considers the entire segment of "wealthy" family groups, it invests a lot of resources in developing communication policies to describe its supply and advertise its brand.

If we consider this distinction, it is clear that the examples and the cases mentioned in the previous paragraph make reference to the second typology. More precisely, the two categories can be further divided on the basis of their strategic origins: there can be dedicated or multi-family offices with internal, independent or bank origins, as shown in the following matrix. It is important to define these categories with accuracy so as to proceed in the next chapter with the analysis of the possible spaces for Italian banks to start or continue to operate in the segment of wealth management by means of a family office structure.

The internal family office has been set up directly by one or more families, who have decided not to delegate the management of family matters. It is worth noticing that "all family offices become multi-family within the fourth generation because of the number of the family members and of the difference in the value of sub-groups"[15]. "In addition there is a natural expansion process of the family nucleus up to include external families through marriages with the original family". Examples are Bessner Trust Co., New York; Pitcairn Trust Co., Jenkintown; Laird Norton Trust Co., Seattle; Signature Financial Management, Inc., Norfolk. These multi-family offices are the natural consequence of the increased number of members from generation to generation, each of them with its own character and propensity to risk, along with new family nuclei created by marriages.

The experience acquired in the course of time as internal dedicated family office has sometimes allowed the office to extend its field of action, by providing its competencies to other groups of entrepreneurs, generally characterized by a similar wealth profile. In Italy, examples of this evolution are Secofind, originally set up to serve the necessities of the Zambon family. Also the Alettis have opened their own family office to the public: since May 2003 they have been providing their advice through Francesco Alletti Montano & Co.

---

[15] Interview to Charlie Haines, partner of Charles D. Haines, LLC, a multi-family office located in Birmingham (Alabama, USA) effected by Bloomberg in 2002. See public information at www.wealth.Bloomberg.com, with reference to the document "Money changes everything", 2002.

Whenever the family decides to adopt the dedicated solution, they have to solve some fundamental issues as early as upon setup: the decision of where the company should be physically located is of major importance and it may create a lot of difficulties when the business and/or services required by the family are diversified and present in different countries, so that it is necessary to make a comparative analysis of the fiscal and legal advantages of the overall family business. Moreover, the impossibility to employ a large number of people in the staff, because of the extremely high costs implied by this kind of structure, significantly reduces the potential field of action and often requires outsourcing even when this is not strategically or economically convenient. Finally, external people might be introduced in the company staff because of their unbiased view of best solutions, especially in case of family conflicts.

Independent family offices prevailingly originate from legal or notary consulting firms who have decided to extend their field of action, or from managers who have left their previous employment to create a new structure.[16]. An example of independent multi-family office is TAG Associates in New York, founded in 1983 by former partners of Ernst & Young for the purpose of initially providing services to the managers of Warner Communications. Still nowadays among their major clients there are the senior executives of AOL Time Warner[17]. To avoid conflicts of interests, investment financial management has been delegated to third parties, whereas the family office deals with the coordination of all the accessory services.

In Italy, Mamy's aims at managing the family business assets both as dedicated and multi-family office by means of trust companies. Again, they coordinate the most important financial aspects, whereas the operational aspects are outsourced to external institutions. Other examples are Skema, Consultique and Tiche. The last differs from the typical family office: its average service access threshold is lower (i.e. €1m) and does not manage the relationship between banks and customers directly. In fact, it consists of five professionals who provide best solutions for any kind of issue, but delegate clients themselves for the dialogue with financial institutions.

---

[16] Therefore they can be assimilated to the independent financial planners in Fig. 6.1.

[17] More specifically, over a 20-year period the company experienced a considerable growth, thus confirming the potentials of the business, and now counts 60 employees, who manage the assets of 80 families for a total of over US$ 3bl assets under management.

Both in the case of dedicated and independent players, frequent contacts need to be established with several financial operators: trade banks, asset managers, corporate and investment bankers, thus reducing the internal supply to merely consulting and non-financial services. If, on the one hand, management independence is very high, on the other, costs, as we shall see here after, for a complete management are generally higher than for a bank. The multi-family office is often the favorite solution because, thanks to the larger extension achieved by managing more clients, it charges lower fees and at the same time provides services that cannot be accessed by a sole private operator.

From the point of view of this chapter, bank family offices are those of major interest. Their origins are multifold. As a matter of fact, they may derive from small banks that, starting from the necessity to manage the wealth of the owner family, have created an in-house division able to provide services to other family groups. In Italy, Finanziaria Canova started with the Marzottos and the De Agostinis and only later decided to adopt a SIM structure (stock brokerage company) in order to contact clients with transparency, guaranteed by the control of supervisory authorities and enforced regulations. Another example of an initially dedicated bank family office is Orefici Sim, owned by the Vedanis. Intermarket Sim, instead, operates for the Fernet-Branca family. In Europe, Pictet has been the first bank to create a Multi-Family Office service, whereas it was founded to manage the wealth of the bank's founder families. Driven by the same motivations, also the Swiss bank Julius Baer has set up a multi-family office. In both cases, a separate structure has been created to formally protect the separation between the parent bank and the family office. In this case, Pictet Family Office Ltd and Julius Bear Family Office Ltd have been respectively set up.

Therefore the common element is the creation of an external structure through the successive spin-off of already existing private banks. In this respect, trusts are widely utilized and generally adopted by great merchant banks as well: Citigroup Private Bank for example operates in the family office area through Cititrust[18].

A particularly innovative structure has been finally adopted by JPMorgan: a virtual family office[19], which outsources only some or all of the ser-

---

[18] Reference should be made to chapter 8 for direct witness regarding the case Citigroup.

[19] "Many families have traditionally relied on a family office to coordinate, control, and organize their wealth. Advances in technology have facilitated the growth of an attractive alternative: a "virtual" family office, in which some or all family office functions are outsourced to third-party providers. This can make the family

vices available. The online forum here becomes the meeting point of specialists who are called to solve family management issues. Another virtual solution is Pepper International, managed by Carol Pepper, whose portal has a number of major professionals available that are specialized in fiscal, legal and real estate advisory.

Possible strategic and organizational choices are therefore multiple and often embrace more than one matrix. Let us take the example of CFO SIM[20], whose group of shareholders includes both entrepreneurial families and external managers. Moreover, being a SIM, they are authorized to develop direct asset investment and risk management activities.

Here below, Table 6.1 shows the family office matrices which have been dealt with in this paragraph for the purpose of providing a scheme of the different solutions that can be adopted. The poor presence of dedicated family offices is not to be attributed to their poor development, but to the difficulty in finding information about private structures which quite often prefer not to be publicly known.

Table 6.1 The family office positioning matrix: major players in the Italian market

Family Office Typology	Family Office Matrix		
	Internal	**Bank**	**Independent**
Dedicated Family Office	- Famiglia Manuli	- Pictet (originally)	-
		- Orefici SIM	
		- Intermarket srl	
Multi-Family Office	- Francesco Aletti Montano & Co.	- Pictet (ad oggi)	- Tag Associates
	- Secofind	- Julius Bear	- Mamy's
	- Bessner Trust Co.	- Orefici Sim	- Skema
	- Pitcairn Trust Co.	- Finanziaria Canova	- Consultique
	- Laird Norton Trust Co.	- JP Morgan	- Tiche
	- Signature Financial Management, Inc.	- Citigroup	

6.4 The Family Office Cost Structure

If the goal of this chapter consists in focusing the opportunities available for Italian banks within the evolution of wealth management and the seg-

---

office structure an even more convenient and cost-effective way for families to keep track of their wealth. Whatever course you choose, we can help you deal with ongoing financial needs or provide multi-disciplinary solutions through our family office expertise." www.jpmorgan.com.

[20] Reference should be made to chapter 9 for direct witness regarding this financial institution.

ment of family offices, then we cannot avoid analyzing the costs and margins of this structure. Because of service discretion and customization, as shown for access thresholds, the typology and the amount of fees cannot be defined univocally.

On the whole, fees must be distinguished into management and intermediation fees[21]. The former can be divided into:

- management standard fee: a non recurrent yearly fixed fee[22];

- over performance fee: it is used in the case of profitable management. The fee is lower than the management standard fee and is applied in the case the client manager obtains performances exceeding the given benchmark. Generally a minimum threshold is established under which no fee can applied;

- performance fee: it differs from the previous one as the percentage is applied to the performance irrespective of its being over or under the benchmark. Sometimes it is added to management standard fee.

Intermediation fees can be divided into:

- standard fee: it is applied to transacted volume; then it depends above all on the number of transactions developed in the portfolio, on its movements. Usually it is applied in case of profitable management;

- yearly-based non recurrent fee;

- yearly-based maximum fee: it establishes that the client is not due to pay over a given amount.

The above fees, which once could not be discussed by the client, are now subject to constant negotiation. In addition, non recurrent or maximum fees have been established to protect the client from conflicts of interest.

These fees must be added to all the services that do not strictly belong to the area of private banking: for example, advisory in the field of extraordinary finance, risk advisory or fees for the services provided by legal or notary firms. According to what has been agreed between the client and the family office, two solutions are generally adopted. In the first instance, hourly-based fees are calculated separately from project and service fees. In the second instance, upon formalization of the client-family office relationship, the costs for such services are roughly estimated by fixing a sole

---

[21] See Delia-Russell and Di Mascio 2002.
[22] For example, in the case of Tiche the minimum fee is about Euro 5,200 + VAT.

fee covering all of them. Such estimate is then reviewed upon client's or financial planner's request or according to terms agreed. The latter solution is adopted when the range of services requested by the client is so wide and heterogeneous that any punctual analysis would turn out to be particularly burdensome and complicated in terms of time and accounting procedures.

The family office fees are therefore higher than those of private bankers and wealth managers. It is worth noticing, however, that final costs tend to vary according to client service demand: the family office quite often does not provide the whole range of products and services available, but only a limited selection. Moreover, in the case of demand for exclusively in-house services, the costs for outsourced consulting, research and negotiation drop considerably. As families prevailingly demand for their wealth financial management, the fact that banks can actually manage most of the transactions in-house, undoubtedly represents a competitive advantage as they can provide the same services at lower prices.

As for service pricing, the choice between internal dedicated or multi-family offices is particularly important. In the first case, in fact, fixed costs incidence is high and no scale economies can be exploited nor can any investment on staff training and technological platforms be spread among more clients. Moreover, due to the reduced size of the company compared with multi-family offices, in terms of assets under management, upon negotiation for outsourcing services, the bargaining power is likely to be lower and thus causing higher pricing. Finally, from the emotional point of view, setting up a dedicated family office requires a "non-return" choice in the short run: dismantling an ad-hoc structure would in fact provoke a high waste of resources.

As a result, to access a dedicated family office, the client should own at least US$100m in liquid assets[23], which would enable the client to amortize the high fees charged by the manager and totaling a minimum annual amount of at least US$200,000, to be added to the other professionals, back-up staff, technological equipment, management fees (usually close to 60 basis points), structure operating costs and various benefits. By summing the two components, we obtain a total cost of about 140 basis points, which must be added to administrative expenses for structure maintenance.

In the case of the multi-family office, instead, thanks to operating cost reduction, the average access threshold drops to US$20m in liquid assets,

---

[23] Reference is made to the interview to Sarah Hamilton, founder of Fox Exchange, effected by Bloomberg in October 2002. For more information visit www.wealth.Bloomberg.com.

amount that enables operators to target a far more extended reference market.

In the future growing competition will affect margins/fees applicable by wealth managers. The reduction should involve management fees as well as distribution costs and administrative expenses. The phenomenon is already in progress according to data provided by Prometeia: in fact if we take the 2001-2002 period, in Europe average revenues fluctuated between 130 and 140 basis points per family, which are far higher at a parity of service than in the United States, where cost reduction started at an earlier stage. Therefore in the next five years, the European market is expected to come closer to the American one and thus reduce individual management fees by at least 30 basis points, as shown in Table 6.2.

Table 6.2 Analysis of expected evolution in management revenues over the next five years

	Administration	Production	Distribution
Current revenues (140 bp)	20 bp	45 bp	75 bp
Next-5-year revenues (110 bp)	20 bp	35 bp	55 bp

Source: Accenture, 2001 processing of Prometeia data.

If we enter the details of the single components[24], administration fees should remain pretty stable, because competition in the past few years has already reduced prices considerably. Major competition should develop within service production: the huge number of assets managers, fund managers, hedge funds and financial advisors will lead to keen competition, with the consequent exit of some players who will not be able to attract customers because they fail to achieve the break-even point or to have a reliable track record. Today it is important for the multi-family office to invest in brand creation/consolidation and public visibility, in high reputation maintenance and in planning a benefit and incentive scheme for human resources so as to keep major professionals within the company structure.

To conclude, important changes will also affect distribution, with a general reduction of service costs. Fees will remain high anyway because of consulting fees, which will have an ever increasing incidence within wealth managers' supply.

---

[24] See evaluations by Delia-Russell and Di Mascio 2002.

6.5 The Family Office Opportunities in the Italian Market and the Role of Banks

6.5.1 A General Overview

As we have seen in paragraph 6.1, the research carried out by Cap Gemini and Ernst & Young in 2002 and 2003 shows that wealth management has the highest growth rate in the whole industry of financial services, thanks to the increase in the number of HNWIs despite the international downturn in High-Tech.

This is confirmed by the evolution in the number of dedicated family offices in the USA, which rose from 500-1,000 in the mid '90s to over 3,500 in 2002[25]. This figure can further increase if we consider the operators who, due to family discretion requirements, are not publicized and thus excluded from official statistics. According to another study by Cerulli Associates – an advisory and research firm in Boston dealing with the evolution of the worldwide market of financial institutions – in June 2001 private family offices were estimated from 3,000 to 5,000 units in the United States.

Multi-family offices set up far more recently (2001-2002) seem to be only 50 according to Fox Exchange estimates. These, however, should be added to the several professional and advisory firms that, by reducing their access threshold to US$5m, are trying to combine their traditional range of services with other advisory activities.[26] The above 50 family offices have exploited the presence in a new segment characterized by high access barriers and have shown substantial growth rates with, sometimes, an average increase of 5 new Relationship Managers per year. At the same time, the annual guaranteed remuneration has been raised to US$250-300,000 for specialized managers. The need for best quality standards and the high demand for services have driven 17 US financial institutions providing wealth management services to plan an increase of 430 new Relationship Managers between 2001 and 2003.

---

[25] Data are extracted from Fox Exchange and Datamonitor, "European High Net Worth Customers", London, 2001.
[26] The inclusion of this category of operators is questionable: as one of the fundamental criteria for the family office is the long-term approach toward future generations and, to provide this kind of service, the wealth must be of huge proportions, the focus should be limited to U-HNWIs.

In Europe, always according to Fox Exchange, over 200 families have formally structured dedicated offices for the management of their wealth and the number is still on the way up. Development opportunities for the family office in Europe, and in particular in Italy, seem quite promising especially in the case of multi-family offices, which, by establishing far lower access thresholds than private offices, represent an interesting solution for family business[27].

In the forthcoming future, it is likely there will be an increase in the volumes and number of family offices worldwide along with mergers and acquisitions among companies operating in wealth management or in similar industries in order to increase their critical masses, to consolidate their brands and create formerly absent in-house competencies. As already mentioned in the paragraph about cost structure, the family office can tackle the reduction of management fees successfully, only by means of a consolidated positioning within the market. External growth may represent a desirable solution.

If we analyze the top ten family offices worldwide, we can draw important indications: on the one hand, the turnover is undoubtedly high; on the other, all the cases refer to companies located in the United States, to confirm the far more recent development of the European market. Moreover, in the past four years M&As have been quite numerous: 5 out of 10 family offices have been involved by a process of external growth (see Table 6.3).

Table 6.3 The top ten family offices in the USA (2002 data)

Company	Seat	Acquisition by	Assets Under Mgt ($bl)
Atlantic Trust Pell Rudman	Massachusetts, Delaware	AMVESCAP	8
Family Wealth Group	New York, Delaware, Minnesota, California	Schwab	8
Rockfeller & Company	New York, Delaware		4
Whittier Trust Company	California, Nevada		4
TAG Associates	New York	CF Capital Mgmt	3
Asset Mgt Advisors	Wyoming	SunTrust	2.5
Laird Norton Trust Co.	Washington		2.2
Pitcairn Trust	Pennsylvania		2
Vogel Consulting Group	Wisconsin		1.5
Frye-Louis Capital Mgmt	Illynois	Credit Suisse	1.3

Source: www.trustandestates.com

---

[27] The growing interest of Italian family business is confirmed by the numerous conferences held on this subject over the past few years. The main internet sites dedicated to family offices and sector associations mention more than 10 conferences in 2003.

A deeper analysis of the US operators shows that in some cases (e.g. Asset Management Advisors and SunTrust) the two structures were both operating in the area of wealth management through trusts according to the family office approach. Elsewhere, (e.g. the case of Credit Suisse which acquired Frye-Louis Capital Management in 2001) the acquisition was an important opportunity for developing competencies that had not been formalized yet within the banking group. Frye Louis has had the chance of a much faster growth; Credit Suisse has obtained the access to highly specialized know-how experiences that are often an exclusive prerogative of family offices.

The main reasons for these mergers and acquisitions can be summarized into the following factors. By merging with another financial player, family offices can achieve the necessary critical mass to make further investments in company growth, acquire more innovative technologies and have huge financial resources so as to diversify their supply and attract high-standing professionals into their team. Moreover, sometimes mergers allow bridging gaps in some strategic areas or entering different geographical territories. One example is that of Tiedemann Trust Company: they intended to extend their competencies and service supply to approach the business of family offices and to propose themselves as a centralized operator for wealthy clients.

In the case of acquisition by banking groups, family offices may benefit from the bank fame and brand to attract a larger group of clients that are no longer restricted to the same geographical area. In fact, a portion of the bank HNW customers are likely to take advantage of the family office to delegate the wealth management of their family business and concentrate in a unique player tasks that used to be performed by various professionals. On the other hand, the bank can acquire resources and competencies otherwise hardly attainable in-house and operate in a segment characterized by highly interesting margins compared with retail and affluent segments[28].

The risk of the conflict of interests should never be neglected. The team of financial planners must be completely free in their management choices: they might decide, for example, to use client current account services provided by a bank that is not the parent one if the price-quality ratio is better elsewhere. This example highlights a quite delicate matter: it is essential

---

[28] TAG Associates aimed at approaching the business of investment banking in segments that were complementary to theirs. As for consulting firms, the merger between Mahoney Cohen, an accounting firm, and Neuberger Berman Trust, a firm of legal advisors, notaries and investment managers, aimed at better customer satisfaction by coordinating their institutional activities and thus widening their supply.

for the family office to achieve a balance in which bank budgeting criteria and service standardization must be carefully avoided; if not so, despite remarkable cost reductions, the family office would start abandoning customization which is a distinctive feature of quality wealth management.

Once the position has been consolidated in the domestic market, many family offices may take the decision to set up branches in other countries and to attack markets where this phenomenon is still practically unknown: Latin America and Asia represent quite appealing realities for the almost total absence of integrated management services of wealth management and for the fast achievement of a dominant position in the area and where very high fees can be easily guaranteed.

6.5.2 Private Banking Distinctive Features in the Italian Market

Private banking and, above all, wealth management make up a remarkably fragmented area. As a result, organization models of the different operators may be quite diverse. Nevertheless, the market can be divided into three large categories of operators:

- international merchant banks;

- specialized private banks;

- trade banks.

The fact that several HNWIs have chosen to aim at service quality upgrade to improve customer satisfaction has led international merchant banks to have great success also in Italy[29]. Thanks to their considerable dimensions, the contemporary presence in different national contexts and their wide public visibility, these players can fully exploit their know-how and competencies to provide wide ranging services and advice, which include renowned skills in asset management and investment banking. A great competitive advantage is in fact provided by the possible exploitation of important synergies with the other corporate divisions, so as to be able to tackle family business requirements exhaustively. As for organizations models, these groups have generally developed an in-house division or business unit for both affluent clients and HNWIs. Some have introduced a family office in their structure, which is available by using the group trust company[30].

---

[29] An example in the European market of wealth management is given by BNP Paribas, Barclays, UBS, Deutsche Bank, Credit Suisse, Ing, Citibank.
[30] As shown in the previous paragraph, an example is given by Citigroup and Credit Suisse. For a more detailed analysis of organization models of investment

As for small financial boutiques, such as the Italian Banca Aletti, Banca Leonardo and Banca Akros, the core business used to be investment banking, but over the past few years it has been extended to include the different aspects of wealth management. In this case, the small dimension has allowed them to establish a closer and exclusive contact with clients, by aiming at service strong customization. These elements, on the one hand, urge for the upgrade of all human resources in the company, as the manager is the final point of contact with the client and represents the bank professional profile, reliability, preparation and availability; on the other they urge for a careful and dedicated presence in their restricted territorial area.

Finally, in trade banks private banking structures are being subject to strategic re-organization. Some have already introduced divisions or business units distinguished by client category (e.g. Unicredit Private Banking); others have preferred to provide more standardized private banking services for affluent clients, thus assigning the complicated matters of wealth management to an already existing financial boutique and then incorporated in the group structure. An example is given by Banca Steinhauslin, part of Gruppo MPS since 1999 and incorporated since 2003.

The capillary distribution over the territory and the deep knowledge of the cultural and financial dynamics of family business make diversification toward more specialized services focused on the complex family-firm relationship particularly attractive for trade banks. In this respect, policies should be developed to achieve better coordination between private and corporate divisions. This explains why it is important to understand which organizational solutions are actually feasible, especially if the final goal is the creation of a family office.

6.5.3 Choosing the Best Organization Structure

The development of wealth management in Italy relies on three possible alternatives:

- create a new division or business unit;
- create a new external structure;
- acquire already existing wealth managers or family offices.

The creation of a new wealth management service inside or outside the bank structure may raise some questions in the event the goal is a real qualitative change in the range of services, aimed at embracing the three main branches of wealth management, corporate banking and advisory. As a matter of fact, necessary competencies are multiple and investments in IT systems and recruitment of human resources are extremely high. For example, the decision to adopt all the most important technological resources requires not only a good knowledge of IT requirements but also the ability to recruit the personnel capable of best exploiting the potential of the new software. The decision for an inside or an outside structure will bear remarkable consequences.

The first alternative enables the bank to lightly reduce costs compared with the outside organization. In this case, in fact, it is not necessary to develop new brands differing from those of the parent bank and costly structure duplications can be avoided as would happen for back office, accounting and administration activities. For these reasons, the in-house alternative has been the favorite choice for Italian trade banks. It is worth noticing, however, that if the changed image offered by a wealth management division is to be fully exploited, the bank should make remarkable investments in inside and outside communication.

The other business units must be involved in the process of change by avoiding, if possible, any hesitations about the roles developed by the personnel during and after the transition period. A relation of permeability and collaboration should be established between the wealth management division and the other divisions above all for corporate banking and credit management services, thus avoiding possible conflicts. Colleagues from private and corporate banking might not be motivated to send part of their clients to wealth management as they fear to lose their relation with the client and thus fail to achieve budget objectives. For this reason, the bank should arrange for a specific remuneration scheme including for example bonuses for the indication of potential clients and the fee mechanism for advisory and services required by the wealth manager.

Equally important is effective communication among clients, who must be informed of the excellence and the exclusiveness of the service, so as compensate the possible migration from the old private manager to the wealth manager, without renouncing the comforts of the bank capillary presence over the national territory. To this aim, it might be advisable to arrange an adequate migration mechanism for the family, perhaps by organizing a combined period to avoid sudden changes and the loss of the experience acquired by the private banker in family business. A monitoring mechanism is then essential to assess whether the migration mode is taking place without dissensions. The bank should avoid traumas for the clients, which in the end might lead to bad reputation. A testing time should be started initially on a limited sample of families so as to check whether any errors have been made in the course of the business plan.

The wealth management division will be directly responsible for the coordination of in-house and outsourced services, strategic advisory for family business and for outside communication initiatives like event organization.

Fig. 6.3 shows an example of organization structure with an inside wealth management business unit. As we can see, a critical aspect of the family office is that the division cannot be fully independent from the rest of the bank[31]. The bank willing to implement this organization structure must reassure the client by acting in full compliance with maximum transparency during the entire process of decision-making and showing the client that the risk of conflicts of interest is being carefully and constantly kept under control.

Fig. 6.3 An example of business unit organization structure

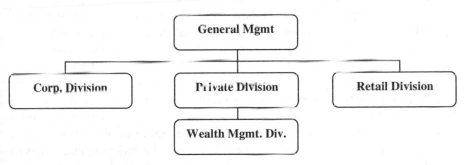

The second alternative shares a lot of problems with the already examined inside structure. In particular, it is essential to arrange an adequate business plan formalizing the connection with the parent bank, the fee structures and the incentives for the indication of potential clients. Cost increase produced by the completely separate management of this organization is offset by the formal management independence. Once again, possibly opportunistic and damaging behaviors for clients' interests should be carefully kept under control through the activity of corporate governance. Finally, an external structure requires an attentive marketing policy serving the creation of a successful quality-oriented image designed for HNW clients.

Fig. 6.4 exemplifies an organization model with the creation of an outside wealth management structure. The main plus of the decision to ac-

---

[31] See the previous paragraph.

quire an external wealth management company or family office is the possible formal separation from the rest of the group. The outstanding discretion and the independent management of operations and resources make this organization model the favorite solution for merchant banks and specialized private banks.

Fig. 6.4 An example of organization model with an outside wealth management structure

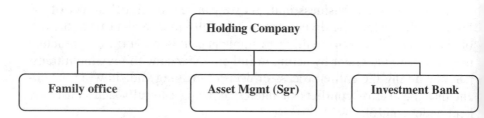

With the third alternative the risk of an erroneous strategic model is far lower than in the case of the creation of a new structure. The costs resulting from the implementation of new technologies and the recruitment of specialized human resources, or from the total upset of the existing structure and the management of the complex wealth management process, are obviously reduced or even non-existent[32]. The bank then will have to carry out an attentive analysis of the economic advantages considering on the one hand the costs of a totally new structure and on the other the price to be paid for the acquisition of an already existing family office. Of great importance in this respect is the ability of the parent bank to best exploit the value added of the family office by respecting its independence so as to ensure good profitability and the collaboration of high-standard professionals.

6.5.4 The Centralized or Decentralized Management Model

The possibility of entering the wealth management market as family office also depends on the management model the bank intends to implement. In the centralized model commonly utilized by trade banks and by those specialized in private banking the roles of the relationship manager and the asset manager are totally different. Although financial and organizational costs are lower because wealth management is centralized in a sole structure where multiple synergies can be exploited, service customization

---

[32] Reference should be made to the previous paragraph for a more accurate analysis of the advantages resulting from growth via external acquisition.

based on client requirements is not as simple and the time to market is longer. As a matter of fact, once the client's main guidelines have been perceived, the relationship manager must involve the asset manager as the former is not able to develop the necessary strategy independently. Whenever new options arise or organization/administration problems are to be solved, the relationship manager must contact the client again and start a new decisional phase. Generally, the wealth management dedicated structure is a management trust (Sgr), which is responsible for the implementation and creation of a portfolio on the basis of the indications provided by the relationship manager. This organization model is adopted by UniCredito and Banca Intesa.

Table 6.4 The matrix of strategic and management solutions for a bank family office

Strategic/management model	Strategic solutions		
	Inside BU creation	Outside BU creation	FO Acquisition
Centralized Model			
Decentralized Model			Ideal solution for family office

The decentralized model best suits the family office. In fact, here client management and wealth management are assigned to a team that can rapidly change asset strategies on the basis of the constant dialogue with the client. Service customization is very high as asset management is within the wealth management division. On the other hand, as observed in the case of Banca Aletti & Co., it may become difficult to attentively control and monitor the rationality of the process. In other banks, corporate governance will have to manage major organizational problems. Some specialized private banks, like that of the group Deutsche Bank, have opted for this choice due to the lack of a management trust (Sgr), whereas in the case of Steinhauslin the use of the group asset management might be an optimal solution, especially when the client does not require specific service customization.

It is worth noticing that both the centralized and the decentralized models can be matched with an organization based on an inside or outside structure, as shown in Table 6.4.

As a result, according to the various possible combinations, the creation of a family office will be more or less difficult. On the basis of our analysis, it is apparent that the choice of the outside organization model, perhaps with the acquisition of an already existing family office, along with a decentralized management model seems to be the ideal condition to operate in the area of wealth management.

6.6 Conclusions

As illustrated in the previous paragraphs, the creation of a family office structure is a very complicated process despite the remarkable growth potential. Constant concentration on quality and excellence, great flexibility and management independence represent some of the outstanding critical aspects.

It is true that for many banks the alternative to total customization of the service for HNW family business is a partial improvement of the service quality. This solution is hardly feasible, especially if the bank intends to consolidate its market positioning in the long term. In particular, in the next few years wealth management fee margins will mainly result from extra-wealth management advisory services, which represent the real novelty in relation to HNWIs private banking.

The bank that intends to enter the area of family office is bound to work out a value proposition and a business plan including an accurate definition of the organizational relations with the other bank divisions or group companies, the development and control plans for goal achievement and communication among the employees and the clients. Moreover, it is important to establish ahead of time the main alliances and strategic relations with providers of outsourced services. The family office, in fact, should be able to develop an image reflecting a service quality, innovation and customization-oriented approach as well as a transparent management of the various processes.

To achieve all this, human resources acquire a strategic importance: the team of financial planners must be an important reference for the client and the family office must keep the best professionals by establishing a system based upon career motivation, creativity stimulation and personal contribution to avoid excessive turnover in the team. To this aim, it may be useful to establish communication relations with research institutes and universities with a view to capturing the best talents and seizing the economic and social aspects of wealth management.

All this requires extremely refined infrastructure, organization and strategy. In particular, technology is the key item to compete and to be able to inform and successfully communicate with the family.

7 The State of the Art of the Multi-Family Office

Edmondo Tudini

7.1 Objectives and Methodology

The primary goal of the survey object of this chapter consists in identifying the main features of the business model characterizing the players involved in the international industry of the multi-family office (MFO), by focusing our attention on the following aspects: i) governance ii) target market; iii) range of supply and iv) operating mechanisms.

First of all we had to solve the problem of how we could identify a sample of firms definable as MFOs, that is of firms whose core business is the supply of services dedicated to high net worth families (HNWFs). As a matter of fact, as MFOs have only recently developed and spread, there are no category associations or dedicated databanks. The only source of information is the family office exchange[1] (FOX), an American consulting company assisting HNWFs in the selection of advisors for their wealth management. Over the past few years, FOX has become the most important information center on the MFO industry; in particular their site provides a list of 43 companies defined as MFOs. Out of these 43 firms, 37 are US companies[2]; therefore, limiting the analysis to this sample would have meant concentrating our attention exclusively on the American context. To broaden the scope of our survey, we tried to identify some European MFOs to be included in the sample. To this aim, we made reference to the firms that had attended as MFO representatives the most important conferences recently held in Europe on the subject of family office[3]. Thanks to this further effort we managed to identify another 25 firms (20 in Europe and 5 in the USA) to be included in our sample, finally composed by 68 MFOs, of which 44 in the US and 24 in Europe[4].

The list of the information sources considered for the identification of the sample is provided by Table 7.1, whereas the complete list of the con-

---

[1] For further information about FOX visit www.foxexchange.com.

[2] As for the remaining 6 firms: 4 are European, 1 is Australian and 1 is Canadian.

[3] All of these conferences are characterized by extreme confidentiality. It is very difficult to retrieve material regarding participants' papers.

[4] The sample structure is consistent with the larger number of MFOs in the US compared with Europe.

tacted firms is provided by Table 7.2. Private Banks have been intentionally excluded from the sample even though they provide services for HNWFs; this is due to that the specific goal of the research study consists in identifying the distinctive features of the typical business model of pure MFOs[5].

Table 7.1 Information sources utilized for the identification of the sample of firms to be contacted

Information Source	Organization	Web site	N. of identified firms
Family office exchange (FOX)		www.foxexchange.com	43
Conference – FAMILY OFFICE: Quels services pour pérenniser les fortunes familiales françaises?- Paris (2003).	Edition Formation Enterprise (EFE)	www.efe.fr	2
Conference – The European Family Office Conference – London (1999-2002)	Campden Publishing Ltd[6]	www.campdenconferences.com	8
Conference – The 3rd Annual Geneva Conference on FAMILY OFFICE- Geneva (2002)	MGI – Management Global Information	www.mgi-direct.ch	7
Conference – The Wealth Management Congress– London (2003).	IBC UK Conferences	www.wealthmanagementcongress.com	4
Conference – Family Business & Family Office – Lugano (2002)	MGI – Management Global Information	www.mgi-direct.ch	3
Conference – Family Business & Family Office – Milan (2002)	SDA Bocconi, MGI, AIDAF	www.aidaf.it	1

To collect necessary information for our survey, a questionnaire was e-mailed to sample firms (Annex 1). The questionnaire includes 14 open questions divided into three sections: the first is dedicated to the analysis

---

[5] The several firms that operate within financial groups with the specific task to provide HNWF-dedicated services were not excluded from the sample.
[6] The list of participants at the four editions of the "European Family Office Conference" held in London between 1999 and 2002 has been directly provided by Campden Publishing Ltd.

of the governance of sample firms, the second to the identification of their supply and the third to the analysis of operating processes, with specific reference to remuneration mechanisms and customer relationships[7]. The choice of open questions was considered the most suitable as the objective of the research, as already mentioned, was not verifying the positioning of sample firms in relation to a given business model, but identifying the basic features of an extremely recent and still vaguely outlined business model.

Table 7.2 The sample

US MFOs	
Asset Management Advisors	Tag Associates LLC
Atlantic Trust Pell Rudman	Vogel Consulting Group, S.C.
Pitcairn Trust	Arlington Partners Family Office
Family wealth Group (US Trust)	Capital Analysts of Jacksonville, Florida, Inc.
Cymric Family Office Services	Chaffee & Westenberg Companies
Deloitte & Touche Family Office LLP	Hawthorn
Gresham Partners, L.L.C.	Heritage Financial Management
Laird Norton Trust Company	Joseph W. Roskos & Co.
Oxford Financial Group, Ltd.	Frye Louis Capital Management, Inc. (Strategic Advisor)
Rockefeller & Co., Inc.	Legacy Trust Company
Sentinel Trust Company, LBA	Lincoln Financial Advisors
Sterling (a National City Company)	Fiduciary Trust Company
Synovus Family Asset Management	Plante and Moran Family Wealth Advisors
Thompson Jones LLP	Tanager Financial Services, Inc.
Tiedemann Trust Company	Anchin Block & Anchin LLP
Wetherby Asset Management	Benning Financial Group
Whittier Trust Company	Erskine Family Offices LLC
Northern Trust	Private Advisory Services
Inlign Wealth Management LLC	FXM Inc.
Fleming family & partners	Donlvy -Rosen & Rosen, PA
Tocqueville Asset Management L.P.	Bessemer Trust Company
Smart and Associates LLP	Geller & Company

---

[7] The questionnaire was prepared by extracting the most significant questions among the ones proposed by FOX to the MFOs that intend to join their network. www.foxexchange.it

Table 7.2 Continued

European MFOs	
Sauerborn Trust AG 3	SFF Family office
Shield Management Services Limited	Barons Financial Services
Coddington Financial Services Pty Ltd	Nean wealth Advisors
Key Trust Company Limited	Private Client Bank Family Office Services
Marcuard Family Office	Daco partners investing & consulting SA
Pictet Family office Ltd	Homburger
Julius Baer family office Ltd	Erhard &Cie financial Consultant AG
Siriu Asset Managemnet Ltd	Genevaprivateoffice SA
Financière MJ	LGT Trust (Lux)
FidesTrust Vermogenstreuhand GmbH	Leboeuf, Lamb, Greene & Macrae
PHI Trust	CFO Sim
Mamy's Family Office Strategies	Macfarlanes

Out of the 68 contacted firms, questionnaires were returned by 16 US and 5 European MFOs[8]. Considering the limited number of replies, we tried to obtain further information about the sample firms initially identified by visiting their web sites. This further analysis allowed us to obtain significant information about another 11 firms, 9 in the States and 2 in Europe.

Table 7.3 Firms whose relative information was obtained by visiting web sites

Firm name	Firm web site
Asset Management Advisors	www.amaglobal.com
Oxford Financial Group, Ltd	www.ofgltd.com
Laird Norton Trust Company	www.lntco.com
Bessemer Trust Company	www.bessemer.com
Sentinel Trust Company, LBA	www.sentineltrust.com
Tag Associates LLC	www.tagassoc.com
Vogel Consulting Group S.C.	www.vogelcg.com
Sauerborn Trust AG	www.feri-family-office.de
Marcuard Family Office	www.marcuardfamilyoffice.com
Cymric Family Office Services	www.cymricfamilyoffice.com
Whittier Trust Company	www.whittiertrust.com

At that point available information regarded a group of 31 MFOs, most of which were US firms. In the attempt to redress our sample, we tried contacting the European firms about which we had no data available. In

---

[8] Not all the firms provided exhaustive replies.

particular, 7 telephone interviews were made with as many representatives of European MFOs. The research was carried out on a sample of 38 firms (25 American and 13 European firms)[9]. Table 7.4 provides the list of the sources utilized for information collection.

Table 7.4 Sources utilized for collecting information about sample firms

Information sources	N. of firms USA	N. of firms Europe	Total
E-mailed questionnaire	16	4	20
Telephone interviews	0	7	7
Web sites analysis	9	2	11

7.2 Cautious Interpretation of Results

As explained in the previous paragraph, due to the absolute novelty and the still vague outline of the issue object of our analysis as well as to the difficulty met in collecting necessary data, our research is based on information obtained by resorting to different sources and in a rather de-structured manner. The presentation of results has therefore required a remarkable effort of synthesis by the author.

No doubt, this represents a limit of our survey and some caution is necessary upon results interpretation. In this sense, consistently with the objectives of the research, results must be read with a systemic rather than punctual logic so as to seize the clearly emerging typical elements of the MFO business model.

The survey described in this chapter is only a first step toward the real comprehension of MFOs' operating logic, which is bound to require further studies and analyses.

7.3 The MFO Governance

The first area of analysis regards the governance of sample firms. In particular retrieved information involves the following aspects:

---

[9] Due to confidentiality motivations and upon MFOs explicit request, we are allowed to reveal neither the names of the firms returning our questionnaire nor the names of the people interviewed.

- independence;
- firm origins;
- management background.

Independence, the first aspect, should theoretically represent one of the distinctive features of the MFO business model. In fact, one of the strengths of MFOs in HNWFs advisory should be represented by their possibility of acting without any conflict of interest as they are independent, that is not connected by shareholding or partnership agreements with possible third-party providers.

Independence derives from that in this situation the MFO management would not directly or indirectly benefit from choosing a given investment strategy or service provider.

In other words, the MFO independence should guarantee an action constantly aligned with clients' interests. Needless to say that this guarantee will vanish as soon as the MFO enters a group structure that is naturally characterized by the presence of synergies bearing possible conflicts of interest. In this case, the MFO, due to the lack of independence, is in the same position as the private division of a universal bank or of a private bank inside a banking group.

With reference to our 38 sample MFOs, the analysis has identified 28 independent firms and 10 group firms[10]. In the latter category 6 firms belong to a banking group and 4 to an investment group (Fig. 7.1).

Fig. 7.1 Independence of sample firms

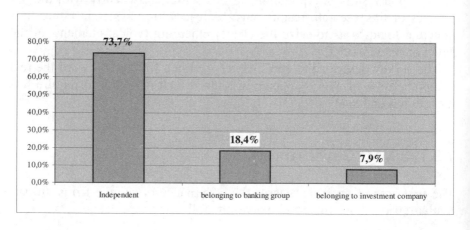

---

[10] Our survey revealed no formal partnership relations between sample MFOs and possible third-party service providers.

Therefore independence is confirmed to be a distinctive feature of the MFOs business model. Moreover, there seem to be no particular differences between the American and the European contexts, where the incidence of independent MFOs is about the same.

Table 7.5 MFOs inside a group structure[11]

Firm name	Parent banking group	Investment group	Merger/acquisition date	Set-up date
Asset Management Advisors	Sun Trust Banks		Acquisition 2001	
Atlantic Trust Pell Rudman		AMVESCAP	Acquisition 2001	
Julius Baer family office Ltd	Julius Baer Bank			2000
TAG Associates		GF Capital Management	Merger 2002	
Hawthorn	PNC Bank		Acquisition 2000	
Frye-Louis Capital Management, Inc.	Credit Suisse		Acquisition 2001	
Family wealth Group		Schawab	Acquisition 2002	
Pictet Family office Ltd	Pictet Bank			1999
SFF Family Office SA	Sandoz FF Holding Bancaire et Financière SA			2000
LGT Trust	LGT Group			1999

Such evidence should not lead to underestimate the recent entry of important financial groups in the MFO industry (Table 7.5), which has been effected through the setup of ad hoc companies or by acquiring already existing MFOs. In fact, the phenomenon on the one hand suggests the great appeal of the HNWF market and on the other that the same market is being perceived also by the big groups as a specific niche to be serviced with specific strategies

Firm origins, the second aspect, are considered by our survey above all to verify whether the firms currently operating in the market as MFOs derive from dedicated family offices, that is to say from offices originally set up by a sole family to meet their requirements. Such distinction is relevant as the firms originating from a dedicated family office might have acquired distinctive competencies that allow them to offer a wider range of services to client families.

---

[11] Data contained in the table are publicly available on the web sites of the companies involved.

Out of the 38 sample MFOs, 11 derive from dedicated family offices. All of them are American, which indicates the change from dedicated to multi-family office is a typically American phenomenon, so far almost unknown in the continental reality. The reasons are to be attributed to the larger presence and the longer-dated tradition of the family office industry in the USA rather than in Europe[12], where this innovation started developing as late as in the late '80s[13].

Fig. 7.2 Origins of sample firms

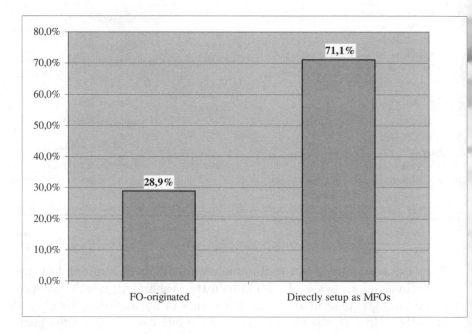

Moreover, given the relevance of the phenomenon in the USA (Fig. 7.3), an evolution toward the MFO model is reasonably expected also for some of the European family offices of longer dated tradition.

---

[12] The family office industry has very old origins in the United States; the first family office dates back to the Rockfeller family in 1894 and as early as in the '40s family offices were already quite numerous. J. Grote, Money Changes Everything, Bloomberg Wealth Manager , October 2002.

[13] The widespread presence of family offices in Europe is a quite recent phenomenon and is now developing fast; in particular, according to some estimates nowadays in Europe there are more than 200 family offices, Merryl Linch, Cap Gemini Ernst & Young, World Wealth Report, 2002.

Fig. 7.3 Origins of US sample firms

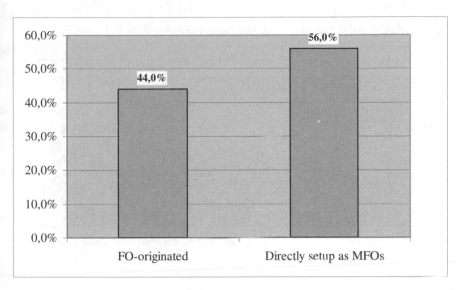

Management background is the third aspect considered by our research, where the term background refers to the professional experiences acquired by the individuals with an outstanding role in the management of sample firms. Here the goal consists in seizing the necessary or, better, the most suitable competencies to manage an MFO. In this sense the background of the firm management may represent an important indicator.

Despite some inevitable approximation, we can state that the experiences formerly acquired by MFO managers can be grouped into the following four macro-categories:

- financial experiences (banks and investment bankers);

- legal experiences (law firms specialized in business law and fiscal matters);

- managerial and entrepreneurial experiences (entrepreneurs and managers);

- accounting and advisory experiences (consulting firms, auditors, professional firms).

By means of this classification we tried to understand the typology of prevailing background in each of the sample firms[14]. Fig. 7.4 synthesizes

---

[14] For firms whose data were collected by visiting websites, the management background was identified on the basis of the following criterion: if at least 50% of the

the results obtained with reference to the whole group of MFOs object of our analysis[15].

Fig. 7.4 Management background of sample firms

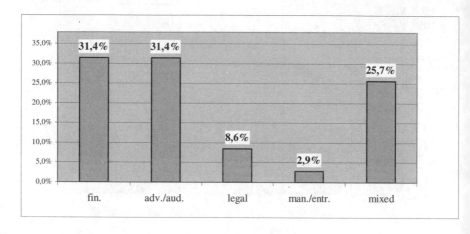

Fig. 7.5 Background: comparison between the USA and Europe

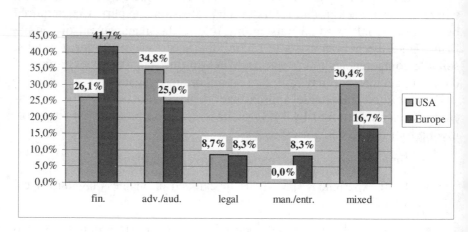

Most of the MFOs reveal a financial or advisory prevailing background, while it is rare to detect the legal or the managerial component as prevailing. In addition, about one fourth of the sample firms show a management

---

of the members of the management team (as described in the site) had a common background, then this background was considered as prevailing; otherwise it was considered as mixed.

[15] Data were collected about 35 firms (USA: 23; Europe:12).

team with mixed competencies that are not prevailing for any of the categories being considered.

In addition, the data examined as a whole do not allow seizing important features that distinguish the various categories of sample MFOs with respect to the variable considered. In this sense the geographical variable (Fig.7.5), the firm origins (Fig. 7.6) and independence (Fig 7.7) seem to acquire some relevance.

In Europe MFOs managers present above all a financial background, whereas the advisory background is prevailing in the United States, even though about one third of firms reveal only mixed competencies (in Europe only 18.7% of cases). Another interesting element of differentiation consists in that while in Europe the managerial background is prevailing in only 1 out of the 12 MFOs considered, in the United States this does not occur in any of the 23 sample firms.

With reference to the origins variable, which is significant exclusively in the United States, Fig. 7.6 highlights how the financial background is prevailing in only 1 out of the 11 FO-originated firms; here the differences between US and European MFOs are partially explained by such evidence.

Fig. 7.6 Prevailing background: differences in the USA

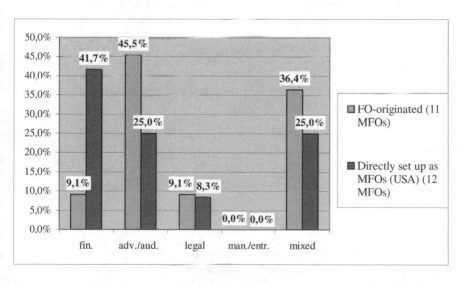

Finally, as for the distinction between independent firms and group-affiliated firms, the financial background is obviously prevailing in the latter (Fig. 7.7).

Fig. 7.7 Background: comparison by independence

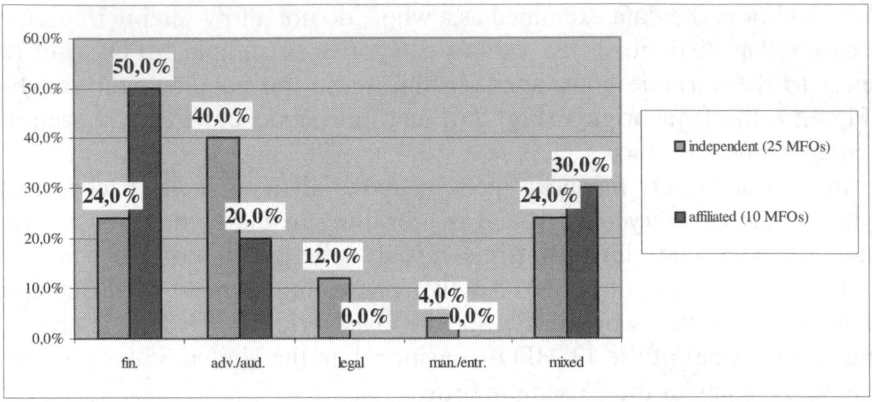

7.4 The MFO Target Market

To better outline the MFO market (generally identified as the segment of all the HNWFs interested in the services provided by such operators), some data were collected on the following two aspects:

- the minimum amount of manageable assets[16] to have access to the services provided by MFOs;

- the amount of manageable assets the client family entrusts to the MFO professional management.

The access threshold to the services provided varies among our sample firms[17] from a minimum of US$3m to a maximum of US$25m, whereas the average value is equal to US$12.7m. In particular, about 75% of sample firms establish their access threshold between US$5m and US$15m (Fig. 7.8).

---

[16] The concept of manageable assets is broader than that of liquid assets; in fact it makes reference to all the assets the client family is ready to entrust to the MFO professional management and which may be object of active management (purchase/sale). Manageable assets do not include family business capital shares (unless divestment is explicitly planned) and the enjoyment assets the family intends to keep. This accepted meaning of manageable assets is rather widespread and shared in the industry of wealth management. Grote 2002.

[17] Data were collected about 36 firms (USA: 24; Europe:12).

Fig. 7.8 Access threshold

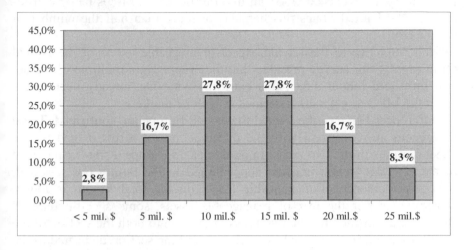

Fig. 7.9 Access threshold: differences between the USA and Europe

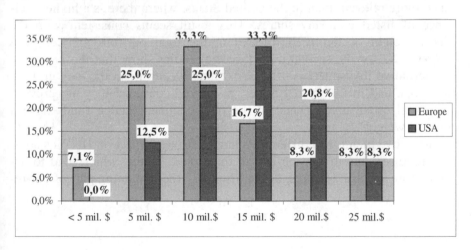

Our data confirm that the MFO target market is represented by a quite specific (the most affluent) niche within the larger market of wealth management services[18]. Despite the unquestionable clarity of this evidence, it will be advisable to consider some of the existing differences between Europe and the United States, which are once again relevant (Fig. 7.9)[19]. In

---

[18] See the previous chapter by Ventrone.

[19] With reference to this specific aspect, independence and origins seem not to be relevant.

particular, for the European firms the access threshold is significantly lower: it does not exceed US$10m in 8 out of the 12 MFOs being considered; in the United States this happens in more than half the number of sample firms.

With reference to the second aspect, manageable assets of the typical client family, our survey revealed that they represent a multiple of the access threshold (about 3.5x); this confirms what has already been stated about the MFO target market defined as a niche market.

Differences between the United States and Europe are confirmed. These differences are consistent with the different mix of assets owned by the client families in the two areas. In particular, in Europe a significant share of the HNWFs wealth is often concentrated in the family business and, thus, the incidence of manageable assets on the total wealth is lower. Moreover, as for the mix of manageable assets, some specific features should be underlined for the two areas in relation to both the section of the wealth invested in traditional asset classes and the section dedicated to the prevailing typology of alternative investments.[20]. As for the first aspect, in Europe the incidence of bonds and securities on HNWFs' total wealth is much more relevant than in the United States, where there is a higher incidence of listed company shares. This result seems consistent with the higher weight of family businesses in the total portfolio of European HNWFs. As for the second aspect, recent studies show that the incidence of alternative investments on HNWFs' total wealth is on the way up both in Europe and in the United States: in the old continent they are prevailingly real estate investments, in the new continent hedge funds have a relevant weight[21].

The above mentioned differences have a strong impact on HNWFs advisory requirements in Europe and in the United States, which tend to acquire more specific features, as confirmed by the remaining part of our research.

---

[20] Merryl Linch, Cap Gemini Ernst & Young, World Wealth Report, 2002.
[21] Family Office Exchange Studies, Alternative Investing Practices by Family Enterprises Study, 2003.

Fig. 7.10 The manageable assets of the typical client (36 replies)

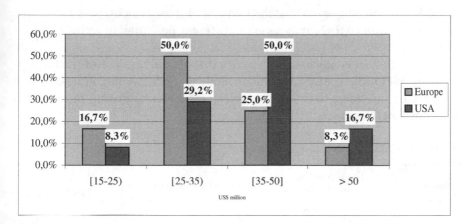

7.5 The MFO Supply of Services

The array of services provided by MFOs can be broad and cover different areas; in fact the specific objectives of the MFO are: i) reduce, by providing highly specialized in-house services, the number of services providers utilized by HNWFs to preserve and increase their wealth (accountants, business consultants, lawyers, banks and investment firms); ii) guarantee the coordination of these subjects, so as to provide the client with an integrated service that allows reducing inefficiencies and fully exploiting all market opportunities. The "advisory" aspect represents a fundamental component of the MFO supply.

More specifically, the business areas in which the MFO may provide its contribution can be divided into the following macro-categories[22]:

- investment management;
- accounting and global reporting;
- tax planning and retirement plan;
- trusteeship;
- business consulting and corporate finance;
- charitable gifting;
- family's management;

---

[22] For a deeper analysis of the potential range of MFO supply see Hamilton 2002.

- concierge.

Each macro-category is matched with multiple services (see Table 7.6) in which various MFOs may assume different positions in terms of make or buy.

In this sense, it is advisable to specify that also in the case of the buy option, the MFO role is anyway fundamental, as it is determinant in selecting the service provider, defining the objectives and monitoring the selected operator's performance.

Table 7.6 MFO provided services: an example

Investment Management (IM)	Accounting and Global Reporting (AR)	Tax Planning and Retirement Plan (TR)	Trusteeship (T)
Risk tolerance assessment	Financial statement preparation	Integrated tax planning (enterprises/individuals/investments)	Trust building
Strategic asset allocation	Cash flow analysis	International tax saving strategy development	Trust administration
Asset management	Balance sheet certification	Estimated tax calculations/payments	
Alternative investments	Net worth statement preparation	Retirement planning	
Real estate planning	Bill paying	Retirement tax planning	
Manager's selection	Reconciliation of all account activity	Proprietary wealth migration strategies	
Monitoring	Easy to read monthly or quarterly reporting		
Risk management			
Performance valuation	Consolidated reporting for managed and unmanaged assets		

Table 7.6 Continued

Business Consulting and Corporate Finance (CC)	Charitable Gifting (G)	Family's Management (FM)	Concierge (C)
Strategic management of business	Advice on gifting to other family members	Family governance definition	Travel planning
			Special event planning
Board representation	Advice on charitable entity structure	Family meeting coordination	Yacht/plane administration
Maintaining controls			
Selection of organizational form	Gift administration	Coaching and/or counseling	Home computer training
	Family foundation administration		
Compensation planning		Family dispute resolution	Family financial education
	Charitable trust advice		
Research and development credit			Auto, boat, vacation home purchasing
Merger and acquisition opportunities			
Buy / sell arrangements			
Banking relations			

In the course of our research we tried to understand which areas were controlled by each of the sample MFOs. In particular, the analysis allowed us to distinguish *typical areas,* that is areas controlled, despite different definitions in terms of make or buy, by almost all of the sample firms and *accessory areas*, that is areas controlled by only some of the sample firms (Fig. 7.11).

Typical areas can be divided into 4 macro-categories of services:

1. investment management;

2. accounting and global reporting;

3. tax planning and retirement plan;

4. trusteeship.

Accessory areas are represented by:

1. business consulting and corporate finance;

2. charitable gifting;

3. family's management;

4. concierge.

In this sense, we tried to establish whether there was a form of connection between the typology of accessory services and the different categories of MFOs identifiable on the basis of the variables concerning the firm geographical territory and its origins.

Fig. 7.11 Services provided by sample firms

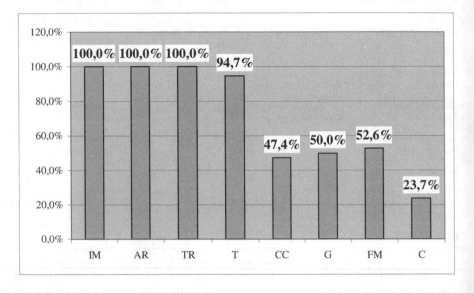

Fig. 7.12 reveals remarkable differences between the US and the European situation.

In Europe, consistently with the prevailing mix of the HNWF wealth, corporate finance and business consulting services are more relevant and are provided by most of the sample MFOs (75% in Europe against 30% in the USA).

As for the other business areas, instead, US firms seem to have a better positioning as their supply is on average broader and more complete. More precisely, concierge services are an exclusive prerogative of American MFOs. Hence, data seem to confirm the existence of a country effect, which is connected with the size variable of the average assets under management, which produces significant differences in the characteristics of European and American MFOs.

Fig. 7.12 Comparison between the USA and Europe

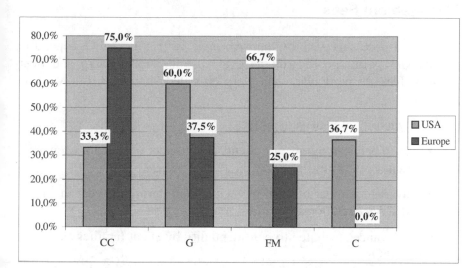

In addition, within the US MFO industry there seem to be some differences resulting from the MFO origins (Fig. 7.13). More precisely, MFOs originated by dedicated family offices present an average more extended supply, especially with regard to concierge and family's management services

Fig. 7.13 Differences within the US MFO industry

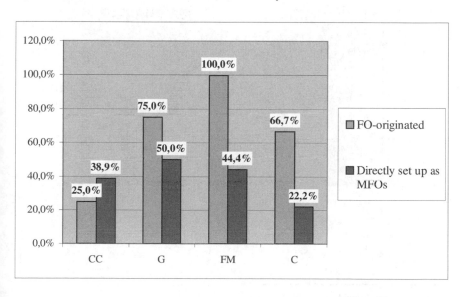

7.6 Operating Mechanisms: Customer Relationship and Management Fees

The last aspect surveyed by our research is that of MFOs operating mechanisms, with specific reference to customer relationship and management fees. In particular, data were collected about the following aspects:

- typology of management fees;

- ratio between number of clients and number of staff for each MFO (client to staff ratio);

- average number of meetings with client during the year in case of full service relationship;

- relevance attributed to confidentiality by client families as viewed by MFOs.

As for the typology of management fees, the research revealed that the sample MFOs adopt remuneration schemes based on the alternative application of different kinds of fees: asset based fee, hourly based fee, project and service based fee (Fig. 7.14)[23].

Fig. 7.14 Management fees

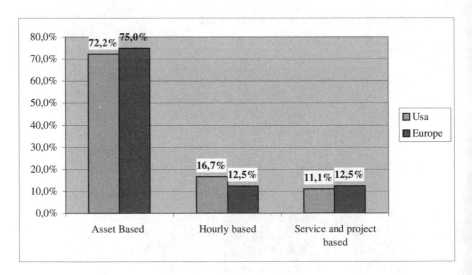

---

[23] Data were collected about 27 firms.

The management fees most commonly applied are asset based (21 MFOs), whereas the application of the other two kinds of fees is much more limited (7 MFOs).

More precisely, the typical remuneration mechanism provides that clients pay the asset-based fee on the basis of the complexity of the service received and of the size of the assets entrusted to the MFO management. If special services, which are not specifically included in the general agreement stipulated between the client and the firm, are provided on an occasional basis, an additional fee will be obviously applied. Here below follows the remuneration mechanism adopted by one of the sample MFOs for providing the full range of advisory services.

Table 7.7 An example of the typical remuneration scheme adopted by MFOs

Client manageable assets	Asset based fee	Special service based fee
Initial US$20m	0.85%	Special fees are applied for all services not specifically provided by general agreement stipulated with clients. Here price is agreed by parties prior to service supply.
Following US$20m	0.65%	
Following US$25m	0.40%	
> US$65m	0.25%	

The widespread application of the remuneration scheme just described seems to suggest the existence of scale economies in the management of the customer relationship.

As for customer relationship, the first element to be considered is the client to staff ratio[24], which represents an indicator of maximum synthesis of the degree of customization of the service provided. In this sense, confirming the high advisory content of MFO services, the average value of this indicator is rather low (2.6) in our sample[25]. Yet, some dispersion is revealed around this average value (the root-mean-square deviation is 1.1), which suggests caution in the interpretation of data and which can be probably explained by different make or buy choices made by each operator. As for the differences between American and European MFOs, Fig. 7.15 clearly shows that the client to staff ratio is lower for the former than the latter

This evidence is probably connected with the different average size of client wealth in Europe and in the United States. European firms need to have a larger number of clients to cover their operating costs.

---

[24] The client to staff ratio is the ratio between the number of clients and the number of employees.

[25] Data have been collected about 32 firms (USA:22; Europe:10).

Fig. 7.15 Client to staff ratio

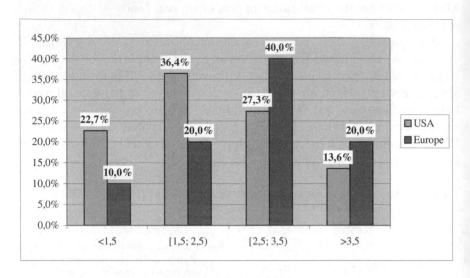

As for the average number of meetings with the client over the year[26], it seems closely correlated with the number of human resources dedicated to each client as measured by the client to staff ratio (Fig 7.16).

Fig. 7.16 Client to staff ratio and average number of meetings with client

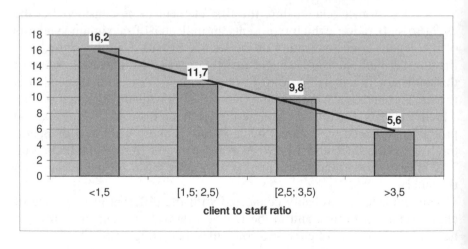

The average number of visits is higher in the USA than in Europe. In particular, in the US the number ranges from 6 to 20 visits/year (average

[26] Data were collected about 27 firms (USA: 19; Europe:8).

12.6), whereas in Europe the same value ranges from 2 to 15 (average 7.2). This evidence seems to confirm the impression of a lower degree of customization for the services provided by European MFOs as against American ones. In this sense, despite the absence of certain data regarding the management fees applied by European and American firms, we believe we can assume that in Europe, given the smaller size of client family assets and the presence of scale economies at the level of the individual client, MFOs are forced to apply lower fees not to make their supply too onerous. This obviously results in the necessity to cut operating costs and thus in lower customization and/or smaller range of services.

Finally, as for the last aspect surveyed by our research, the relevance of confidentiality in the customer relation management, results cannot be questioned: the capacity to guarantee confidentiality is a critical factor for success in the MFO industry. In fact 100% of sample firms[27] believe that confidentiality is perceived by the client as an element of utmost importance (in a 1-10 scale the value is between 9 and 10 for 100% of sample firms).

7.7 Conclusions and Possible Development Trends for the MFO in Europe

The research allowed us to better outline the international industry of MFOs. As a matter of fact, thanks to the analysis of the various aspects, we were able to identify some features which were common to all of the sample firms and, as such, distinctive of their business model.

MFOs aim their services at a very specific client segment composed by families who own a particularly large wealth (in terms of manageable assets, some dozen million dollars) hence the target market of this industry is a restricted niche within the wider market of wealth management.

In order to meet the requirements of such an elite group of clients, MFOs propose themselves as wide-spectrum advisors, who assist client families in finding the best solutions to all of the issues regarding the management of their wealth. In particular, apart from providing specific in-house services, MFOs develop a fundamental role in the selection and coordination of all the third-party service providers the family requires to meet their requirements. The important advisory content, confirmed by the high number of resources dedicated to each client and the wide ranging selection of the supply turn out to be fundamental aspects of the MFO busi-

---

[27] Data were collected about 28 firms.

ness model. In this sense, a source of competitive advantage is certainly represented by the possibility of having high standard and wide ranging competencies available that allow providing a full scale services. This must be added to the ability to conquer the client's trust, which turned out to be an absolutely unavoidable critical factor for success.

With specific reference to the extension of the supply, the research allowed us to identify some macro categories of services controlled, though with some different characteristics in terms of make or buy, by all of the sample firms and as such distinctive of their business model. More precisely, the macro-categories are:

1. investment management;

2. accounting and global reporting;

3. tax planning and retirement plan;

4. trusteeship.

On the whole, the MFOs supply is not confined to these macro-categories of services, but includes areas that are even more specific and that can be defined as "accessory", as they are not controlled by all of the operators present in the market.

A further distinctive feature of the MFO business model is "independence", which characterizes most of the firms in our sample. The possibility of acting in absence of any conflict of interest distinguishes the supply of the MFO from that of other operators in the market of private banking. Moreover, our survey revealed that in the past few years a growing number of big financial groups have entered the MFO industry in order to extend their client segment just in the area of private banking and that the number of not independent operators is becoming larger and larger.

If what has been stated so far has a general application, the research also allowed us to identify some significant differences in the business model adopted by the firms in the surveyed sample. In particular, a country effect has emerged in correlation with the size effect. In other words the business model of the European firms presents some specific features in comparison to the American firms. The crucial element seems to be the difference in the target market of the two areas. In Europe, on the average, the manageable assets owned by the client family, also due to the larger presence of family business, are lower than those of the American families. Moreover, relevant differences regard the assets mix, especially in relation to alternative investments.

All this has a strong impact on some of the MFO characteristics in Europe and in the Unites States. In particular, the most relevant differentiation elements revealed by our research regard the nature of the accessory services and the degree of customization guaranteed to the client.

With reference to the first aspect, the research revealed that in Europe, consistently with the characteristics of client family assets, MFOs provide advisory in the areas of corporate finance and business consulting much more often than in the United States, whereas with reference to the other categories of accessory services, the US firms on average present a more comprehensive supply, especially in terms of family's management and concierge.

As for the second aspect, service customization seems to be more developed in the United States, where resources dedicated to each family (client to staff ratio) are more numerous and where meeting with clients are more frequent. This difference in service customization, as already explained in the course of the research, seems to be correlated with the different size of the family wealth in the two areas (USA and Europe) and with the presence of scale economies at the level of the individual client, suggested by the remuneration scheme typically adopted by MFOs (decreasing asset-based fees).

The relevance of the country variable suggests some reflections about the possible development in the MFO industry in Italy, where the HNWFs and the environmental context present some particular aspects. In this sense, the relevant factors appear to be the following:

- the central role of the family business within the HNWF wealth;

- the poor transparency of the relation established between the HNWF and third-party service providers, especially bank providers;

- the poor cultural propensity to delegate the management of relevant sections of family wealth;

- the presence of an extremely onerous fiscal system.

The above mentioned factors obviously have a strong impact on the characteristics of the demand for advisory services by Italian HNWFs and thus on the chances of development of the MFO industry in this country.

First of all, in Italy the ability to establish a full-disclosure client relationship, due to the confidentiality and the diffidence characterizing HNWFs, is more difficult than elsewhere and therefore this capacity represents the first discriminating factor for the success of the operator willing to act according to the MFO model. In this sense, the position of banks is definitely unfavorable compared with that of the other service providers contacted by Italian HNWFs (lawyers, accountants and advisors) because of their tradition and because banks typically operate in situations of conflict of interest. On the other hand, though, they have more expertise in the financial field and thus the possibility of making scope economies that allow them to provide a wider range of services at extremely competitive prices. It is evident that in Italy no integrated wealth management is feasible if no relevant contribution is given in terms of advisory in the areas of business consulting and corporate finance that, consequently, become crucial. Just as crucial is the capacity to offer best solutions in relation to fiscal matters; in fact the necessity to reduce fiscal pressure is perceived as an essential feature by Italian HNWFs. This particular need may actually offer the key to win the distrust that typically torments the relationship between HNWFs and service providers. This explains why professionals (lawyers and accountants) that traditionally assist Italian families and their businesses in solving fiscal matters are in fact in a privileged position in comparison to financial institutions that usually concentrate their services in the area of investment management. In particular, tax advisory should be founded on integrated tax planning, with necessarily an international scope so as to guarantee the exploitation of all tax saving opportunities available on a global scale. Therefore service internationalization seems to be a critical factor for success.

In the light of these considerations, it is the author's opinion that the development of the MFO industry will be possible provided that the operators take into account the specificity of the client family requirements. In this sense, professionals that traditionally assist HNWFs and have established consolidated relations with them seem to be in a favorable position. In particular, a winning organization model might be represented by an association of professionals with different competencies and at different locations over the national and European territory. Less favorable, always in the author's opinion, is the position of banks; their possibility of acting as MFOs rather than mere service providers is subject to their capacity to win the diffidence that historically separates them from HNWFs. Banks probably will be able to play a major role with clients that are more sensitive to the cost of advisory services and whose wealth is composed by prevailingly financial assets. In this case, in fact, their specific expertise and the possibility of making economies may represent an important competitive advantage.

Finally, always in the author's opinion, the Italian context seems to be a fertile land for the birth and the growth of dedicated family offices. As in the United States, in Italy an important role in the development of the MFO industry is likely to be played by some of those operators that will decide to provide other families access to their supply.

Annex 1 –Questionnaire

1. Firm Background and Ownership

When was the firm founded?

What is the firm governance?

Has the ownership changed over time? If so, describe the story and the nature of major ownership changes.

Originally, was the firm operating as a "dedicated family office"? If so, when did it begin to provide services to other clients?

Which is the dominant background[28] of the key personnel (partners and relationship managers assigned to clients) of your firm? Could you provide their biographies?

2. Profile of Clients and Services provided

Is there a minimum amount of manageable assets[29] that a family/individual must own to access the services of your firm? If so, which is this amount?

On average, which is the amount of manageable assets owned by the typical client of your firm?

Could you list the service areas in which your firm provides its advice?

Could you list some services with reference to each area?

3. Client Relationship Management and Remuneration Scheme

Which is the client to staff ratio[30] in your firm?

How frequently do you visit your client? Who typically represents the firm?

On average, ranging from one to ten, how important is confidentiality to your clients?

How do you charge for your services?

---

[28] The background is referred to the previous working experience of key personnel of your firm.

[29] The manageable assets are the assets that the potential client is ready to entrust to the management of the Multi-Family Office.

[30] The ratio between the number of employees and the number of clients.

Could you describe the typical compensation scheme in the case of full-service relationship?
Do you accept fees from any service providers?

8 The Art of Family Office: The Case of a Multinational Bank Branch

Corrado Griffa

8.1 The Strategic Goals of a Very High Net Worth Family

The strategic goals usually indicated by families owning a very high net worth (i.e. U-HNWFs with an over €50m net worth), include their wealth preservation and growth, a balance between enterprise and portfolio operations, a unitary view and management of these interests in the long run, the entrepreneurial independence of individual family members, the availability of suitable resources to start up or expand family members' business activities at any time.

In our opinion and on the basis of our professional experience, the correct interpretation of family goals is the starting point for a suitable organization of the family wealth structure.

Often implicitly and in a de-structured manner, the family perceives the necessity of a dedicated structure able to coordinate and direct some essential activities:

- management of financial, real estate and industrial assets belonging to the family and to its members; the possibility of a unique reference structure capable of acquiring an overall view of large-sized assets that are not always under the investor's careful supervision is considered an important aspect, which is becoming increasingly hard to find in a world of growing complexity;

- maintenance and review of investment goals; objectives need reviewing in front of changes in both external (macro and micro economic)and internal conditions (evolution of the family and personal situations of its members);

- recurring control of investment policies;

- performance valuation and review with indication of possible changes;

- identification and evaluation of financial investment opportunities;

- identification and presentation of investment alternative strategies (financial, real estate and industrial investment);
- recurring review of family wealth organization structure.

Once the above described points have been identified as essential and agreed upon, the family members will have to answer an important question: should they create their own professional structure (dedicated or captive family office) or rather exploit and share the services provided by an outside family office with the other customers of the same family office?

We believe the answer should take into account the following aspects:

- What is the nature of the portfolio? If the portfolio is largely diversified, the best solution is the outside family office; if the portfolio is largely concentrated (a sort of private equity fund), the private family office would probably suit it better, with professional resources exclusively concentrated on this typology of assets;

- Do investors prefer a direct, constant hands-on contact on their investments or do they prefer a less involving, more passive attitude with *ex-post* control? In the first instance the outside family office would be less effective than the dedicated one and vice-versa.

- The captive structure implies higher startup and fixed costs, whereas the outside structure has exclusively variable costs. Dismantling a dedicated structure is costly and requires times and modes that are not always short and simple; "unplugging" the supply of external services is very easy and immediate.

- The availability of professional resources and the capacity to retain them in the long term is a critical aspect for the captive structure. This does not mean attracting good, reliable professionals; this is only the first step; what is more difficult is retaining them by motivating and rewarding them (not only economically).

- The critical mass (in terms of assets entrusted to the family office) is high and the cost-benefit aspect has to be considered in the case of the captive option.

- The need for a consolidated view of the family wealth, including the necessity to pursue fiscal efficiency (when performance consolidation is connected with the existence of a "global custody" relation, which is rarely feasible in a captive structure).

Trust, intellectual independence and experience are essential elements of the concept of family office and of the relative operating process; the family office able to best combine the three components is very likely to be "the winner" in the course of time and become the ideal "fellow-traveler" for the family that has decided to use its services.

8.2 Preliminary Analysis of Family Needs

An appropriate evaluation process of the structure will include a due diligence of the family current status and future expectations. On the basis of our experience, it should cover the following aspects:

a) Current status and pursued goals

- Is this the case of the entire family wealth or just a part of it?

- What are the nature and the background of the family wealth? How many generations are involved? Are there any particular restrictions as to wealth structure and destination? What is the wealth historical importance and what is the family value system?

These aspects are important because some values must not be dispersed: lifestyle and life approach are intangible assets that do or may last in the course of time.

- What are the financial goals being pursued? Are there any particular or specific goals? Diversity often means preciousness: although it is not always possible to content everybody and everything, it is always necessary to study each aspect and bear each of them well in mind in the definition of the overall picture.

- What are the family goals as to their wealth? We have often analyzed situations where new generations did not know precisely the size, the structure, and the immediate or latest goals of family wealth; it is up to the previous generations to prepare the young ones by sharing family goals and any possible destination of the accumulated wealth.

- Are there any particular goals in terms of wealth destination, such as charitable gifting, scholarships, research, etc.?

b) Shared views and critical mass

- Are any of the goals shared by one or more family members?

- Do common goals represent a "critical mass"?

- Which non-financial goals and investments can be achieved collectively? Keeping a wealth together is possible only if common goals are fully understood, accepted and shared; if not so, everyone had better pursue his/her own path in terms of portfolio investments so as to achieve individual goals more effectively: pursuing collective goals may become a sometimes excessive limit to the detriment of their performance and effectiveness.

- On this basis, a plan will be necessary to proceed more effectively.

c) Analysis of options

- Analysis of current service providers (plus and minus)

- Can family requirements be met by current managers? Good managers must be used for what they are able to do well; it is often useful to specialize managers in the tasks they can best perform, rather than ask everybody to do everything, maybe in competition.

- Any possible alternatives must be analyzed, including the use or creation of a dedicated investment structure.

- All of the options and relative characteristics (capital required, costs, commitment, resources, etc.) must be indicated by finding an agreement on the best possible option.

d) Following steps

- A plan will be developed to achieve established goals by analyzing implementation costs.

- Identification of family leadership: who leads and directs the entire process? We believe it useful, and often unavoidable, to have a reference within the family, a player involved in the investment process and able to interact with the other family members better than a manager or even a family officer just because he/she is part of it and directly interested in the best result of the entire process.

- A management process will be developed for the plan and its different steps.

- Current and potential problems and critical aspects will be highlighted.

- All steps will be precisely scheduled.

8.3 Essential Features

Once the preliminary analysis has been completed, the family will have to concentrate their attention on the essential features of the solution to be adopted. This analysis will cover the following aspects:

- definition and identification of explicit and implicit costs relating to the different solutions (captive family office versus external family office);

- inspiring guidelines for the investment policy of the family office, which may include specific restrictions to the various investments;

- operating modes with which to proceed to investments or disinvestments;

- information sources on which useful analyses and evaluations should be based as to investments and disinvestments;

As for Italian investors, possible structures might alternatively include the following:

- trust company

- srl

- SIM

  SGR

- dedicated Sicav

- virtual structure

In our experience, many families have adopted the virtual solution (more often provided by outside advisors close to the family: the lawyer or the accountant rather than the historical notary); regulated structures like SIM, SGR and SICAV are characterized by high costs (in particular for startup and development), but they can meet typical technical requirements (financial market operations); the trust company shows very good features in case of external services (such as those provided by Citigroup Private Bank to a multitude of families).

Figure 8.1 describes the typical structure of the service provided by our bank through the group trust company (Cititrust).

Fig. 8.1 The case of Cititrust

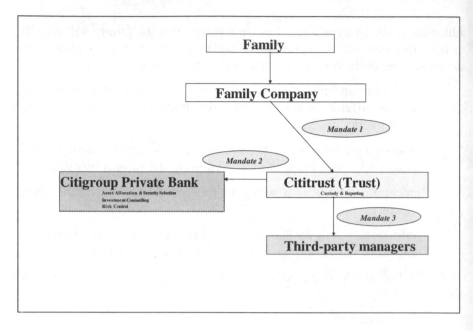

Fig. 8.2 Activities of a family office

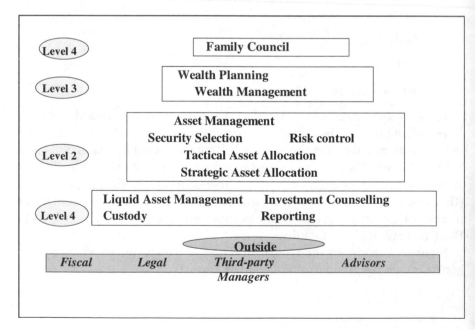

Figure 8.2 illustrates the typical activities developed by the family office, they include:

- level 1: liquidity management, custody, reporting, investment counselling

- level 2: strategic and tactical allocation, risk control, manager selection, investment

- selection (securities);

- level 3: family wealth planning and management.

The family office will utilize a number of professional managers that will be selected according to investors' experiences, preferences and expectations, to managers' professional experiences and to the best balance between the characteristics of the same managers. Similarly, at operative level, the family office will utilize one or more financial intermediaries for financial transactions (investments, disinvestments).

8.4 The Legislative Framework

Synthetically, an Italian private investor (i.e. each individual within the family) can invest in all the different investment products issued in Italy and abroad, such as:

- Italian shares and bonds (government, company)

- Italian investment funds

- harmonized foreign investment funds (OICVM)

- non-harmonized foreign investment funds (non-OICVM)

- foreign bonds

- foreign shares

- Italian alternative funds (e.g. hedge funds, closed-end funds, private

- equity")

- foreign alternative funds

Non-OICVM products and foreign alternative funds are subject to annual tax-return and returns are taxed by personal and graduated rates, to capital account valuation (capital gains), foreign exchange account valuation. Dividends on foreign shares are subject to annual declaration and returns are taxed (except for different application of taxation bilateral treaties).

For all of the other forms of investment returns are subject to a 12.5% tax rate (tax is differently applied according to the kind of product), with no need for annual return.

The investor can opt for one of the following taxation systems:

1. saving management: interest receivable, received dividends, capital gains and capital losses are annually consolidated on the relative accrual basis (*pro-rata*) and subject to a 12.5% rate. In the case of foreign alternative investments, a personal and graduated rate will be applied. No need for annual return.

2. saving administration: interest receivable, received dividends, capital gains and capital losses are subject to a 12.5% tax rate applied upon single operation, on a strictly chronological basis. Annual return is compulsory for foreign dividends. As for foreign alternative investments, a personal and graduated rate will be applied.

3. tax return system: a personal and graduated rate is applied with an integrated declaration of single investments and relative returns.

Therefore there is a competitive advantage for the management system as well as for domestic rather than foreign forms of investments.

The presence of multiple management relations with multiple managers might result fiscally inefficient for the investor if, for example, a management relation presents a (taxable) gain and another a loss (which can be recovered over a four-year period in case of future profits). The investor might therefore consider the possibility of starting actual fiscal consolidation, which would allow him to compensate profits and losses. This possibility requires the investor to have a sole management relation with an authorized intermediary (who operates as the global custodian in the presence of a global custody relationship and as withholding agent) with partial or total delegation to third-party managers. This is a feasible alternative for large-sized wealths, typically represented by family office customers.

8.5 A Case Study

We believe it might be interesting to synthesize our recent experience with an Investor who was able to define his objectives as to the family financial assets.

The path we pursued together involved the following aspects:

1. definition of return typology – absolute or only relative to a reference parameter – best suiting the investor's goals and guidelines. In this context, an absolute return was defined, by limiting tolerance to possible negative performances. The Investor retained it was important to focus on the interest/dividend binomial: investments had to provide a constant/predictable flow of coupons for the bond section and a constant/predictable flow of dividends for the share section, on the basis of the story of every single security;

2. possible utilization of leverage in order to improve the portfolio aggregate profitability. In this case specific restrictions have been applied;

3. definition of dynamic asset allocation able to vary in relation to specific events/situations/scenarios; here a distinction was made between:

   - diversification to be implemented partially through discretional management (active) and partially through indexed investments (passive);

   - tactical management to be implemented through an investment advisory relationship provided by the reference financial institution;

4. as for the bond section, the defined iterative process was focused on the aspects of financial duration and on the fixed/variable partition of the bond portfolio;

5. as for share section, very precise restrictions were defined as to the possible exposure to currency risks, also by resorting to ad hoc instruments;

6. potential investments in derivate products by establishing specific restrictions regarding the following:

   - maximum percentage of total portfolio

   - levels

- type of products
- exclusively covered/closed end positions
- profits must be locked in
- position manageability (number, type, amount)

7. potential investments in structured products with definition of evaluation criteria:
    - maximum percentage of total portfolio
    - capital protection factors
    - duration
    - product liquidity
    - possible credit enhancement

8. potential investments in alternative products as per following:
    - maximum percentage of total portfolio
    - investment specific goals
    - investment typology/characteristics
    - contribution to strategy, goals, expected profitability

9. definition of investment time horizon; our Investor accepted a long term horizon viewed as the sum total of multiple short terms;

10. definition of investment style, that is:
    - contrarian vs. consensus
    - out of benchmark trap

The results of the path pursued are obviously specific of the Investor and they cannot be considered as the rule to be adopted *erga omnes*; on the other hand, its specific nature confirms the necessity to be flexible and available to find the solution best suiting the Investor's objectives.

9 The Art of Family Office: The Case of a Specialized Intermediary

Andrea Caraceni

9.1 Introduction

In this chapter we intend to examine the figure of the Family Banker, who has been experiencing a striking evolution in the course of time and according to the specific nature of the economic context.

More specifically, we intend to give an insight of the current Italian situation by restricting our observation field to the requirements of one category of customers, i.e. families owning and managing their own business. In this context the banker has to take care of family wealth on one side and of business financial issues on the other.

Our analysis is divided into four sections: the first analyzes the meaning of Family Banker, the second introduces the concept of Family Office (FO), the third examines the FO service supply and the fourth offers an example of Family Office: the Corporate Family Office SIM S.p.A.

9.2 The Family Banker

The role of the Family Banker consists in providing a sole service which is positioned somewhere between asset management and corporate finance. This role is generally played by financial institutions and independent advisors.

Financial institutions are generally characterized by the specialization and the neat separation of the above activities. This prevents them from playing the Family Banker's role in the best possible way.

On the other hand, the positioning of banks that apply the model of the *Haus Bank* enables them to compete in this particular market niche; the *Haus Bank* must also manage with utmost care the conflict of interest emerging from its being family advisor and creditor at the same time.

Among the independent advisors that assist the family, a major role is certainly played by accountants, then lawyers and marginally notaries. Unfortunately all of these professionals are strongly specialized in issues that are typical of corporate finance but only marginally present in asset management (e.g. fiscal matters).

A new player has recently appeared on the Italian financial stage: the Family Office. This institution originated in the United States and has been developing in the Anglo-Saxon world since the XIX century. It is a multidisciplinary structure dealing with the integrated management of family wealth, by providing a multitude of services: from financial advisory to succession strategies, from the control of generation changes to wealth profitability optimization, from tax planning to administrative management.

In Italy the FO turns out to be more deeply concentrated on the management of merely financial aspects concerning the family wealth and, as a result, the family business, which represents an extremely high share of the total wealth (over 50% on the average).

Consequently, at present the Haus Bank and the Family Office are the models that can be utilized to play the role of the Family Banker:

Compared with Haus Banks, FOs turn out to have the following strengths:

- professionality focused on the specific market segment;

- independence from commercial strategies of the head structure;

- best management of privacy;

- absence of potential conflicts of interest;

- family need sharing and trustworthy client relationship.

9.3 The Family Office

We shall now deepen the analysis of the FO viewed as the structure developing the Family Banker's role and then focus our attention on the three research areas: the goals pursued by FOs, the taxonomy of FO typologies and the different legal structures that can be adopted.

9.3.1 Goals

The goals pursued by FOs can remarkably vary.

The first and fundamental goals are risk management/control and wealth reporting. To this aim, necessary wealth administration management (accounting and data aggregation and formal information check up) must be combined with a strong control of both investment risks (risk management) and performances in relation to the objectives previously established.

The second goal is wealth preservation and/or creation. Generally the first item is prevailing: defending the wealth families have created with their own business. On the other hand, families achieving the second or third generation also feel the necessity to best exploit their accumulated capital in order to create new wealth.

Another goal of outstanding relevance consists in assisting the family in the management of the financial issues involving the family business. In this particular area, the FO must constantly and exclusively assume the role of client advisor to avoid any kind of conflict of interest. Here the primary goal is choice optimization in a financial area that is growing increasingly complex from the technical point of view (derivatives, options, structured products, financial engineering, etc.) and where different solutions have to be analyzed with great competence.

Finally, quite important is management centralization and rationalization with regard to the further issues the individual families retain necessary. In other words, there is the constant need for the most professional management of the most disparate activities.

9.3.2 Taxonomy

FOs can be classified on the basis of their shareholders, the requirements they meet, the clients and the services supplied. The different combinations of these aspects lead to the identification of specific models.

Fig. 9.1 FO different typologies

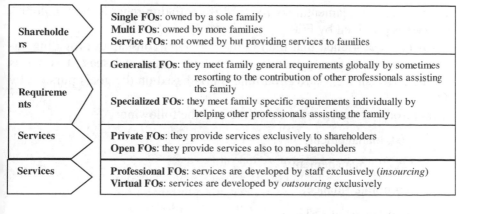

Shareholders	**Single FOs**: owned by a sole family **Multi FOs**: owned by more families **Service FOs**: not owned by but providing services to families
Requirements	**Generalist FOs**: they meet family general requirements globally by sometimes resorting to the contribution of other professionals assisting the family **Specialized FOs**: they meet family specific requirements individually by helping other professionals assisting the family
Services	**Private FOs**: they provide services exclusively to shareholders **Open FOs**: they provide services also to non-shareholders
Services	**Professional FOs**: services are developed by staff exclusively (*insourcing*) **Virtual FOs**: services are developed by *outsourcing* exclusively

9.3.3 Legal Structure

The legal structure of Family Offices can be quite varied.
Some important distinctions can be outlined with reference to its being:

- formalized or not formalized;

- onshore or offshore;

- regulated or not regulated by financial authorities.

Formalized or not formalized structures, but not regulated by financial authorities and located offshore have no relevance in our study.

Formalized structures regulated by financial authorities located onshore or offshore represent the ideal structure to compete in an extremely selective market.

Being regulated by financial authorities, the last typologies are, in fact, characterized by transparency in structures and operating modes and offer further guarantees in terms of regulations and contracts with respect to all of the interest holders: client families and owner families.

Moreover, as for investment advisory, an activity that is not subject to any restrictions by official regulations but that is highly critical and delicate, these structure typologies are able to provide their clients better guarantees. Finally, it is worth underlining that financial advisory, reserved to financial intermediaries for some years, has then been deregulated but it now seems that new community guidelines are going to have this reservation reinstated.

9.4 Services

A further and fundamental source of differentiation regards the typologies of services provided by FOs.

If it is unquestioned that the FO main activity consists in providing advisory services to family members on a wide range of issues, it is not as easy to establish a classification unless it is based on the goals pursued by FOs.

Therefore services can be classified into the following:

- risk management;

- wealth management;

- corporate finance;

- non-financial services.

9.4.1 Risk Management

This activity includes:

- global reporting of the family total wealth;

- performance measurement and valuation based on the most recent methodologies of risk management, so that families can fully understand the risks connected with their own investments and verify *ex post* their risk-weighted returns;

- analysis of returns after tax so as to take into account the different fiscal impact of the various investments in relation to the fiscal position of each recipient;

- privacy management, that is a sort of screening action between service providers and the family, in order to avoid information leakage regarding the identity, the wealth size and the strategies adopted;

- analysis of investment risks, above all aimed at identifying the acceptable risk and loss ceiling in relation to both the family total wealth, where the value of the family business is also included, and the family financial requirements. This activity, which today is prevailingly manual and poorly automated, is bound to be strongly developed thanks to the widespread utilization of the FO Platform: IT platforms are in fact being developed to allow collecting information and data in an automated and ordered manner as well as integrating the individual services FOs are provided with by a network of highly specialized institutions and professionals.

9.4.2 Wealth Management

Wealth management may be aimed at wealth preservation or creation on the basis of the established investment goals. This process is absolutely similar to what has been previously stated as to risk analysis; it starts from the identification of family requirements and lifestyle to proceed with the definition of expected assets and liabilities and finally risk-weighted profitability parameters, which represent the investment goal of the global wealth.

The process of assets allocation must be divided into its typical segments: securities investments, real estate, private equity, alternative investments and finally shelter goods.

Finally it is important to make a further consideration in relation to the possibility of using benchmarks in family wealth management. In this respect, it is worth noticing that families using these services are investors of such huge amounts that they can be assimilated to institutional investors/qualified operators, even if current regulations do not allow defining them as such. On the other hand, as for the individual investments, the possibility of identifying benchmarks that are consistent with the goals established in the global investment strategy turns out to be very low, if not null, in the presence of assets whose evaluations are hard to find and/or refer to sector indices (art works, luxury estates, collector's cars, etc.).

9.4.3 Corporate Finance

This activity ranges from financial risk management to asset and liability management, from credit management to the management of extraordinary finance.

The activity aims at providing families with regular advisory specialized and focused on all the financial issues as well as at assisting the entrepreneurial family's traditional advisors in matter of taxation and company law, etc.

A fundamental aspect is the perspective from which corporate finance advisory is to be developed, a perspective that consists in fitting this activity into the area of the family's more general investment strategies as well as into business risk sharing. If on the one hand corporate finance advisory must take into account the family overall strategies, on the other it is important to analyze and manage financial risks resulting from both the family business and the management of family wealth. If, for example, the family business exports to North-American markets by exposing itself to dollar exchange risks, investment decisions regarding the family wealth will have to consider this structural position in the evaluation of dollar investments.

9.4.4 Non-Financial Services

In this field the areas of interest are the most disparate: they range from the management of family cars and housekeeping to the management of insurances and philanthropic gifting.

Services can be thus divided into:

- personal services (social security, holiday bookings, etc.);

- management of specific goods or categories of goods (boats, estates, etc.);
- company administration (accounting and secretarial functions, etc.);
- management of specific activities (charitable gifting, etc.).

9.5 The Case of Corporate Family Office SIM S.p.A. (CFO SIM)

As for the main variables in FOs classification, CFO SIM is characterized by its being:

- a multi FO;
- a generalist FO, as they want to meet the family global needs by outsourcing;
- a specialized FO in financial issues that are tackled by their own professional staff;
- an open FO, as they provide services not only to shareholders but also to clients.

The choices regarding the body of shareholders, the legal structure, the services to be provided originate from CFO SIM guidelines, which in their turn originate from a Family Office really capable of developing the role of the Family Banker, with all the distinctive features previously discussed. In the first place, our study will describe CFO SIM guidelines along with the motivations of its foundation. In the second place, the study will explain how such guidelines and motivations have been made concrete by selecting a body of shareholders, a legal structure and by specializing in the supply of specific services.

9.5.1 Basic Guidelines

The inspiring principles of CFO SIM are professionality, independence, confidentiality and family need sharing.

Professionality is viewed as the deep and specific knowledge of the particular market segment of entrepreneurial families. If financial advisory is the core business of CFO SIM, family need sharing leads the company to offer services that are complementary, but also essential, to those of banks and of the entrepreneur's advisors.

The independence of the banking system leads to free judgment and to the absence of conflicts of interest, a crucial aspect in the fair development of the Family Banker's functions. Confidentiality, then, is a congenital feature of the company, which was set up with the characteristics of the trust company and the specific purpose of developing FO functions.

Consequently, CFO SIM is a Family Office that has decided to manage family wealth directly and administer and/or manage its assets. Within the context of the other services demanded by shareholder and/or client families, CFO SIM provides advisory services by supporting family decision-making directly, managing the relationship with third-party providers of outsourced services and guaranteeing client-vs.-provider privacy. The company supplies wide-ranging financial advisory services as they aim at becoming the family global financial advisor: their strength lies in that they add their financial competencies in the management of FO typical business areas, such as the management of financial variables connected with charitable gifting.

9.5.2 Motivations

The set up of this new structure results from sometimes dissimilar and sometimes similar motivations of entrepreneurial families and managers, who are both members of the body of shareholders. The most relevant reasons follow here below:

Fig. 9.2 Motivations for the set up of CFO SIM

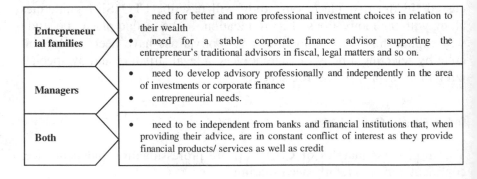

9.5.3 Shareholders and Governance

A typical feature of CFO SIM is the body of shareholders who can only be of two typologies: entrepreneurial families and managers. Therefore entrepreneur-shareholders make sure that the company services are targeted to the family typical requirements. Managers make sure the company is developed in that particular market segment composed by Italian entrepreneurial families and that clients' and shareholders' interests are not mixed together.

Moreover the body of shareholders is open to the access of new partner-families or partner-managers.

Fig. 9.3 Shareholders and activity of CFO Holding and CFO SIM

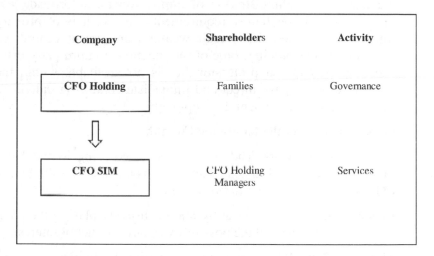

9.5.4 SIM Legal Structure (Securities Intermediation Company)

The choice of the SIM legal structure depends on a number of factors: the wish to access the market directly without intermediaries in order to guarantee privacy and confidentiality during operating stages; the possibility of providing advisory services regarding investments and corporate finance in full compliance with current regulations (as previously mentioned, the reservation to financial intermediaries might be reinstated by community authorities and it is therefore important to operate as SIM in this area). Moreover, the control of supervisory authorities (CONSOB and Banca d'Italia), along with other obligations provided for by the sector regulations (compulsory certification, presence of a person in charge of internal audit reporting directly to the Board of Directors and to the Board of Auditors), are a guarantee of transparency and reliability toward all of the interest holders, clients and shareholders in primis. Finally the choice of operating as a SIM emphasizes the company focus on the financial aspects among the different issues tackled by the Family Office.

9.5.5 Services

The activities developed by CFO SIM are different. As to the most strictly financial, and thus fundamental, services, the company has chosen the insourcing option. They can be summarized as per the following:

- management or administration of family wealth, tailor-made services depending on family requirements. In fact it is of primary importance to keep the overall wealth management centralized (possibly by outsourcing some of the functions to third-party managers, when required professionality is not available within the SIM) in order to have direct and immediate control on individual managers and management development;

- global reporting of the family total wealth;

- performance valuation and measurement according to the latest methodologies of risk management, that is essential for the family to become aware of the return/risk ratio;

- financial advisory by constantly and exclusively playing the advisor's role so as to avoid the possibility of any conflict of interest.

- Moreover CFO SIM carries out such additional activities as:

- management of insurance and social security issues as highly correlated with the financial ones and examinable through the same risk management methodology;

- company secretariat and assistance to improve communication with all interest holders (by introducing, for example, the figure of the independent advisor);

- administrative management of goods;

- family secretariat to solve problems the family considers important;

- conveyance of know how and advice for the design and possible implementation of a Family Office.

Fig. 9.4 Guidelines shape CFO SIM

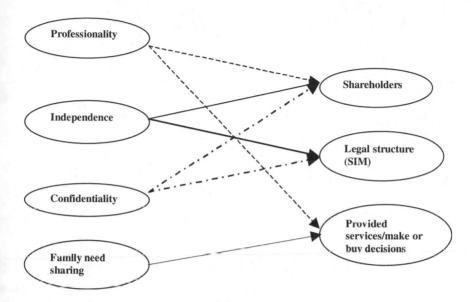

CFO SIM has thus taken possession of the strengths that constitute the advantage of the Family Office in comparison with the *Haus Bank* in order to best develop the role of the Family Banker.

References

A.I.F.I. (2000) Capitali per lo sviluppo. Un'analisi del mercato internazionale del private equity e del venture capital, Il Sole 24 Ore, Milan

ABI – Prometeia (2000) La gestione dei servizi finanziari alle PMI nell'esperienza delle banche europe, Rome

ABI (1994) Economia e redditività dei servizi di pagamento, Rome

Accenture (1998) Voice of the Millionaire: HNWIs buying behavior analysis, New York

Ang JS, Wuh Lin J, Tyler F (1995) Evidence on the Lack of Separation Between Business and Personal Risks Among Small Businesses, Journal of Small Business Finance, n.4

Aronoff C (1998) Megatrends in family business, Family Business Review, 3 (X): 181-185

Aronoff C, Astrachan JH, Ward JL (1996) Family Business Sourcebook II. Business Owners Resources, Marietta, Georgia

Autorità Garante della Concorrenza e Del Mercato – Banca D'Italia (1997) Indagine conoscitiva sui servizi di finanza aziendale, supplemento al Bollettino n. 39, Rome

Avery RB, Bostic RW, Samolyk KA (1998) The Role of Personal Wealth in Small Business Finance, Journal of Banking and Finance, n.22

Bank Of America (2003) Company information

Bank Of Italy (2001) Fiscal Rules, Research Department Public Finance Workshop, Rome

Bank Of Italy (2002) The Impact of Fiscal Policy, Research Department Public Finance Workshop, Rome

Bank Of New York (2002) Annual Report

Baravelli M (2003) Strategia e organizzazione della banca, Egea, Milan

Beckard R, Dyer WG (1988) Managing Continuing in the Family Owned Business, Organisational Dynamic

Benson B (1990) Your family business: a success guide for growth and survival, Business One Irwin, Homewood

Bento AM, White LF (2001) Organizational Form, Performance and Information Costs in Small Businesses, The Journal of Applied Business Research, n.4

Berger AN, Udell GF (1998) The Economics of Small Business Finance: The Roles of Private Equity and Debt Markets in the Financial Growth Cycle, Journal of Banking and Finance, n.6-8

Bitler MP, Markowitz TJ, Vissing-Jorgensen A (1991) Why must Entrepreneurs Hold Large Ownership Shares? Optimal Contracting in Privae and Newly Public Firms, The Rand Corporation, Working Paper, November, University of Chicago and NBER

Bloomberg (2002) Money changes everything, London

Bradley M, Jarrel AG, Kim EH (1984) On the Existence of an Optimal Capital Structure: Theory and Evidence, The Journal of Finance, n. 3, July

Burns P, Whitehouse O (1993) Financial Characteristics of Small Companies in Britain, in The 3i European Enterprise Center, Special Reports n.8 September

Cap Gemini and Ernst & Young (2003) World Wealth Report

Caselli S (1998) La valutazione del costo per la clientela, in Carretta A, De Laurentis G (1998), Il Manuale del Leasing, Egea, Milan

Caselli S (2000) Lo sviluppo del corporate e investment banking in Italia: profili strategici e organizzativi, in Forestieri G (2000) Corporate & Investment Banking, Egea, Milan

Caselli S (2001) Corporate Banking per le PMI, Bancaria Editrice, Rome

Caselli S, Gatti S (2003) Il corporate lending. Manuale della gestione del credito alle imprese: organizzazione, valutazione e contratti, Bancaria Editrice, Rome

Caselli S, Gatti S (2003) Venture Capital. A Euro-System Approach, Springer Verlag, Berlin, London

Caselli S, Gatti S (now publishing) I cambiamenti della finanza d'impresa e l'articolazione dei servizi di corporate finance, Ricerca Enbicredito ABI – Ministero del Lavoro

Caselli S, Gatti S (now publishing) La finanza strutturata in Italia, Newfin, Università Bocconi

Cavalluzzo KS, Geczy C (2002) The Choice of Organizational Form: Taxes, Liability, Agency and Financing, Working Paper, Georgetown University and University of Pennsylvania

Cavalluzzo KS, Sankaraguruswamy (2002) Executive Compensation in Privately Held Small Corporations, Working Paper Georgetown University,

Cenni S, Landi A (1996) I prodotti della banca, in Onado M(1996) La banca come impresa, Il Mulino Bologna

Chami R (2001) What is Different About Family Business?, International Monetary Found, WP/01/70, May

Cipollone P, Guelfi A (2003) Tax credit policy and firms' behaviour: the case of subsidies to open-end labour contracts in Italy, Temi di discussione, n. 471, march

Citigroup (2002) From Banker to Partner – The Citigroup Private Bank's New Private Banking Model, May

Cohn M (1992) Passing the torch, 2nd Edition, McGraw Hill, New York

Corbetta G (1995) Le imprese familiari. Caratteri originali, varietà e condizioni di sviluppo, Egea

Corbetta G (2001) Le imprese di medie dimensioni, Egea, Milan

Corbetta G (2002) Le medie imprese, Egea, Milan

Corbetta G, Bolelli F, Caselli S, Lassini U (2001) Gli spazi di collaborazione fra banca e imprese familiari, Rapporto di Ricerca SDA Bocconi- Banca Intesa BCI, Milan

Corbetta G. (1995) Patterns of development of family businesses in Italy. Family Business Review. 4: 255-265

Corticelli R (1979) La crescita dell'azienda. Armonie e disarmonie di gestione, Giuffrè

Credit Suisse Group (2003) Company information profile

Cressy RC (1996) Commitment Lending under Asymmetric Information: Theory and Tests on UK Startup Data, in Small Business Economics, n. 5

Cressy RC, Olofsson C (1997) European SME Financing: an Overview, in Small Business Economics, n. 9

Danco LA (1982) Inside the Family Business, Prentice-Hall, New York

Datamonitor (2001) European High Net Worth Customers, London

De Cecco M, Ferri G (1994) Origini e natura speciale dell'attività di banca d'affari in Italia, in Temi di discussione, n. 242, Banca d'Italia, Rome

De Geus A (1997) The Living Company, Harvard Business School Press

Delia-Russell T, Di Mascio A (2002) Wealth Management, Il Sole 24 Ore, Milan

Dessy A (2001) Capitale di debito e sviluppo delle imprese, Egea, Milan

Deutsche Bank (2003) Company Information

Dyer WG jr. (1986) Cultural Change in Family Firms: Anticipating and Managing Business and Family Traditions. Jossey-Bass, San Francisco

Elliehausen GE, Wolken JD (1990) Banking Markets and the Use of Financial Services by Small and Medium-Sized Businesses, Staff Studies, n.160, Board of Governors of the Federal Reserve System, Washington

Eurisko (2003) Multifinanziaria

Family Office Exchange (2002) It's about so much more than managing money

Family Office Exchange (2002) Managing Change in the 21st Century

Family Office Exchange (2003) Alternative Investing Practices by Family Enterprises Study

Fenn GW, Liang N (1998) New resources and New Ideas: Private Equity for Small Businesses, Journal of Banking and Finance, n.6-8

Filotto U (2002) La nuova web bank, Bancaria Editrice, Rome

Forestieri G (1997) Il sistema bancario italiano verso un modello di corporate banking: mito o realtà?, in Baravelli M (1997) Le strategie competitive nel corporate banking, Egea, Milan

Forestieri G (2003) L'investment banking: origini e sviluppo, in Forestieri G (2003) Corporate e Investment Banking, Egea, Milan

FOX Exchange (2002) Defining the Family Office

Garofano G (2003) Il family office: una struttura organizzativa per la gestione dei grandi patrimoni familiari, tesi di laurea, Università Cattolica, Milano

Generale Bank & Meespierson (1999) Cross-Border Notional Pooling in Euroland & Financial Risk Management. A Benefit and a Necessity, in Treasury Management International, n. 72

Gersick KE, Davis JA, McCollom M, Lansberg I (1997) Generation to Generation: Life Cycles of the Family Business. Harvard Business School Press, Boston, MA

Gibb A and Davis L (1995) In pursuit of Frameworks for the Development of Growth Models of the Small Business, in International Small Busienss Journal, October-December

Grant Thornton (2001) Family business Services, Company Information

Grote J (2002) Money Changes Everything, Bloomberg Wealth Manager, October

Hagopian Y and Horrel P (1998) Cashing in on the euro-Opportunities and Threats for Corporate Treasurers and Banks, in International Cash Management

Hamilton S (2002) The Multi-Family office Mania, Trusts & Estates, November

Haynes GW, Avery RJ (1996) Family businesses: Can the Family and the Business Finances be Separated?, The Journal of Entrepreneurial and Small Business Finance, n.1

Hollander BS and Elman NS (1988), Family-owned businesses: an emerging field of inquiry, Family Business Review. 1 (II): 145-164

Iovenitti P (1998) Strategie mobiliari per la continuità e la successione d'impresa, Egea, Milan

JP Morgan-Chase (2003) Company information

Kane A, Marcus JA, Mc Donald LR (1984) How Big is the Tax Advantage to Debt, in The Journal of Finance, n. 3, July

Kets De Vries MFR (1988) The Dark Side of CEO Succession, in Harvard Business Review, January-February

Kets De Vries MFR (1993) The Dynamic of Family Contrlled Firms: the Good and Bad News, in Organizational Dynamics, Vol. II, Winter

La Chapelle K and Barnes LB (1998) The Trust Catalyst in the Family-Owned Business, in Family Business Review, 1 (I), pp. 1-17

Lansberg I (1988) The succession conspiracy, Family Business Review, 2 (I), 119-143

Lazzari V (2000) Il risk management quale servizio di corporate banking, in Forestieri G, Corporate & Investment Banking, Egea, Milan

Lea JW (1991) Keeping it in the family, New York, Wiley

Lel U and Udell GF (2002) Financial Constraints, Start-up Firms and Personal Commitments, Kelley School of Business, Indiana University, Working Paper

Lombard Odier Darier Hentsch (2002) F2F – Family to Family, Geneva

Magretta J (1998) Governing the Family-Owned Enterprise: An Interview with Finland's Krister Ahlstrom, in Harvard Business Review, vol. 76, n. 1, pp. 112-123

Manzone B and Trento S (1993) Il trasferimento intergenerazionale delle imprese, in Banca d'Italia, Temi di discussione, n. 205, July

Mazzola P (2003) Il piano industriale, Università Bocconi Editore, Milan

Mazzotti E and Moneta A (2000) Investment Banking, Merchant Banking e Asset Management, Franco Angeli, Milan

Mediobanca (2003) Dati cumulativi delle principali banche europee, Milan

Merrill Lynch - Cap Gemini Ernst&Young (2003) World Wealth Report

Merryl Linch, Cap Gemini Ernst & Young, World Wealth Report, 2002.

Mintzberg H (1978) Patterns in Strategy Formation, in Management Science, n. 3

Mintzberg H (1985) Of Strategies, Deliberate and Emergent, in Strategic Management Journal, n. 3

Mottura P (1987) Condizioni di equilibrio finanziario della strategia d'impresa, in Finanza, Marketing e Produzione, n. 1, March

Mottura P, Caselli S, Gatti S (2000) I servizi di electronic banking per le piccole e medie imprese, Newfin Università Bocconi – Unicredito Italiano, Milan

Musile Tanzi P (2001) Il manuale del private banker, Egea, Milan

Musile Tanzi P (2003) Il manuale del private banking, Egea, Milan

Musile Tanzi P (2003) L'evoluzione degli assetti organizzativi nel private banking: le implicazioni di open architecture system, W.P. Newfin, Università Bocconi, March

Musile Tanzi P (2003) Private Bank perfomance valuation, W.P. SDA Bocconi, n. 92/03, June

Neubauer F and Lank AG (1998) The Family Business. Its Governance for Sustainability. Routledge, New York

Paisner M (1999) Sustaining the family business; Reading, Perseus Book

Paternello A (1995) La domanda dell'utente impresa, in Scott WG, Manuale di marketing bancario, Utet Torino

Perrini F (1998) Finanza per la successione. Private equity e imprese familiari, in Economia & Management, n, 2

Price Waterhouse Coopers (2003) Family business Center, Company Information

Price Waterhouse Coopers Consulting (2001) Global Trends in Performance Measurements

Reid GC (1993) The Survival of Small Business Enterprises, Routledge, London

Resti A (2003) Il private banking, Edibank, Roma

Roach C (1989) Segmentation of the Small Business Market on the Basis of Banking Requirements, in International Journal of Bank Marketing, n. 2

Rutherford MW and Oswald SL (1999) Antecedents of Small Business Success, Paper presented at the Academy of Management Chicago 1999 Conference: Change and Development Journeys into a Pluralistic World, 6th-11th August, Chicago

Shenker MC and Astrachan JH (1996) Myths and realities: Family businesses' contribution to the US economy – A framework for assessing family business statistics. Family Business Review. 2: 107-124

Simon H (1996) Hidden Champions: Lessons from 500 of the World's Best Unknown Companies, Harvard Business School Press, Boston, MA

Tagliavini G (1999) Costo del capitale, analisi finanziaria e corporate banking, Egea, Milan

Testa, Huwitz & Thibeault, LLP – Successful succession planning: Thinking about tomorrow today, in www.altassets.net

The Boston Consulting Group (2002) Prospering in Uncertain Time, Global wealth 2002

Thompson J.D (2002) L'azione organizzativa, Isedi, Torino

Tosi HL, Pilati M, Mero NP, Rizzo JR (2002) Comportamento organizzativo, Egea, Milan

Trust and Estates (2002) The Multi-Family Office Mania, November

UBS (2003) UBS Family business Group, Company Information

Unicredito Italiano (2002) Bilancio e Relazione

University of Bath (2002) Global Cash Europe 2001, Bath, UK

Ward JL (1987) Keeping the Family Business Healthy. Jossey-Bass, San Francisco

Ward JL (1988) The special role of strategic planning for family businesses. Family Business Review, 2 (I)

Ward JL (1991) Creating Effective Boards for Private Enterprises, San Francisco, Jossey-Bass Publishers

Ward JL (1997) Growing the Family Business: Special Challenges and Best Practices, in Family Business Review, 4 (X), pp. 323-335

Winker P (1997) Cause and Effects of Financing Constraints at the Firm Level, in Small Business Economics, n. 9

List of Contributors

Corresponding Address

Professor Stefano Caselli
Professor Stefano Gatti

Institute of Financial Markets and Financial Intermediaries
"L. Bocconi" University
Via Sarfatti, 25
20136 Milan
Italy

stefano.caselli@unibocconi.it
stefano.gatti@unibocconi.it

Stefano Caselli
  Associate Professor in Banking and Finance at "L. Bocconi" University, Milan, Italy. Professor at Banking and Insurance Department of SDA Bocconi, Bocconi School of Management, Milan, Italy. He's developing research activity, managerial education and strategic consulting in: corporate and investment banking, leasing and asset finance, credit risk management, SME's financing.

Stefano Gatti
  Associate Professor in Banking and Finance at "L. Bocconi" University, Milan, Italy. Professor at Banking and Insurance Department of SDA Bocconi, Bocconi School of Management, Milan, Italy. He's developing research activity, managerial education and strategic consulting in: corporate and investment banking, project financing, corporate finance and company valuation.

Andrea Caraceni
  CEO Corporate Family Office SIM S.p.A., Milan, Italy.

Guido Corbetta

Full Professor in Strategic Management in Family Business at AidAF – Alberto Falck Chair, at "L. Bocconi" University, Milan, Italy. Senior Professor at Strategic and Entrepreneurial Management Department of SDA Bocconi, Bocconi School of Management, Milan, Italy.

Corrado Griffa

Vice President, The Citigroup Private Bank, Milan, Italy.

Gaia Marchisio

Coordinator of AidAF – Alberto Falck Chair in Strategic Management in Family Business at "L. Bocconi" University, Milan, Italy. Assistant Professor at Strategic and Entrepreneurial Management Department of SDA Bocconi, Bocconi School of Management, Milan, Italy.

Paola Musile Tanzi

Full Professor in Banking and Finance at University of Perugia, Italy. Professor at Banking and Insurance Department of SDA Bocconi, Bocconi School of Management, Milan, Italy.

Edmondo Tudini

Ph.D. student in Business Administration at "L. Bocconi" University, Milan, Italy. Assistant Professor at Banking and Insurance Department of SDA Bocconi, Bocconi School of Management, Milan, Italy.

Daniela Ventrone

Ph.D. student in Business Administration at "L. Bocconi" University, Milan, Italy. Assistant Professor at Banking and Insurance Department of SDA Bocconi, Bocconi School of Management, Milan, Italy.

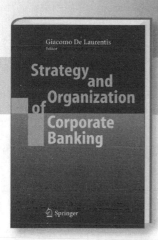